Animal Assisted Therapy in Counseling

D0061282

Animal Assisted Therapy in Counseling

Cynthia K. Chandler

Routledge
Taylor & Francis Group

NEW YORK AND HOVE

Published in 2005 by
Routledge
Taylor & Francis Group
270 Madison Avenue
New York, NY 10016

Published in Great Britain by
Routledge
Taylor & Francis Group
27 Church Road
Hove, East Sussex BN3 2FA

© 2005 by Taylor & Francis Group, LLC
Routledge is an imprint of Taylor & Francis Group
Formerly a Brunner-Routledge title.

Printed in the United States of America on acid-free paper
10 9 8 7 6 5

International Standard Book Number-10: 0-415-95173-9 (Hardcover) 0-415-95202-6 (Softcover)
International Standard Book Number-13: 978-0-415-95173-9 (Hardcover) 978-0-415-95202-6 (Softcover)
Library of Congress Card Number 2004028796

Library of Congress Cataloging-in-Publication Data

Chandler, Cynthia K.
    Animal assisted therapy in counseling / Cynthia K. Chandler.
        p. ; cm.
    Includes bibliographical references and index.
    ISBN 0-415-95173-9 (hb : alk. paper) -- ISBN 0-415-95202-6 (pb : alk. paper)
    1. Pets--Therapeutic use. [DNLM: 1. Bonding, Human-Pet. 2. Animals, Domestic.
3. Counseling--methods . 4. Cultural Diversity. 5. Psychotherapy--methods.] I. Title.

RC489.P47C48 2005
616.89'165--dc22   2004028796

Taylor & Francis Group
is the Academic Division of T&F Informa plc.

Visit the Taylor & Francis Web site at
http://www.taylorandfrancis.com

and the Routledge Web site at
http://www.routledgementalhealth.com

*This book is dedicated to Rusty, Dolly, and Snowflake,
who are my companions, friends, and cotherapists.*

Contents

ACKNOWLEDGMENTS   XI
ABOUT THE AUTHOR   XIII
ABOUT THE AUTHOR'S THERAPY ANIMALS   XV

1 An Introduction to Animal Assisted Therapy   **1**
Description of AAT   5
The Human–Animal Connection   5
Benefits of AAT   8
Risks Involved with AAT   8
Historical Highlights of AAT   10
AAT-C: A New Frontier Therapy   12

2 Research in Animal Assisted Counseling   **15**
Psychophysiological Health   16
Anxiety and Distress   17
Dementia   17
Depression   18
Motivation   19
Self-Esteem Enhancement   19
Children in Pediatric Hospitals   19
Children with Developmental Disorders   19
Children and Adolescents with Emotional and
    Behavioral Problems   20
The Elderly and Nursing Home Residents   21
Physically Disabled Persons   22

CONTENTS

Psychiatric Patients   23
Conclusions   24

3   Selecting an Animal for Therapy Work   25
Therapy Dogs   26
Selecting a Puppy for Therapy Work   29
Therapy Cats   30
Therapy Horses   31
Small Therapy Animals   31
Therapy Farm Animals   33

4   Training a Pet for Therapy Work   35
Socialization   36
Touch Desensitization   39
Obedience Training   40
Teaching Special Skills and Trick Training   43

5   Evaluation of a Pet for Therapy Work   49
American Kennel Club Canine Good Citizen Test   50
TDI Testing Requirements   51
Delta Society Pet Partners Evaluation   51
Pet Partners Aptitude Test   52
Pet Partners Skills Test   52
Tuskegee Behavior Test   54

6   Risk Management in Animal Assisted Counseling   57
Professional Disclosure and Informed
   Consent to Participate in AAT   59
Client Screening for AAT   59
Recognizing Stress in Therapy Animals   59
Understanding Your Pet's Communication   61
Preventing Injury and Infection during AAT   66
Preparing a Pet for a Therapy Visit   69
Ethical Considerations for AAT   70
Dangers for Animals in Elderly Residential Care Facilities   70
Dangers for Animals in Institutionally
   Based Residential Programs   71
Concerns for Animals in Visitation Programs   71
Concerns for Wild (Nondomesticated)
   Animal Programs   71

7   Animal Assisted Counseling Techniques   **73**
Animals as a Surrogate for Therapeutic Touch   74
Animal Assisted Rapport Building   75
Animal Assisted Psychosocial Goals and Techniques   79
Animal Facilitated Life Stage Development   85
A Typical Animal Assisted Counseling Session   89
Introducing the Pet Practitioner   90
Animal Assisted Basic Relational Techniques   91
Accessing Feelings through the Use of AAT   93
Animal Assisted Family History Gathering   99
Animal Assisted Interventions and Clinical Diagnoses   101
Animal Assisted Metaphor   102
Animal Assisted Play Therapy   106
Play Therapy Yard   109
Animal Assisted Group Play Therapy   109
Equine Assisted Counseling   110
The Therapeutic Zoo   120
Termination Issues in AAT-C   123
Documentation and AAT   124
Program Evaluation and AAT   125

**8   Sensitivity to Cultural Differences and
      Populations with Special Needs**   **127**
Cultural Differences in Attitudes about Animals   129
AAT-C with Elderly Clients   130
AAT-C with Hospitalized and Hospice Clients   132
AAT-C with Clients in Prisons or Detention Centers   133
Residential AAT Programs in Prisons   134
Juvenile Detention Programs with AAT   135

**9   Crisis Response Counseling with
      Therapy Animals**   **139**
Therapy Dogs Make the Best Crisis Response Pet Practitioners   140
The Nature of Crisis   141
Crisis Response Safety   141
Become a Recognized Crisis Response
   Counselor with Your Pet   142
The Nature of Crisis Response Counseling   143
Form an Animal Assisted Crisis Response
   Counseling Team   147

CONTENTS

10 Establishing a School-Based Program for Animal Assisted Therapy and Education **151**

Guidelines for AAT Program Development 152
Types of AAT School-Based Programs 153
How to Solicit Funding for Your AAT Program 154
How to Report on the Progress of Your AAT Program 157

11 Establishing and Maintaining a University-Based AAT Training Program **159**

Seeking Approval and Establishing Policy
for an AAT Program 160
Obtaining AAT Credentials 161
Being a Role Model: Practicing AAT-C 162
Developing a University Course 162
Involving the Community 163
Establishing a Center 164
Creating Student Internships in the Community 164
Serving as an Educational Resource 165
Gaining National and International Recognition 165

12 An Intercultural AAT Experience: Examining the Human–Animal Connection in South Korea **167**

A History of the Human–Animal
Connection in South Korea 169
The Human–Animal Connection in the 21st Century:
A New Era for South Korea 170
International Information Exchange and
Relationship Building 172
Defining the Role and Scope of
AAT in South Korea 173

APPENDIX A 177
APPENDIX B 179
APPENDIX C 181
APPENDIX D 185
APPENDIX E 193
APPENDIX F 201
APPENDIX G 207
REFERENCES 221
INDEX 229

Acknowledgments

I would like to thank the Denton County Juvenile Detention Postadjudication Program of Denton, Texas, and Rocky Top Therapy Center of Keller, Texas, for graciously allowing me to participate in and to photograph their services and facilities. I would like to thank the counselors who contributed stories about their work with their therapy pets. I would like to thank my colleagues at the University of North Texas who have encouraged and supported me in the development and growth of the animal assisted therapy program. I especially want to extend my gratitude to my mother Billie and my father Orbie Chandler and my siblings Bonnie, Betty, and Charlie for providing me with a foundation for appreciating the many gifts that animals bring into our lives. And finally, I would like to thank each and every one of my dedicated friends who have always been there to support, encourage, and guide me through life, most especially Bev, Bobbie, Laura, Susie, Linda, Ben, Rebecca, and Denette.

About the Author

Cynthia Kay Chandler was born in Ft. Worth, Texas, on July 17, 1956. Her first 7 years of school were undertaken in El Paso, and then her family relocated to Muleshoe, Texas, where she graduated from Muleshoe High School in 1974 (I could not resist throwing that fun piece of trivia in). She received her doctoral degree in educational psychology in 1986 from Texas Tech University.

Dr. Chandler has been working as a full-time professor since 1989 in the University of North Texas (UNT) counseling program in the Department of Counseling, Development, and Higher Education. This counseling program is consistently ranked as the best in the state of Texas and in the top 20 in the nation. She developed and directs the Center for Animal Assisted Therapy at the university and developed the first and only course in this subject at UNT. Other graduate courses she teaches at UNT include biofeedback therapy techniques and practicum; women's emotional health; basic counseling techniques; counseling practicum; assessment; and counseling research. She developed an advanced biofeedback-training program and instituted and directs the Biofeedback Research and Training Laboratory at UNT.

Dr. Chandler is a licensed professional counselor, a licensed marriage and family therapist, and a nationally certified biofeedback and neurofeedback therapist, as well as an approved supervisor in each of these four fields. She is a nationally certified Pet Partner with Delta Society with her dogs Rusty and Dolly and her cat Snowflake, a licensed Delta Society Pet Partners instructor, an Animal Assisted Therapy instructor, and an animal team evaluator.

Dr. Chandler has several publications in nationally refereed professional journals, has coauthored two books, and has presented at professional venues across the U.S., Canada, Austria, Greece, and South Korea. She coleads the annual statewide Training Institute in Counselor Supervision and organizes and leads several community workshops every year to train volunteers and professionals to become registered Delta Society Pet Partners.

About the Author's Therapy Animals

I could not engage in any animal assisted activity or therapy were it not for my trusted therapy partners Rusty, Dolly, and Snowflake. They are first and foremost beloved family members, my companions, and my friends. Without their loyal and dutiful efforts I would not be writing this book. Rusty is a red on white parti-color American Cocker Spaniel born in Denton, Texas, on June 6, 1999. He has an abundance of dark red freckles on his face and large red furry patches all over his body including over both eyes, with solid red, long, droopy ears. He has extraordinarily curly fur for an American cocker. I brought Rusty home when he was 7½ weeks old and named him after a player on my favorite baseball team, Rusty Greer, who then played left field for the Texas Rangers. Rusty's full AKC registered name is Chandler's Rusty Ranger. His personality is friendly, affectionate, and playful with robust energy.

Dolly is an American Cocker Spaniel and looks almost like Rusty only smaller, with straight, long, flowing fur. She was born near Lubbock, Texas, on September 30, 2002. She joined my family when she was 7 weeks old. Her personality is friendly, affectionate, and playful, but she is more quiet and reserved than Rusty. She exhibits a hint of delicate, feminine petite in her demeanor and prances along as if bouncing like a ballerina off of the tips of her toes. Her AKC registered name is Chandler's China Doll.

Snowflake is a solid white domestic American short hair cat. His left eye is green, and his right eye is blue. His nose is a bright pink as are the pads of his paws. He is large and husky with a very playful personality. He is a stray cat that wandered up into my yard in Denton, Texas, as a kitten and had no one to claim him, so he joined our family. He was named Snowflake because of his unique appearance. Snowflake's uniqueness is compounded by the fact that he is deaf, most likely from birth. The veterinarian estimated his age at about 8 to 9 weeks when he arrived at our home, and thus his approximate birth date is toward the end of February 2001.

Chapter 1

An Introduction to Animal Assisted Therapy

Description of AAT   5
The Human Animal Connection   5
Benefits of AAT   8
Risks Involved with AAT   8
Historical Highlights of AAT   10
AAT C: A New Frontier Therapy   12

> "Our task must be to free ourselves by widening our circle of compassion to embrace all living creatures and the whole of nature and its beauty."
> — Albert Einstein

Imagine you are 13 years old and because of poor decisions you have made you find yourself in a residential juvenile detention facility. On this first day of your confinement, your own clothes have been replaced by a drab set of brown coveralls, your street shoes have been taken, and you have to wear thick, institutional orange socks and flimsy slippers. You are escorted everywhere by stern looking adults in security uniforms comprised of black T-shirts and camouflage pants with large, black army boots. The cinder block walls are painted pale gray and form long cold corridors interrupted only by an occasional heavy metal door and interior window of thick glass with wires running through it. The loud sounds you hear are the clicks and clangs from the security locks on the doors opening and then closing behind as you travel deeper into the abyss of freedom lost. The order barked from your adult security escort to pass on through the door startles you, interrupting your concentrated yet futile thoughts to regain some sense of control over the situation. You are scared. No, it's more like you are petrified. You are no longer sure of yourself as you thought you were a few days ago. Your mind is in a flurry. "Should I run, but where would I run to and how would I get out? Should I act defiant showing them how tough I am and that I am not going to give in to their attempts to dominate me? Or, should I just cry, because that is what I really want to do? No, I must not show them how scared I am. I must not let them control me. I will … I will … Wait a minute. What is that jingling noise? Is that, is that, a dog? Yes, it is a dog! Can I pet him? Is it a boy or a girl? What's his name? Hi, Rusty! What are you doing here? Oh, look he likes it when I scratch his ears. I think he really likes me. You know, I have a dog at home. His name is Scooter. He's just a mutt. But he is really smart. I have taught him some tricks. Can Rusty do tricks? Oh wow that is so cool, he gave me a high five! You say Rusty is a counselor here? Wow, a dog counselor. So, can I have counseling with Rusty? Great! Thanks for letting me pet Rusty." Now you are not so scared. Maybe this place is not where you want to be, but maybe, just maybe you can make it through this dark period of your life all right, especially since the people here bring dogs for you to pet and play with.

Sometimes life is painful. Sometimes we do not feel as safe and secure as we would like. Sometimes we need comfort and affection to help us through tough times. We need a broad support system. We need people to help us. And yes, sometimes we really need a dog. Or we need a cat, or a horse, or some other animal to help us through our pain and to move us toward a better place in our life. Animal assisted therapy (AAT) is one way animals can be very helpful to people. And working with therapy animals in the profession of counseling is what I want to talk to you about in this book. Animals who assist in the therapy process are referred to by a number of different and interchangeable titles including therapy animal, therapy pet, pet practitioner, pet facilitator, and so on. Regardless of the variation in descriptive titles, each therapy pet serves the same basic purpose, that of working in partnership with a professional human therapist to provide compassionate and stimulating therapy designed to facilitate human client recovery.

Animal assisted therapy in counseling (AAT-C) is the incorporation of pets as therapeutic agents into the counseling process. This can be done in a variety of ways and by utilizing a variety of techniques. AAT-C is appropriate for numerous settings including schools, hospitals, agencies, and private practice. The most common and most preferred application model of AAT-C is for counselors to work in partnership with their own pet, a pet that has been evaluated and certified as appropriate for such work. This model is preferred because you are most familiar with your own pet and can best predict the pet's emotional and behavioral reactions. In addition, the strong and healthy bond demonstrated between you and your pet can contribute greatly to the therapeutic process, especially by reassuring a client that the therapist can be trusted because the client observes positive interactions between the pet and the therapist. A second application model of AAT-C is for a counselor to obtain the assistance of a trained animal handler who has a certified therapy pet. This model requires the trained animal handler to facilitate interactions between the therapy pet and the client under the counselor's guidance and supervision. This model allows counselors to provide AAT-C for a client without having their own therapy pet. Also, trained animal handlers may be able to facilitate animal-related tasks that are outside of the counselor's skills, such as involving a client with animal training, grooming, and other appropriate animal-related activities. The disadvantages of this second AAT-C application model include the necessity of obtaining permission from the client to involve another person in the therapy process, securing a confidentiality agreement from the animal handler, and having confidence in both the animal handler and the therapy pet. A counselor who wishes to utilize the second model, to employ the assistance of an animal handler with a therapy pet, has the additional obstacle of finding such an animal therapy team located conveniently nearby. There are organizations that provide training, evaluation, and certification for persons who wish to work with their therapy pets, and most of these organizations have a website that can assist in contacting a certified animal therapy team. The national organization that currently provides the most rigorous training, evaluation, and certification process for AAT teams is Delta Society (http://www.deltasociety.org). Another popular animal therapy certification organization is Therapy Dogs International (TDI; http://www.tdi-dog.org).

AAT-C is one type of application in the broader field of AAT, thus it is important to first briefly introduce the overall construct of AAT. AAT promotes positive human–animal interaction and incorporates the talents and traits of a therapy animal into a therapeutic setting to facilitate the recovery of a patient seeking physical or mental health services. Under the careful guidance of a trained therapist, the animal contributes to the client's recovery process. Examples of AAT in physical therapy would be having a patient walk a dog down a hallway or pet or brush a cat, activities designed to increase muscle strength and control. AAT in a mental health counseling session could involve a child victim of abuse gently petting and talking to a dog or cat to teach the concept of appropriate touch and gentle relations; the warm and caring attitude of the therapy pet and human therapist combined reinforces the child's positive experience. Why involve pets in therapy? Because therapy pets can alter the dynamics of the therapy process in several ways:

1. The client may be more motivated to attend and participate in therapy because of a desire to spend time with the therapy pet.
2. The client's focus may be temporarily shifted away from disabling pain because of the interaction with the therapy pet to the extent that the client can work harder and longer in therapy and potentially gain more benefit per session.

3. The client may receive healing nurturance and affection through physical contact with the therapy pet.
4. The client may experience soothing comfort from petting or holding the therapy pet.
5. The client may experience unconditional acceptance by the therapy pet.
6. The client may experience enjoyment and entertainment from interaction with the therapy pet.
7. The client may be able to form a more trusting relationship with a therapist who demonstrates he or she can be trusted by the way the therapist interacts with the therapy animal.
8. In many instances, based on the unique characteristics of the client's condition or needs, the client may be able to perform activities and achieve goals that would not otherwise be possible without the assistance of a therapy pet.

As a result of the unique dynamics presented, participation of a therapy pet in the therapy process may reduce the stress of therapy for the client and allow for quicker and greater recovery.

While it is true that the field of counseling has been assisting clients' recovery quite well without the assistance of animals, it is important to consider what potential benefits for the client might be gained with the addition of a pet practitioner. A highly functional client with little to no resistance to the therapeutic process may not gain significantly from the work of a therapy pet. This client may find the pet's presence entertaining and comforting; however, there may be no significant difference in the therapeutic outcome with or without the therapy pet with this type of client. On the other hand, a client that has some clinical dysfunction may benefit significantly from the assistance of an animal helping in a therapy session, as may a client who is resistant to therapy. It is with these dysfunctional or resistant clients that counselors are seeing the most dramatic positive effects of working with a therapy animal as compared to the same work without a therapy animal. While somewhat limited in number, there are empirical studies demonstrating some of these positive effects, which are reviewed in the next chapter.

The psychosocial and psychophysiological benefits of AAT have been well documented (Fine, 2000a; Wilkes, Shalko, & Trahan, 1989). For example, studies have reported quicker recovery and increased longevity for cardiac patients who owned a pet (Friedmann, Katcher, Lynch, & Thomas, 1980; Friedmann & Thomas, 1995). Reductions in levels of blood pressure, stress, and anxiety in children occurred when a researcher was accompanied by a pet (Friedmann, Katcher, Thomas, Lynch, & Messent, 1983). Decreased depression and increased socialization occurred in elderly persons interacting with residential or visiting therapy pets (Holcomb, Jendro, Weber, & Nahan, 1997; Perelle & Granville, 1993). And more socially appropriate behaviors occurred for children with developmental disorders who interacted with a therapy pet (Redefer & Goodman, 1989). Also fewer behavior problems occurred in children with emotional and developmental disorders when they interacted with a therapy pet (Kogan, Granger, Fitchett, Helmer, & Young, 1999). AAT has been incorporated into numerous health care professions including nursing, counseling and psychology, physical rehabilitation, therapeutic recreation, and speech therapy (Gammonley et al., 1997). It has been shown to be beneficial in a variety of settings, such as schools, counseling agencies, hospitals, nursing homes, hospice care, developmental disability facilities, juvenile detention centers, and prisons (Burch, 1996,

2003; Delta Society, 1997). Much has been written on the subject of AAT, yet more controlled research studies are needed to support and expand on existing clinical findings.

Description of AAT

It is important to comprehend the difference between animal assisted activity (AAA) and AAT. Most people tend to lump AAA and AAT into one category called animal assisted therapy. However, technically speaking, AAA involves mostly social visits with a therapy animal, whereas AAT strategically incorporates human–animal interactions into a formal therapeutic process.

AAA involves goal-directed activities designed to improve patients' quality of life through utilization of the human–animal bond (Gammonley et al., 1997). Animals and their handlers must be screened and trained. Activities may be therapeutic but are not guided by a credentialed therapist. AAA usually involves such tasks as visiting with patients and friendly petting with some playful activity. It may also include education about or related to the animal itself. However, compared to AAT, AAA is a less formal human–animal interaction.

AAT utilizes the human–animal bond in goal-directed interventions as an integral part of the treatment process. Working animals and their handlers must be screened, be trained, and meet specific criteria. A credentialed therapist, working within the scope of a professional practice, sets therapeutic goals, guides the interaction between patient and animal, measures progress toward meeting therapy goals, and evaluates the process. AAT may be billed to third-party payers just as any other kind of reimbursable therapy (Gammonley et al., 1997).

AAT is considered an adjunct to existing therapy. A therapist can incorporate the animal into whatever professional style of therapy the therapist already enacts. AAT therapy can be directive or nondirective in its approach. AAT sessions can be integrated into individual or group therapy and used with a very wide range of age groups and persons with varying ability. AAT is a practice modality and not an independent profession. Persons guiding AAT must have the proper training and credentials for their professional practice, such as those for a licensed professional counselor.

A therapy animal currently has no federal recognition or protection as a service or assistance animal has. Service animals are specially trained to assist the disabled and must be allowed, by law, to accompany their owner, handler, or trainer into any facility. However, a credentialed therapy animal, though not protected by federal regulation, may be invited into many places a nonworking animal is not because of its status as a professional working animal. A professional vest or neck scarf worn by the therapy animal identifying it as a working professional goes far in gaining acceptance into many places.

The Human–Animal Connection

There seems to be a natural tendency for humans and pets to form a relationship with one another, even if the animal is not that person's pet. This natural tendency is what fosters such quick rapport and empathy between the client and therapy pet.

The pet practitioner does little but be itself, and has the client's trust well before the client trusts the human therapist.

The typical relationship between a therapy pet and a client can be rapidly formed and easily terminated although some grief issues may need to be addressed. The therapy animal–client relationship does not have the depth of attachment that a bond between a pet and its owner may have, but it can still be a strong and positive relationship. The therapy pet most likely serves as a transitional object to the client who takes a subjective experience and projects it onto a real object.

> Animals make good transitional beings because they move and show inten-
> tional behavior, behaving more like a person than a stuffed toy who just lies
> there unless moved by the child. Unlike stuffed toys who provide soft touch,
> animals are capable of giving active affection and seeking out the child. But
> most importantly they can never contradict the attributes projected onto them
> with words.
>
> (Katcher, 2000b, p. 468)

To an extent, a human therapist is also a transitional object for a client in that a client may temporarily project feelings and needs onto the therapist until moving toward greater autonomy. But perhaps therapy pets make the best of all transitional objects. They are affectionate and responsive, unlike a toy or blanket, and uncondi-tionally accepting and nonjudgmental, unlike most humans. As transitional objects, therapy pets combine the best therapeutic attributes of both toys and humans while avoiding the obvious limitations that toys and humans may present.

Some authors have referred to the therapeutic benefit of AAT as based on the concept of a basic human–animal bond (Kaminski, Pellino, & Wish, 2002). However, in *Veterinary Ethics* Tannenbaum raises questions about the use of the term and sug-gests that a true bond possesses the following characteristics (Iannuzzi & Rowan, 1991, p. 155):

It must involve a continuous, ongoing relationship rather than one that is sporadic or
    accidental.
It must produce not just a benefit but a *significant* benefit to both, and that benefit
    must be a *central* aspect of the lives of each.
It must involve a relationship that is, in some sense, voluntary.
It must be bidirectional.
It must entitle each being in the bond to respect and benefit in their own right rather
    than simply as a means to an end.

Based on the above conditions, it is clear that the client and therapy animal's relationship does not meet the elements described by Tannenbaum that are needed to form a true human–animal bond, a bond that is more likely to be formed between a pet and its owner. It is more likely that the benefits gained by a client in therapy with a therapy animal are a result of a different type of relationship between the client and pet than that of an owner and a pet.

The client–therapy animal relationship is likely formed on the basis of a shared connection that relates the client and therapy animal. This shared connection is situa-tional and characteristic. While pet owners typically form a permanent attachment to their pet, the relationship between a therapy pet and client is less about an attachment and more about trust and affiliation. A client initially finds a therapy pet easier to trust than a human therapist, in that the pet characteristically does not judge or deceive; and in seeking affection and interaction, the therapy pet displays that it is vulnerable and desires a nurturing association much like the client may experience in a therapeutic situation. The client trusts the unconditional, genuine presentation of the therapy pet and affiliates with the pet's vulnerability and the pet's desire for nurturance; this may expedite the formation of a strong relationship between the therapy animal and the client.

Given that the client may more closely associate with and relate to the therapy animal than the human therapist, at least in the earlier stages of the therapeutic process, this connection between client and therapy animal may facilitate the conditions that foster client recovery. The client's connection with the therapy animal may contribute to a warmer and safer atmosphere for the client. The client may experience the therapy pet as a temporary support mechanism during sessions, feeling comforted by the pet's presence or from touching or holding the pet. The client may experience quicker and deeper trust for the human therapist seeing how the therapy animal and human therapist interact. The therapy animal can be an additional mechanism to convey the human therapist's empathy for the client, especially when the human therapist reflects the interactions between the client and the therapy animal. It is of primary importance that human therapists establish rapport and convey empathy for clients in order to form a therapeutic relationship. This therapeutic relationship is necessary for client recovery to occur. A therapy animal can enhance the establishment and continuation of a therapeutic relationship between the client and the human therapist.

The relationship between the therapy pet and the client is not meant to be a substitute for the relationship between the client and the human therapist. In fact, it is meant to do just the opposite, to facilitate the relationship between the client and the human therapist. As the client observes the closeness between the counselor and the counselor's pet, the client's fondness for the pet spills over to the counselor. It is always imperative that the human counselor develop and maintain good rapport with the client. The incorporation of a therapy pet into a counseling session should not serve as an excuse for failing to foster a close, caring relationship between a human therapist and the client.

If a client has had a traumatic experience with an animal similar to the pet practitioner, then the natural tendency to connect with the pet can be impaired. Clients with severe impairment, such as a fear or phobia of dogs, should not be encouraged to be around the pet unless the client requests closer contact. If a client who previously wanted no contact with the pet later requests some contact, such as wanting the pet in the therapy room and so forth, then the client should be allowed to set the parameters for that contact with the therapist's assistance. A client must not be pressured to be around a therapy pet of which the client is afraid. However, opportunity for the client to establish contact with the therapy pet should be left open. I have found that more often than not, those few clients who were initially afraid of my therapy dog and requested no interaction with the animal eventually requested the dog's presence during the therapy session and even initiated interaction with the pet before long. This process often took several weeks, but, observed from a comfortable distance, the dog's friendly demeanor and extremely well-behaved manner won the client over.

Benefits of AAT

There are numerous benefits to incorporating pets into the therapy process. These benefits extend to the client, the pet practitioner, and the pet's human cotherapist. The benefits of AAT to the client include a strong entertainment component. A dog fetching a ball and performing tricks or a cat chasing a feather toy across the floor evoke a smile in the client. Opportunities to interact with a social animal that seeks and outwardly displays pleasure with contact, such as a purring cat in a lap or a dog displaying its tummy for petting, can facilitate personal and social development in a client. Petting an animal can also create a soothing and calming effect for the client. A dog's or horse's ability to be attentive to commands and training cues can facilitate skill development in a client, as well as strengthen client self-concept and self-esteem. AAT is a multisensory experience for the client that may enhance attention to tasks and integration of therapeutic experiences. The presence of an animal adds significant kinesthetic, tactile, auditory, visual, and olfactory stimulation to an environment, and a more alert individual may integrate information to a deeper, more meaningful level (Figure 1.1).

The benefits to the pet practitioner are based largely on the animal's innate needs. The therapy work provides a stimulating activity for a highly intelligent creature. The therapy pet gets to spend more time with its cotherapist owner. The pet practitioner avoids being left at home alone and getting bored. The therapy animal is often a healthier and happier animal due to the amount of time it spends with its cotherapist owner and the rigorous health and training requirements for the therapy animal.

There can be multiple benefits of AAT to the human cotherapist. The handler gets to spend more quality time with the pet. The handler gets to share with others the affection, gifts, and talents of the pet. The pet contributes to a warm and friendly work atmosphere. Some clients will respond better to therapeutic intervention that involves a therapy animal than to therapy without an animal. There are some basic therapeutic goals and interventions that can actually work better with pet practitioner facilitation. When word gets out about the pet practitioner, many clients will prefer going to the therapist with the animal than to other therapists in the area. And another potential benefit may be that the care and training costs associated directly with a professional pet practitioner may be tax deductible as a business expense.

Risks Involved with AAT

There are some risks involved in practicing AAT for the client, the pet practitioner, and the pet's human cotherapist. But a counselor may prevent these risks by following proper risk management procedures. Specific methods for risk management are covered in a later chapter. One type of risk is injury to a client. Examples of how injury may occur to a client who interacts with a therapy pet include the following: a horse can step on a client's foot during mounting, a cat can scratch a client during play, a large dog can knock a client down while running to fetch a ball, and so forth. Therapy animals are trained and screened for proper temperament, so injury to a client by a pet practitioner would most likely be inadvertent yet is still a possibility. Another risk is that the client can become attached to the therapy animal, and thus grief and loss issues may have to be addressed upon termination of services. Also,

Figure 1.1 Therapy dog Rusty responds to a request by a juvenile in a detention facility to perform a "sit pretty" trick: A self-esteem building exercise for the juvenile.

the client may be allergic to or afraid of the therapy animal. Thus careful screening and evaluation of clients is necessary. In addition, some clients having had little or no contact with a pet before may prefer not to be around animals.

The risks to the pet practitioner are largely due to threat from the pet's clients. The more fragile the animal, for example a bird or a small dog, the greater the risk of injury from being dropped or hit by a client. A therapy animal can also experience stress and overwork. The pet practitioner must rely on the human cotherapist for prevention of injury and management of stress.

The pet practitioner's human cotherapist has a responsibility to insure the safety and welfare of the client and the pet practitioner. In addition, the therapist must allow ample time in the schedule for caring for the therapy pet. This includes training, feeding, exercising, playtime, rest, health care, and so forth. Also, the time it takes a therapist to get to a destination can increase significantly when accompanied by a therapy animal because many people met along the way may approach and initiate conversations about the therapy animal or their own pet at home. However, the advantage to this is that it increases the opportunity for the therapist to interact with persons they might not otherwise have had an opportunity to meet.

Historical Highlights of AAT

AAT began in the U.S. in 1919 when Secretary of the Interior Franklin K. Lane suggested using dogs with psychiatric patients at St. Elizabeth's Hospital in Washington, D.C. (Burch, 1996). In 1942, the U.S. military used pet therapy at the Pawling Army Air Force Convalescent Hospital at Pawling, New York; this was primarily a working farm for recovering veterans (Hooker, Freeman, & Stewart, 2002). Neither the St. Elizabeth's nor the Pawling programs collected data or performed research studies on the benefits of AAT.

Child psychologist Boris Levinson was the first professionally trained clinician to formally introduce and document the way that companion animals could hasten the recovery of a client in counseling (Levinson, 1997). He published his first work in *Mental Hygiene* in 1962, "The Dog as a 'Co-therapist'" (Levinson, 1962). Levinson discovered he could make significant progress with a disturbed child when his dog, Jingles, attended therapy sessions. He went on to find that many children who were withdrawn and uncommunicative would interact positively with the dog (Levinson, 1969). The pet served as a transitional object to aid in facilitating a relationship between the patient and the human therapist.

Equine assisted physical therapy (known as hippotherapy or physical therapy with horses) began as a formal treatment modality in the 1960s and today seems to be the leader of all animal-related therapeutic modalities in the U.S. It is reimbursed by most health insurance companies and is very widespread. The North American Riding for the Handicapped Association (NARHA) was established in 1969 in Denver, Colorado, and by the year 2003 had over 700 affiliated centers across the U.S. and Canada (M. Kaufman, personal communication, September, 2003). "NARHA is a membership organization which fosters safe, professional, ethical and therapeutic equine activities through education, communication, standards and research for people with and without disabilities" (NARHA, 2003, p. 1). NARHA evolved to incorporate mental health intervention. The NARHA special interest section that sets standards for equine assisted counseling is the Equine Facilitated Mental Health Association, or EFMHA.

In the early 1970s, a former dairy farm was converted into a residential treatment center for children and continues to this day to have great success with children who have varying developmental disabilities and emotional and behavioral needs. This is the Green Chimneys Children's Services in New York. The farm animals of Green Chimneys not only provide companionship to the children but also motivate and facilitate recovery (Fine, 2000a).

The mental health-related AAT work of Boris Levinson was expanded on in the 1970s by psychiatrists Sam and Elizabeth Corson at the Ohio State University Psychiatric Hospital (Hooker et al., 2002). They were the first to integrate animals in the hospital environment and to collect research data. In 1975, they expanded their pet therapy research to nursing homes (inpatient, long-term, residential care for the elderly and severely disabled) where they began to note significant physical, psychological, and social improvements in the nursing home patients as a result of the pet therapy.

TDI was founded in 1976 by Elaine Smith, a practicing nurse, after she moved to New Jersey from England. She had very good luck working with her therapy dogs in her native country and brought the concept with her to the U.S. "Using her German Shepherd, Phila, and her Shetland Sheepdog, Genny, in therapy sessions, Smith got a woman to talk who hadn't spoken in years" (Burch, 2003, p. 11). TDI is the oldest and currently the largest therapy dog organization in the U.S. In the year 2003, over 14,000 dogs and approximately 10,621 handlers in all 50 states of the U.S. and in Canada and a few other countries were registered with TDI (Therapy Dogs International, 2003).

The nursing profession has significantly contributed to the acceptance of AAT into mainstream medicine and health care. Professional nursing practice journals began to publish on the area of AAT in the 1980s (Hooker et al., 2002). In the beginning, most of these were descriptive works on how animals fulfilled the desire of patients to be needed and reduced the stress levels of patients, visiting family members, and staff. Over the next few years, more scientific investigations began to appear in nursing and other health care journals. These documented the physiological benefits of AAT, such as lowered blood pressure in child patients and greater one-year survival rates for adults after experiencing a myocardial infarction or angina.

In 1990, William Thomas presented his AAT-related ideas, referred to as the Eden Alternative (Hooker et al., 2002). His approach was to transform health care facilities into natural habitats with an abundance of plants and animals to provide a nourishing environment for both patients and staff.

The highly respected AAT training organization Delta Society began their Pet Partners program in 1990 (Delta Society, 2003). In 2003, it had over 6,400 therapy animal teams servicing needy individuals in all 50 states of the U.S. and in 4 other countries. Delta Society promotes the work of therapy dogs, cats, birds, small animals (i.e., hamsters and gerbils), horses, and farm animals in a variety of settings, such as schools, nursing homes, hospitals and other health care facilities, and prisons and detention centers. Many facilities will not allow a therapy animal to enter unless it has a national certification, such as that from Delta Society, that reflects that the handler and pet have adequate training and preparation for therapy work. Delta Society is recognized for their rigorous training and evaluation requirements for AAT teams.

The Equine Assisted Growth and Learning Association was established in 1999 in Utah to promote equine assisted therapy in education and mental health (EAGALA, 2003). EAGALA provides standardized training programs to certify equine assisted therapists and sponsors an annual national conference for exchange of research and educational information.

In the 1990s and early 2000s, health care journals published several experimental research articles documenting the benefits of AAT in a variety of health care settings (Hooker et al., 2002). For example, AAT was found to be beneficial in home health care settings as it was used to divert the patient's attention during painful procedures as well as to create more enjoyable nurse visits. It was determined that AAT reduced the strain and stress for patients and visitors in hospice settings (home nursing care for the terminally ill). AAT was found to be helpful for patients with Alzheimer's disease, resulting in increased socialization and social activity and decreased agitation. And research has demonstrated decreased anxiety and depression and increased socialization for hospitalized psychiatric patients with a variety of mental health diagnoses (Barker & Dawson, 1998; Marr et al., 2000; Mcvarish,

1995). Research in AAT continues today in both mental and physical health fields. While existing studies already demonstrate many benefits of AAT, additional studies are needed to both replicate existing work and elaborate on potential benefits that have yet to be discovered.

AAT grew greatly in popularity in the U.S. in the late 1990s and early 2000s partly because the lay public received greater exposure to it through stories published by mainstream newspapers and magazines and television broadcasts. As a result of these media stories, an abundance of schoolteachers and counselors across the nation began seeking out AAT training so they could share the benefits of pet therapy with the populations they served. Following are some examples of these media stories. Cindy Ehlers of Eugene, Oregon, took her Husky, Bear, to visit with students and others traumatized by the 1998 shootings at Thurston High School in Springfield, Oregon, and the violence in 1999 at Columbine High School in Littleton, Colorado (Rea, 2000). Tracy Roberts brought her two Australian Shepherds, Lucy and Dottie, to school to act as teacher's aides in the fourth and fifth grade classes at the Canterbury Episcopal School in DeSoto, Texas (Tarrant, 2000). Lucy and Dottie were reported to be a comfort to the kids and a welcome relief from the stress of school. Dena Carselowey and her Labrador Retriever, Buggs, served as cotherapists at Minneha Core Knowledge Magnet Elementary School in Wichita, Kansas (*Denton Record Chronicle*, 1999). Buggs provided unconditional acceptance the moment a student entered the counselor's office. Often the kids came in to see the dog and stayed a while to talk to the counselor while they petted and played with Buggs. Therapy dog teams volunteered counseling services through the Red Cross in New York, providing comfort and stress relief to victims and families affected by the World Trade Center terrorist attack of September 11, 2001 (Teal, 2002). *Time* magazine published an article on new dog assisted reading programs popping up across the U.S. Reading assistance dogs provided a fun atmosphere for reading practice for reading-challenged children (Barol, 2002). Stories about animal assisted reading programs initiated the development of an abundance of these types of programs across the U.S. in schools and public libraries as well as in community bookstores.

AAT training and service programs are not yet readily offered at the university or college level, but there has been a growing trend in that direction since the 1990s. Currently, only a handful of universities have professional research, training, or service centers or programs in AAT or closely related fields. A list of some of these university centers is provided in the appendix. A key factor in the continued growth and acceptance of AAT in both mental and physical health domains is the participation of major universities in AAT research, training, and service programs. The university system has long been a widely accepted medium for moving new types of health intervention into the mainstream.

AAT-C: A New Frontier Therapy

Despite over 30 years of history in the U.S., AAT-C is still considered a new frontier in promoting client welfare, growth, and development. Few universities in the U.S. to date offer training for counselors in AAT even though child psychologist Boris Levinson empirically demonstrated in the early 1960s that pets help to form a strong connection between client and therapist. Pet practitioners can be especially helpful when working with populations who might be discouraged, unmotivated, resistant, or defiant or who have poor self-insight, deficits in social skills, or barriers to developing relationships. The pets involved with AAT-C can enhance the motivation, encouragement, inspiration, and insight properties of therapy. Those professionals who choose to explore the new frontier of AAT-C may face resistance and criticism from their peers. Levinson was ridiculed and laughed at when he first presented his findings at the American Psychological Association conference in 1961 (Levinson, 1997). Unfortunately, this type of collegial rejection regarding the consideration of nontraditional treatment modalities does occur. A nontraditional modality typically refers to a relatively new intervention focus as compared with more established therapeutic modalities with a long history of research and application. While it is important to examine, assess, and otherwise thoroughly scrutinize any new type of therapy, we must not utilize the need for rigorous scrutiny as a justification for premature dismissal of a potentially beneficial treatment approach. The potential benefits to engaging in responsible practice and research of AAT-C would seem to make up for the potential obstacles that this engagement presents. Those who do become involved in AAT-C will be included among other pioneers who lay the foundation for a therapy that continues to grow in popularity. And it is important to consider the truly wonderful benefit that it is a lot of fun to take your pet to work.

The purpose of this book is to help further the interest of AAT in the counseling field. It is primarily designed for beginners in AAT. It has drawn from a number of worthwhile resources in an effort to consolidate information into one succinct and valuable guide. In previous years, I had to pull information from a number of different places, including my own experience and training, in order to provide students with the knowledge they needed to practice AAT-C. Having placed that information in one source will now make it much more convenient to teach these important training concepts. Wherever possible, I have incorporated real life stories into the book chapters to enhance the subject matter. Some of these stories were shared with me by colleagues, and many are from my own experience working in the field. The book begins by introducing the subject of AAT and reviewing some recent research regarding AAT-C and related areas in Chapters 1 and 2. The book then takes the reader through the steps of partnering with a pet with the selection of a therapy animal in Chapter 3, the animal's training to be a pet practitioner in Chapter 4, and the animal's evaluation and certification process in Chapter 5. Proper risk management procedures to be considered when working with a therapy animal are covered in Chapter 6 along with an examination of ethical concerns related to AAT-C practice. Chapter 7 describes several AAT techniques that can be applied to facilitate the recovery of a client in counseling. Chapter 8 addresses how to be culturally sensitive in the application of AAT-C and describes some specific ideas to address the special needs of certain populations. Chapter 9 describes the complex topic of animal assisted crisis response counseling and how to become a recognized crisis response counseling team with your therapy pet. Chapters 1 through 9 were designed to fulfill the educational needs of my enthusiastic students whom I have the privilege to train to be AAT counselors. Chapters 10 and 11 were specifically added at the request of my colleagues who wanted to know how to set up AAT-C programs in elementary and secondary schools and how to design a university AAT counselor education program to train counselors to practice AAT-C. And finally, Chapter 12 describes an AAT cultural exchange experience I had in South Korea. This chapter exemplifies international differences in the practice of AAT as well as reinforcing the value of sharing learning opportunities and exchanging valuable information with our colleagues all over the world.

I sincerely hope you enjoy reading this book as much as I enjoyed writing it. If the book fails to meet your needs or expectations, then I would be happy to hear from you and I will endeavor to include that information in a possible future edition, depending very much of course on how well this edition sells. If you are satisfied with aspects of the book, then I would also very much like to hear what you liked about it so I may retain and reinforce that information for the future. In any case, if you are reading this book, you must have an interest in AAT and that makes us colleagues who share a mutual interest in a highly valuable profession, and for this I salute you. And, thank you very much for reading my book. Here's wishing you and your pet "Happy Tails!" By the way, you can reach me at the University of North Texas Counseling Program in the College of Education; my e-mail address is chandler@coe.unt.edu.

Chapter 2

Research in Animal Assisted Counseling

Psychophysiological Health   16
Anxiety and Distress   17
Dementia   17
Depression   18
Motivation   19
Self-Esteem Enhancement   19
Children in Pediatric Hospitals   19
Children with Developmental Disorders   19
Children and Adolescents with Emotional and Behavioral Problems   20
The Elderly and Nursing Home Residents   21
Physically Disabled Persons   22
Psychiatric Patients   23
Conclusions   24

"It's funny how dogs and cats know the inside of folks better than other folks do, isn't it?"

— Eleanor H. Porter, *Pollyanna*

With any relatively new up and coming treatment focus, it is important to establish a base of research to validate the value of the therapy. Although many more experimentally based clinical trials in AAT in a counseling setting are required, we shall examine in this chapter some existing research in AAT in mental health or related fields as a baseline for future research endeavors. The research described in this chapter is not meant to be all-inclusive but rather to review important AAT-C-related literature from recent years. For a more comprehensive and historical examination of AAT research, I refer you to Fine (2000a) and to Hooker et al. (2002).

Psychophysiological Health

Psychophysiological health can be enhanced by positive human–animal interactions. Odendaal (2000) measured significant changes in blood plasma levels of various neurochemicals after subjects engaged in a positive interaction with an unfamiliar dog. Neurochemicals associated with a decrease in blood pressure increased; in humans and dogs, endorphin, oxytocin, prolactin, phenylectic acid, and dopamine increased significantly. Cortisol, a hormone associated with increased stress levels, decreased significantly in humans, but in dogs, the decrease was nonsignificant. This nonsignificant result might be because the dogs with their owners found the novel situation initially very exciting. As Odendaal (2000) states

> The results of this experiment support the theory of attentionis egens in human–dog affiliation. Once the physiology is known, i.e., the role that neurochemicals and hormones might play during positive interaction, it is possible to use this information as a rationale for using animals in animal-assisted therapy. (p. 279)

From the results, Odendaal (2000) drew these conclusions:

1. The greatest psychophysiological benefit of the human–animal interaction occurred between 5 and 24 minutes after the start of the interaction, and thus interactions shorter or longer than this may offer no additional benefit.
2. "(A)ttentionis egens needs (affiliation behavior, positive interaction) are described on the neurochemical level and on an interspecies basis ... the dog experiences the same physiological effects as the patient." (p. 279)
3. Neurochemical changes occurred that are associated with decreases in blood pressure, thus if biochemistry measures are not available for a future study, the much simpler blood pressure measure could be a valid indicator of whether the interaction has the desired physiological effects.
4. The six neurochemical changes measured in this study can be used as a profile for affiliative behavior.
5. The physiological parameters "are regarded as effects of a complex biological interaction, and in a sense, the physiological changes are results of the phenomenon of human–dog interaction." (p. 279)

Anxiety and Distress

Barker and Dawson (1998) reported a successful use of a single AAT session in the reduction of anxiety with hospitalized psychiatric patients with psychotic disorders, mood disorders, and other disorders. A comparison group, a single session of therapeutic recreation, only experienced a reduction in anxiety for patients with mood disorders. Thus, AAT was determined to be effective in the reduction of state anxiety levels for psychiatric patients with a variety of psychiatric diagnoses.

The presence of a certified therapy dog, a nine-year-old Golden Retriever, was found to significantly alleviate distress in children undergoing a standard pediatric physical examination (Hansen, Messinger, Baun, & Megel, 1999). Thirty-four children aged 2 to 6 years participated in the study. A two-group repeated measures design was used to examine rating scores of videotaped sessions rated with the Observation Scale of Behavioral Distress. Although distress scores increased for both groups over time regardless of the dog's presence, when the dog was in the examination room, fewer behaviors indicative of distress were exhibited, so the children had significantly different distress scores.

Dementia

A "pets as therapy" program was found to be beneficial with persons with dementia in a psychiatric ward (Walsh, Mertin, Verlander, & Pollard, 1995). Seven participants who were over 65 years of age and who were diagnosed as having some form of dementia, usually of the Alzheimer's type, served as the experimental group. The study was conducted over a 12-week period. The intervention involved an equal amount of supervised visitation time for each subject over a 3-hour period twice per week. The pet therapist was a trained, public relations Labrador for the Guide Dog Association that was very experienced with people, of a quiet temperament, and not likely to become excited. The handler was a qualified obedience instructor of 8 years who owns and trains the dog. Measures included ratings on the London Psycho-Geriatric Rating Scale (LPRS; for the measurement of mental disorganization/confusion), the Brighton Clinic Adaptive Behaviour Scale (BCABS; to assess daily functioning), diastolic blood pressure, heart rate, and ward noise levels. Results indicated significant experimental group changes in reduction in heart rate and a substantial drop in noise levels during the presence of the dog. No significant differences on pre- and post-test comparisons between the experimental and control group were found on the LPRS or the BCABS. Although no significant differences were found between the experimental and control group in blood pressure change, there was a slight drop in mean diastolic blood pressure for the experimental group.

The presence of a therapy dog visiting with residents at three long-term care facilities increased socialization for participants with Alzheimer's disease (Batson, McCabe, Baun, & Wilson, 1998). The mean age of participants was 77.9 years. The therapy animal was a miniature Schnauzer certified as a therapy dog. Patients participated in 10-minute sessions on 2 different days: 1 day with the dog present and 1 day without the dog present; the conditions were randomly presented based on a random numbers table. Sessions were videotaped for later coding. Dependent t-tests analysis revealed significant increases when the dog was present for the following socialization variables: smiles, tactile contact, looks, physical warmth, praise, and duration of leans toward. The researchers also examined several physiological parameters, but no significant difference was found for these: blood pressure, pulse, or peripheral skin temperature.

Depression

Exposure to an aviary was reported to be effective in reducing depression in elderly males at a veteran's hospital (Holcomb et al., 1997). The aviary was $10 \times 8 \times 4$ feet and contained 20 songbirds representing about 10 different breeds. The walls of the aviary were Plexiglas to allow for easy viewing. It was well lit and clearly visible from any point in the activity room. A video camera taped interactions of hospital residents with the aviary, and judges viewed and rated the videotaped interactions on a six-point scale. Interactions rated included length of time focused on the aviary, intensity of aviary observation, ignoring the aviary, glancing at the aviary, talking to the birds, and talking with others about the birds. Statistical covariance analysis demonstrated a significant relationship between improvements in depression, as measured by the Geriatric Depression Index, and greater utilization of the aviary.

AAT with a therapy dog was shown to be somewhat effective in reducing depression in adult college students (Folse, Minder, Aycock, & Santana, 1994). Students were selected for participation based on their scores on the Beck Depression Inventory (BDI) and placed into one of three groups: AAT with directive group psychotherapy, nondirective group AAT only without psychotherapy, and a control group. The greatest differences were discovered between the AAT only group and the control group, with BDI scores reducing significantly for the AAT only group. Nonsignificant mixed results were found between the AAT psychotherapy group and the control group. It was thought that the nondirective interactions with the therapy dog in the AAT only group uplifted the mood of the group members, whereas the directive psychotherapy with AAT focused clients on painful issues and thus mediated the results of this combined therapy approach. It is important to note that 6 of the 9 participants in the AAT and psychotherapy combined group did show reductions in BDI scores. But the statistics applied to the study compared the statistical significance of pre- and post-test scores and failed to investigate the possibility of clinical significance or effect size. It is possible that, if it had been utilized, the more sensitive effect size statistic may have demonstrated some clinically significant impact for the AAT and psychotherapy combined group.

The positive effects of pet facilitated therapy to impact depression seem to be based on more than just an opportunity for patients to socialize in the presence of novel stimuli. Mcvarish (1995) demonstrated that patients shown photographs of pets did not show the decrease in depression that patients did who interacted briefly with an animal. Participants consisted of 74 inpatients recruited from two psychiatric hospitals. The photograph group included one 40-minute visit with trained volunteers who shared 250 photographs of pets. The pet therapy group consisted of one 40-minute visit of the same trained volunteers who introduced dogs and kittens to the group. It was found that (a) the pet facilitated therapy group showed a significantly greater decrease in depressive symptoms than inpatients who received the animal photograph session; and (b) the animal photograph group showed a significantly greater decrease in depressive symptoms than inpatients who did not receive any treatment as evidenced by a decrease in total mean scores of the BDI and the Brief Psychiatric

Rating Scale. Thus, although social visitation that centers on novel inanimate stimuli (animal photographs) does seem to positively impact depression, what is most important is that social visitation that centers on the presentation of animals has an even significantly greater positive effect.

Motivation

AAT has been reported to serve as a source of motivation for client participation in therapy. Over the course of 2 years, an animal assisted occupational therapy (OT) group attracted the highest percentage of psychiatric inpatients voluntarily choosing to attend an OT group (Holcomb & Meacham, 1989). The types of OT groups offered included Hug-a-Pet (the AAT group), Living Skills, Clinic, Communication, Assertiveness, Special Topics, Chemical Dependency, and Exercise. In addition, it was found that AAT was the most effective of all of the various types of OT groups offered in attracting isolated individuals to participate regardless of diagnosis.

Self-Esteem Enhancement

A Pets as Therapy program was initiated in a women's prison in Australia to train companion dogs for the elderly and individuals with disabilities (Walsh and Mertin, 1994). The prisoners who participated in the program were rated as needing low security and the dogs were kept in an area with this same rating for the dogs' safety. The women built kennels for the dogs and were responsible for the complete care and training of three dogs each. Training for the women included dog grooming as well as dog obedience and guide dog training. In addition, the women engaged in play and exercise activities with the dogs. Pre- and postassessment score comparisons revealed significant improvement in the women participants of the AAT program on the Coopersmith Inventory (for measuring self-esteem) and IPAT Depression Scale.

Children in Pediatric Hospitals

A hospital can be a stressful place for a child, and attempts are made to help alleviate this stress through various types of therapeutic interventions. Kaminski et al. (2002) reported that pet therapy significantly enhanced the mood of children in a pediatric hospital. Parents rated their children as happier after pet therapy than before pet therapy. In addition, parents rated their children following pet therapy as happier than did parents with children who engaged in a play and activity room. Ratings of videotaped interactions by judges rated children involved in pet therapy as displaying more positive affect than children engaged in a play and activity room.

Children with Developmental Disorders

AAT has been effective in helping children with developmental disorders. It has been reported that a dog, when used as a component in therapy, can have a strong impact on the behavior of seriously withdrawn children. A repeated measures analysis of variance of animal assisted interventions with 12 children with autism demonstrated significant improvements in behaviors with fewer autistic behaviors (for example, hand-posturing, humming and clicking noises, spinning objects, repetitive jumping and roaming) and more socially appropriate ones (for example, joining the therapist in games, initiating activities by giving the therapist balloons to blow up or balls to throw, reaching up for hugs, and frequently imitating the therapist's actions; Redefer & Goodman, 1989). The authors caution that it was not the mere presence of the dog that made the difference, but rather therapist-orchestrated child–dog interactions and child–therapist interactions. The types of child–dog activities started with simple ones and gradually increased to more complex tasks over several sessions. Example activities were modeling and verbally encouraging approaching and exploring the dog through touching, holding, and petting activities; engaging the child to pet and touch the dog identifying body parts; feeding; ball-throwing; bubble-blowing; and grooming.

In an attempt to determine if interaction with a live animal was more effective with 10 children with pervasive developmental disorders than interaction with an inanimate object, a repeated measures analysis of variance was utilized to compare three conditions: (a) a nonsocial toy (ball), (b) a stuffed dog, and (c) a live therapy dog (Martin & Farnum, 2002). Researchers reported that when these children were in the presence of the live therapy dog, they exhibited a more playful mood, were more focused, and were more aware of their social environments.

Interactions with a therapy dog have been demonstrated to positively impact children with learning disabilities. A repeated measures control group design was used to observe 8 children with Down syndrome (Limond, Bradshaw, & Cormack, 1997). The children's ages ranged from 7 to 12 years. The experimental session consisted of adult supervised interaction with a real dog for a 7-minute period, while the control group consisted of adult supervised interaction with a toy stuffed dog for a 7-minute period. Significant differences were found for the real dog group over the imitation dog group. Subjects in the real dog interaction group showed more visual attending and verbal and nonverbal initiation and response behaviors. Thus, the real dog provided a more sustained focus for positive and cooperative interactions between both the children and the dog and the children and the adult.

Children and Adolescents with Emotional and Behavioral Problems

A case study of AAT with two emotionally disturbed children was conducted using change measures: The ADD-H Comprehensive Teacher Rating Scale and direct observation as well as videotapes of therapy sessions with the therapy dogs (Kogan et al., 1999). Each participant took part in weekly AAT sessions that were 45 to 60 minutes in duration. The AAT intervention sessions consisted of two main segments, rapport-building time and animal training time. Rapport-building time included brushing and petting the dog and child-initiated discussions with the dog's handler. Then the child worked with the dog and utilized a variety of commands and training techniques with the dog. Improvements were demonstrated in most of the identified goal areas for the two children including decreased negative comments, decreased self-talk related to the fantasy world, decreased distractibility, decreased learned helplessness, decreased pouting and tantrums, improved relationships with peers, and increased eye contact with people.

Mallon (1994a) assessed the effects of visiting with farm animals on children with behavior and emotional problems at the Green Chimneys Children's Services residential treatment facility. Qualitative findings indicated the children visited the farm animals with a high rate of frequency and they went to see the farm animals more frequently when they were sad or angry because visiting the farm animals made them feel better.

Mallon (1994b) utilized a combination of quantitative and qualitative methods to examine the benefits and drawbacks of placing therapy dogs in residential dormitories with children who had conduct disorder. The residential child care program was Green Chimneys Children's Services. Methods entailed questionnaires, observations, and interviews. The results of the study revealed that the primary therapeutic benefits of this program were that the dogs provided the children with opportunities for love, companionship, and affection. Three primary drawbacks were also detected that included (a) some of the children abused the dogs by hitting them, (b) caring for the dogs and cleaning up after them was labor intensive, and (c) not all of the therapeutic staff was supportive of the program. Although concerns were expressed about placing the therapy dogs with the children, it was felt that the benefits to the children outweighed the difficulties. It was recommended that the program have greater supervision to prevent the abuse of the dogs. Also, staff reported that they could have been more supportive if they had greater input into the design of the program and participation in interventions involving the dogs.

Heindl (1996) demonstrated how pet therapy could be useful as an intervention in a community-based children's day treatment program. A randomized control group pretest versus post-test design was used. Two separate one-way analyses of covariance were used to test for differences. The experimental group participated in a 1-hour-per-week pet therapy intervention for 6 weeks. No significant differences were found in self-concept, as measured by the Joseph Pre-School and Primary Self-Concept Screening Test. However, significant differences were found for behavior problems, as measured by the Woodcock-Johnson Scales of Independent Behavior: Problem Behaviors Scale, with a decrease in such behaviors being the result.

The Elderly and Nursing Home Residents

Older individuals often experience a decreased quality of life and increased stress due to age-related life transitions. AAA has been reported to provide a number of positive benefits for the elderly. A review of several studies involving AAA with residential geriatric patients reported several positive findings: decreased blood pressure and heart rate, decreased depression, and increased life satisfaction (Steed & Smith, 2002).

The presence of a dog in a therapy group significantly increased verbal interactions for elderly residents in the nursing home care unit of the Veterans Administration Medical Center (Fick, 1993). Participants attended a therapy group designed to improve social interactions. Analysis of variance comparisons of videotaped session segments of when the dog was present for 15-minute intervals and when the dog was not present over a 4-week period demonstrated that while the dog was present, twice the number of verbal interactions occurred.

A 10-week pet visitation program demonstrated increases in social interaction in nursing home residents ranging in age from 35 to 95 years with a mean age of 75.39 years (Perelle & Granville, 1993). Pet visitation volunteers were students at a nearby veterinary college with training in animal handling. Animals consisted of four cats, two small dogs, and one rabbit. Six of the animals were brought to the facility each week for 2 hours. Nursing home residents were encouraged by the volunteers to stroke or handle the animals. Volunteers also talked with participants about animals and the residents' former pets and answered participants' questions. An analysis of variance comparison of pretest versus post-test scores on the Patient Social Behavior Scale showed a significant increase of social behaviors. After termination of the visitation program, 6-week follow-up scores showed a significant decline; however, these follow-up scores were still significantly higher than the original pretest scores.

AAT was reported to reduce loneliness in elderly residents of a long-term care facility (Banks & Banks, 2002). The 6-week program involved a pet attendant accompanying a dog to residents' rooms at the facility for a 30-minute session that included such activities as holding, stroking, grooming, walking, talking to, and playing with the animal. To circumvent the socialization between the attendant and the resident participant, the attendant's interaction with the participant was limited to a script read at the beginning of each session. The attendant did not interact with the dog or the participant during the visit. The dog was always kept on a leash, and the same dog was used for the same resident for the entire 6 weeks. Analysis of covariance comparisons of pretest and post-test scores on the University of California at Los Angeles Loneliness Scale demonstrated significant improvement for participants in a once per week AAT group as well as a 3 times per week AAT group, but no significant improvement was found for the no-AAT group. The once per week AAT group did not significantly differ from the 3 times per week AAT group. This study provides strong evidence for the social benefits of AAT.

An analysis of variance repeated measures comparison between AAT and no-AAT with elderly residents at a long-term care facility revealed that AAT participants were more likely to initiate and participate in longer conversations (Bernstein, Friedman, & Malaspina, 2000). The researchers reported that the most dramatic differences between the two groups was that the touching of the animals added significantly to resident engagement in and initiation of touching social behavior. They suggested that, "Since touch is considered an important part of social stimulation and therapy, the enhancement of this social behavior by the animals is an important, and perhaps undervalued effect" (p. 213) and "Since touch between people or between people and animals has been shown by others to have beneficial health effects, this source of tactile contact may have some health value for this population, and this aspect should perhaps be studied more directly" (p. 223).

Physically Disabled Persons

AAT has been shown to be effective in increasing self-efficacy and self-confidence for the physically disabled (Tomaszewski, Jenkins, Rae, & Keller, 2001). Twenty-two adults with physical disabilities participated in a 12-week therapeutic horseback-riding program. The physical disabilities included were multiple sclerosis, closed head injury with concomitant physical impairments, spinal cord injury, cerebral palsy, and scoliosis. Comparisons of pretest and post-test scores demonstrated increased physical self-efficacy, as measured by The Physical Self-Efficacy Scale, and behavioral self-confidence, as measured by a behavioral rating scale. This study provided evidence in support of the psychological value of this type of intervention for adults with physical impairments. However, it is important to note that the behavioral rating scale was developed for the purposes of the study and has limited validity and reliability.

Psychiatric Patients

AAT has been demonstrated to be effective in increasing prosocial behaviors in psychiatric patients being treated for chemical dependency and abuse. An experimental versus control group comparison using a repeated measures analysis of variance was performed with 69 subjects in a psychiatric rehabilitation facility; subjects had a mental illness diagnosis as well as a history of chemical abuse or dependency (Marr et al., 2000). The most frequent diagnosis was schizophrenia (48%), bipolar disorder (27%), unspecified psychosis (18%), or depression (7%). By the fourth week of AAT, patients in the AAT group were significantly more interactive with other patients, scored higher on measures of smiles and pleasure, were more sociable and helpful with others, and were more active and responsive to surroundings. The experimental group and the control group were identical with the exception that the experimental group had animals visit each day for the entire group time. Both groups were designed to build a foundation that aids in the development and maintenance of coping skills necessary to resist social pressures to experiment with alcohol or street drugs or to initiate a recovery process if usage had already begun. The animals that participated included dogs, rabbits, ferrets, and guinea pigs. "Patients were allowed to observe the animals or interact with the animals — hold them, pet them, and/or play with them as long as they did not disrupt the group" (p. 44). Patients were not required to participate directly as participation was voluntary, however there was only one patient out of all the AAT subjects that elected to not interact directly with the animals.

Researchers evaluated, in a blind, controlled study, the effects of AAT in a closed psychogeriatric ward over 1 year. Participants were 10 elderly schizophrenic patients and 10 matched patients with a mean age of 79.1 years (Barak, Savorai, Mavashev, & Beni, 2001). AAT was conducted in weekly 3-hour sessions, and treatment encouraged mobility, interpersonal contact, and communication and reinforced activities for daily living, including personal hygiene and independent self-care, through the use of dogs and cats as modeling companions. AAT activities included petting, feeding, grooming, bathing, and walking the animals on a leash inside and outside the facility around the facility grounds. AAT patient participants were provided with their own dog or cat. Control-group patients were assembled for reading and discussion of current news for a similar duration on the same days that AAT was undertaken. Pretest and post-test comparisons on the Scale for Social Adaptive Functioning Evaluation were significantly better for the AAT group than the control group. The authors concluded that AAT proved to be a successful tool for enhancing socialization, activities of daily living, and general well-being for this population.

Conclusions

As demonstrated above, there is a variety of empirical research to support the psychophysiological and psychosocial benefits of AAT. However, after searching through AAT literature, I discovered that there has been much more written praising the benefits of AAT in counseling and related fields that is not grounded in research. An examination of AAT literature leaves one to conclude that there is a plethora of authors who extol the benefits of AAT, but there are currently relatively few empirical research studies that establish the clinical efficacy of utilizing therapy animals in counseling and related therapies.

> ... [O]n first glance it seems surprising that the potential benefits of therapeutic interventions incorporating non-human animals have not been more extensively researched and utilized. Reasons for such neglect possibly include the lack of available empirical evidence to support proposed benefits. A general bias against the value of non-human animal interactions for human psychological wellbeing may further explain the lack of empirical interest in the area. Thus, one bias perpetuates the other, as in: there are no empirical data so the relationship must not be important, and the relationship is only anecdotally supported so is probably not worthy of empirical investigation ... [A]nd given the enormous potential therapeutic benefits to be gained from the incorporation of non-human animals into therapeutic interventions, it is to the detriment or our science and practice that we continue to neglect such opportunities.
>
> (Fawcett & Gullone, 2001, p. 130–131)

Given the current dearth of empirical support for AAT, it is a responsibility for all AAT practitioners to strive to document clinical successes of their AAT program. If you lack the skills and resources to do this, you might try affiliating with a local college or university professor who has experience with research.

Chapter 3

Selecting an Animal for Therapy Work

Therapy Dogs	26
Selecting a Puppy for Therapy Work	29
Therapy Cats	30
Therapy Horses	31
Small Therapy Animals	31
Therapy Farm Animals	33

"Animals are such agreeable friends — they ask no questions, they pass no criticisms."

— George Eliot

A most important decision you will make as part of your AAT career is the selection of your pet therapist. Your hopes are high that your pet dog, cat, horse, and so forth will have the "right stuff" to be a pet practitioner, and beginning your career in AAT depends on it. However, you do not have to delay your own AAT training until you find the "right" pet. In fact, the earlier you start your own training in AAT, the better prepared you will be to select and train a pet for therapy work. Thus, I tell my students that they do not have to have a therapy pet before they take my training course. The training material provided creates a more in-depth understanding of what you will need from a therapy pet so you will be better able to judge a pet's appropriateness or preparedness for work in counseling.

If for some reason the pet you select does not work well as a therapy pet, then the news is still good. You still have a loving, cuddly family member. And, you can always try again with another pet. Like many of us animal lovers, I have many creatures around me, a fish aquarium, two cockatiels, a koi fish pond, an old house cat named Bandit, and my three family pets that work with me as certified professional pet practitioners, my cat Snowflake, my dog Rusty, and my dog Dolly. Like me, you may in fact end up with more than one therapy pet. Though having only one therapy pet can be quite sufficient for your work.

The most common pet practitioners in a counseling setting are dogs, followed closely by cats, horses, tame small animals such as rabbits and gerbils, and aquarium fish. Typically, reptiles are frowned upon in a therapy setting because of their high risk for carrying disease and causing injury to the client and because of the difficulty in providing proper care and a safe environment for the reptile. Farm animals are useful therapy animals, the most common of these being llamas and pot-bellied pigs. There are in fact certified therapy chickens, and there is now at least one certified therapy camel (L. Norvell, personal communication, November 6, 2004). Now let us look at some of these potential therapy animals a little more closely to help you with your therapy pet decision.

Therapy Dogs

There is no special breed of dog for work in a counseling setting. Some breeds are better known for their ease of training, friendliness toward people and other dogs, tendencies toward affection, calm temperament, desire and tolerance for high-energy activity, and so forth (Coile, 1998). However, any breed of dog or a mixed breed can be a great therapy dog if it meets the necessary criteria. In selecting a candidate for therapy work, it is not so much about the breed as it is the breeding. A dog bred from a line that has tendencies toward aggression, fear, hyperactivity, shyness, over sensitivity, and so forth increases the chances that it may inherit some of those negative traits that would make it inappropriate for therapy work. Knowing as much as possible about a dog's biological parents and even grandparents will make it easier to predict potential characteristics in a dog. However, even dogs born from the same litter can have different personalities.

A dog rescued from a shelter can find a new lease on life providing therapy services. If you are considering a dog rescued from a shelter, before you select it ask if the dog's temperament can be evaluated for its potential as a working therapy dog. Many shelters have this capacity or can point you to an animal evaluator or animal behavior specialist in your area. In the absence of a trained professional animal evaluator, your local veterinarian may be able to evaluate the dog's temperament and attitude. The reason it is vital to have the temperament of a shelter dog evaluated is the dog's history is usually unknown. Many shelter dogs were neglected or abused by previous owners, and this history may impair the dog's ability to work as a therapy dog. Another important thing to consider is that you get a dog that you feel a strong connection to because, after all, it is first and foremost a member of your family and you will have a relationship with it that potentially will last for many years.

There are some obvious characteristics you yourself can check for in a shelter animal to see if the animal will potentially make a good therapy pet. For instance, check to see if a shelter dog is hand shy by quickly moving a flat hand toward the dog's face and stopping about a foot from the dog's nose to see if the dog cowers away from your hand. Or wave your hand back and forth in front of the dog's face about a foot away from its nose. A dog that is afraid of quick hand movements is not a good candidate for a therapy dog. A test for sociability is to call the dog to you while standing up and see if it will come toward you. If the dog does not happily move toward you while you are standing or only moves toward you when you make yourself smaller by squatting down, then the dog is fearful and, again, not a good therapy dog candidate. Clap your hands loudly and see if the dog is afraid of loud noises coming from you; if it is then again it may not be a good candidate as a therapy dog. Dogs that are obviously aggressive, shy, or fearful are less likely to be good candidates for therapy work even with socialization and training.

My preference for a therapy dog is the American Cocker Spaniel because this is my favorite breed and I have had American Cocker Spaniels as pets for most of my adult life. Cocker Spaniels are known for their friendly and affectionate attitude. As a sporting breed, they have a history of being very intelligent and very trainable. They have a great deal of energy and are very playful. You might occasionally come across an atypical Cocker Spaniel with a bad attitude that would not be appropriate for therapy, but most Cocker Spaniels are very sweet and lovable.

A very common breed for a therapy dog is a Labrador Retriever. Labradors do not usually calm down until they are two to three years old but after that are typically calm dogs. As a sporting breed, Labradors are very intelligent and easily trained. This is why you see a large number of Labradors as service dogs for the disabled. Labradors are friendly and well mannered, and that makes them a popular choice as a therapy dog. They are also very strong dogs, quite hardy, and can cope well with stress. Golden Retrievers are also very popular as therapy dogs for many of the same reasons listed for Labradors.

As an animal evaluator, I have evaluated and passed a variety of dog breeds: Cocker Spaniel, Great Dane, Irish Wolfhound, Greyhound, Poodle (large and small), French Bulldog, Boxer, Basset Hound, Beagle, German Shepherd, Labrador Retriever, Golden Retriever, German Shorthair, Bichon Frise, Corgi, Sheltie, Border Collie, Dalmatian, Yorkshire Terrier, Lhasa Apso, Rhodesian Ridgeback, Australian Shepherd, King Charles Cavalier Spaniel, and many other breeds and a whole bunch of mixed breed dogs. Thus, there truly is no breed that is not potentially appropriate as a therapy dog.

The canine counselor must have the right temperament for therapy work. It must be affectionate, friendly, and sociable with persons of all ages and ethnicities and both genders. It must tolerate high levels of noise and activity. The dog must not be aggressive toward other dogs, and it is most helpful if the dog is friendly toward other dogs as well. The dog must be relatively calm. It is imperative that the dog be obedient and easy to control. A therapy dog needs to be comfortable with traveling in a car. It must be comfortable away from home when visiting unfamiliar places and greeting unfamiliar persons. And most important, the dog needs to have a fairly good tolerance to stress. Aggressive or fearful dogs are not appropriate for therapy work. Dogs that bark continuously are also not appropriate for therapy work.

Sometimes it is important to match a dog's personality with the population it is to work with. Most professional therapy dogs are versatile enough to serve just about any group; however, certain characteristics of the dog may suggest a better fit between the pet practitioner and a certain clientele. For example, a younger and more playful dog might be more appropriate for work with high-energy adolescents, whereas a more mature and calmer dog may be more appropriate with elderly clients or very small children.

There are a variety of advantages and disadvantages of working with a dog in therapy (Burch, 1996, 2003). One of the more favorable advantages is that most people really like dogs. Most dogs are very extroverted, friendly, and sociable and outwardly demonstrate their emotions, especially with their tails. It is easy to predict how a dog feels about being approached or interacted with because it tends not to hide its feelings. Thus, people can feel more comfortable being able to understand the animal's behavior when around them. Dogs enjoy engaging in activity with humans. Therapy dogs like just about everyone, so a client can feel immediate unconditional acceptance the moment they enter the counseling room. Dogs are a very trainable species. They can learn various obedience commands and fun tricks useful in therapy work. Except for the very small breeds, dogs don't get sick easily and are fairly sturdy, and this minimizes the risk of injury to them. Dogs can make and maintain good eye contact with people, and they are fun and playful. Dogs may remind clients of a dog they have or had at one time, and this may stimulate the sharing process.

There are potential disadvantages to working with a dog in therapy (Burch 1996, 2003). Some people are allergic to dogs. Some have the opinion that dogs belong outside in the yard. Dogs require a certain amount of grooming and training. Food and water must be made available to the dog as needed. Time must be taken to exercise the dog outside so it may relieve itself and stretch its muscles. You must pick up and properly dispose of excrement after a dog relieves itself. Some persons are afraid of dogs. Some facility staff members may be afraid of dogs. Some dogs have the potential to sometimes have behavior problems. Dogs have a shorter life span than humans and must be retired from therapy when age-related ailments create too much discomfort for the dog to get around. Thus a dog that you have relied on as your cotherapist can assist you at most for only about 10 years, or less, depending on the age of the dog when it began and the breed and health of the dog. The termination process with the client is more complicated as the client is most likely to miss the dog when treatment is complete.

Selecting a Puppy for Therapy Work

If you do not have a dog or your current family dog does not seem appropriate as a working dog, you may want to select a puppy that can grow up to work with you. A dog must be at least 1 year of age before it can work as a therapy dog. There is no guaranteeing what a dog will be like when it grows up. But there are ways to put the odds more in favor of it being a suitable dog for AAT. Get a puppy from a highly reputable breeder with many years of experience and who is familiar with the genetic line for several generations back of the puppy you are considering. If you get the opportunity, meet the canine mother and father of the puppy and examine whether they are friendly and sociable.

When you are shopping for a puppy, there are certain tasks you can present to a puppy to test the puppy's temperament and social capacity. Puppy testing has several versions today, but a brief version consists of five basic exercises that all together take only about 20 or 30 minutes. The puppy test can be performed on a puppy that is as young as 7 weeks old (49 days). The puppies should have some identifying characteristic or different colored collar or bow tie so that you can tell them apart and make notes in your head or on paper. The first exercise is to observe the puppy as it interacts with the other pups in the litter. You are looking for a pup that plays well with others; one that seeks interaction with the other pups in the litter but is neither overly rough and aggressive nor overly submissive and fearful.

The remaining four tasks involve seeing the puppies one at a time in an area large enough for you to play and interact with each puppy but out of sight and sound of other dogs, if possible. There are two tasks to determine if the puppy is sociable. See if the puppy comes to you when you clap your hands and call it to you. As it walks away, call it back again. A puppy that comes back to you again and again is a pup that seeks and enjoys social interaction. Another exercise for social interaction as well as affection is to see how the puppy responds to you when you hold it and play with it. A puppy that seeks to cuddle next to you or lick your face and likes to be near you and held by you is an affectionate puppy. This is a fine quality in a therapy dog. A puppy that does not like to be held and does not care to play with you is not a good therapy dog candidate.

The next exercise is a test for dominance, a characteristic not good for a therapy dog. Gently place the puppy on its back and pet its chest for just a moment. The longer it stays on its back willingly, the more likely it will have a personality that will submit to your will. A puppy that immediately fights to turn back over is a willful pup that may try to boss you around. A bossy dog does not make a good therapy dog. The next exercise is a test for fearfulness. Take a soda can and put a few pebbles or pennies in it and tape up the top. This device should make a nice, loud sound when you rattle it. Gently toss the noisemaker about 2 or 3 feet from the puppy, being careful not to get too close to the puppy or to hit it with the can. It is natural and normal for the puppy to be startled by the loud object and jump a few feet away. What you are looking for is a puppy that recovers quickly from the startle and then walks back close to the can or sniffs it out of curiosity. This type of reaction demonstrates a dog that is not overly fearful and deals well with the unexpected. On the other hand, if after you toss the noisemaker the puppy runs away or will not approach the can, you may have a pup that does not deal well with surprises. These five basic exercises can tell you a great deal about a puppy even if the puppy is only 7 weeks old.

For a more professional approach to puppy testing, Clothier (1996) has written a booklet, *Understanding Puppy Testing*, with standardized guidelines and exercises. She recommends that the puppy be tested no earlier than 49 days and no later than 10 weeks after birth. The tester should be someone who is not familiar to the puppies. The test should be performed at a location that is unfamiliar to the puppies and as free of distractions as possible. The test should be performed out of sight and sound of littermates, other dogs, and other people. If the results of the test are inconclusive, the puppy can be retested at 24 to 48 hours later. The exercises Clothier suggests are briefly described as:

- Social attraction — determine the pup's willingness to approach a stranger
- Following — examine the pup's posture and behavior when getting it to follow you
- Elevation — determine the pup's response to being held off the ground with all feet off the floor
- Restraint — test the pup's willingness to be held
- Social dominance — test the pup's willingness to be placed in and maintain a subordinate position on its side or back
- Retrieve — test the pup's willingness to work with a human by engaging in a fetch game
- Sound sensitivity — evaluate the pup's response to a sudden sharp noise (such as banging a metal dog dish against a concrete floor about 6 to 10 feet from the pup and looking for a quick recovery by the pup after the initial normal startle response)
- Sight sensitivity — test the pup's reaction to a sudden visual stimuli (such as quickly opening an umbrella near the pup and looking for a quick recovery by the pup after the initial normal startle response)
- Stability — test the pup's reaction to a large, unstable and unfamiliar object (such as rolling a chair by a few feet away from the pup)
- Touch sensitivity — test the pup's response to unpleasant physical stimuli by gently squeezing the webbing between the pup's toes
- Energy levels — observe the pup's energy level from the moment all testing begins

Therapy Cats

There is no particular breed of cat that is preferred for therapy. To be a feline facilitator in a counseling setting, a therapy cat must be calm and well mannered. It must have a relatively high tolerance for stress. It must feel comfortable with greeting unfamiliar people. It does not need to know any basic obedience commands. But it must be willing to sit quietly in a lap while being petted even by someone it meets for the first time.

There are some advantages and disadvantages to working with a cat in a counseling setting (Burch, 1996, 2003). Many people prefer cats to other therapy animals because of their personalities. Cats are smaller and less threatening, so most people are not afraid of cats. Cats are active and playful, therefore entertaining to play with and watch. A lap cat provides nurturing and affection. Cats will lie in a lap and provide companionship for long periods of time without requiring activity. Shorthaired cats do not require as much grooming as dogs but longhaired cats may. Cats may remind clients of a cat they have or had at one time and this may stimulate the sharing process.

A common disadvantage to working with a therapy cat is that many persons are allergic to cats. Cats can be trained but are not as trainable as dogs and cannot perform a wide range of skills. Cats can be more introverted and may require more breaks or quiet time. Food and water must be accessible to the cat as needed. A cat needs a litter box to relieve itself. Though cats require less care than a dog, they do require more care than small confined therapy animals, such as hamsters or aquarium fish. And some cats can have some behavior problems.

Therapy Horses

Therapy work is most often a second career for a horse. Horses of good temperament and that are still in good health after retiring from their first career are commonly donated to work at equestrian therapy centers. For a helping horse to work in a counseling setting it must be well trained, calm, and friendly toward people and other horses. A therapy horse must not startle easily to noises or unfamiliar objects.

There can be both advantages and disadvantages to working with a horse in a counseling setting (Burch 1996, 2003). A common advantage is that most people love horses but have no or too little occasion to interact with them. The opportunity to be around or work with a horse can be a very motivating force for participation and cooperation. The client can gain self-confidence from being able to control such a large and powerful animal. Horses are very trainable. Horses are sturdy and durable. Because you can ride a horse, horses provide opportunities for clients to work on skills in a way not possible with other animals.

A disadvantage to working with a horse in a counseling setting is that a good therapy horse that fits all the necessary temperament and health requirements is often hard to find. Some clients may be afraid of horses. Some family members of clients may be nervous about the client getting near or on such a big animal. Some people are allergic to horses. A large space is required to work with a therapy horse. A great deal of manure cleanup is required. Client transportation to the facility where the therapy horse is located may be a problem. For safety of the rider, work with a therapy horse usually requires a counseling team as opposed to just the one handler; other team members may serve as side-walkers or may be needed to lead the horse while the rider is in the saddle. Special equipment is required in working with a therapy horse. Horses require a great deal of time and expensive care. The potential injury from working with a therapy horse could be more severe than an injury incurred from working with a cat or dog (Burch 1996, 2003).

Small Therapy Animals

Small therapy animals include rabbits, pocket pets such as gerbils and hamsters, certain birds, and aquarium fish. These petite pet practitioners are very common in school classrooms but can also be very therapeutic in a counselor's office. A counselor who wishes to work with a small therapy animal must insure that the animal is tame

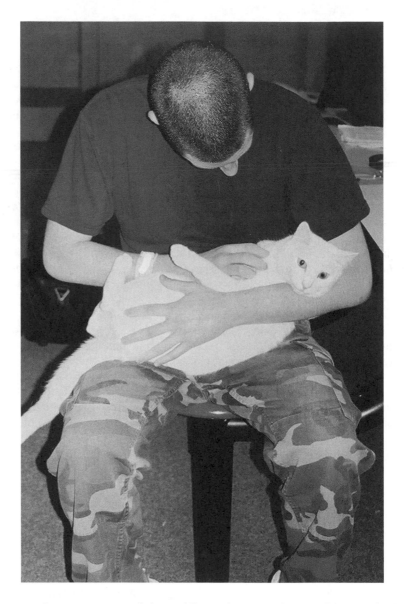

Figure 3.1 Therapy cat Snowflake cuddles with a juvenile in a detention facility: An empathy enhancement exercise for the juvenile.

and free of disease. It is best to acquire such an animal from a pet store that can guarantee its stock is from a reputable source. A small therapy animal must be comfortable being picked up and handled, with the exception of aquarium fish of course. As with other therapy animals, the small therapy animal must be relatively calm and have a good tolerance for stress.

There are certain advantages and disadvantages to working with a small therapy animal in a counseling setting (Burch, 1996, 2003). A very favorable advantage is that small animals are kept in and presented in cages or small baskets and thus do not move around much. Small therapy animals are easier to transport. They are easier and smaller to handle compared to other therapy animals. They often require less care and attention than other therapy animals. Smaller animals are less expensive to purchase and care for. Small animals are especially good for a more subdued or passive approach to therapy. It is practical to have more than one small therapy animal since they take up little space and require less care. Small therapy animals are different from the more common cat or dog and thus very interesting to work with.

A key disadvantage to working with small therapy animals is that they are more fragile and susceptible to injury. Small therapy animals cannot be handled as readily as the larger and sturdier therapy animals. Small therapy animals are not as tolerant of stress as the larger therapy animals. Most small therapy animals, with the exception of some birds, do not have very long life spans. Smaller therapy animals cannot be trained as easily as dogs, cats, or horses. Small therapy animals are not as affectionate as dogs, cats, or horses. Small therapy animals are typically not as responsive to interactions with humans as are dogs, cats, and horses (Burch 1996, 2003).

Therapy Farm Animals

A counseling setting that incorporates farm animal facilitators typically involves a working therapy farm. However, there are exceptions to this, such as a family pet potbellied pig or a pet llama. Pot-bellied pigs are very smart and easy to train. Pigs can learn obedience commands and do fun pet tricks and be taught to use a litter box or a doggy door. Any farm animal is appropriate for therapy as long as it is healthy and not aggressive.

There are some advantages as well as disadvantages to working with farm animals for counseling work (Burch, 1996, 2003). One major advantage is that most people do not have much opportunity to interact with farm animals so they hold one's attention. Farm animals can give a client a sense of competence when working on a farm. Farm tasks lend a sense of accomplishment, and many farm tasks can teach vocational skills. Farm animals do not require intense interaction like dogs do. Farm animals are fun to be around with all of their funny noises and shapes. Farm therapy animals do not require training.

A major disadvantage to choosing to work with farm animals in a counseling setting is that working therapy farms are hard to find. Transportation of a client to a working therapy farm can be problematic. Or, if you own a farm animal as a pet it may be difficult to transport that farm animal to the counseling setting. Most farm animals are large, and injuries incurred from interaction with a therapy farm animal can be more severe compared to smaller therapy animals like dogs or cats. Farm animals are difficult to train and are more unpredictable. Work with therapy farm animals usually requires an adequate number of trained staff members. A person has to be willing to get dirty when working with a therapy farm animal (Burch 1996, 2003).

Chapter 4

Training a Pet for Therapy Work

Socialization   36
Touch Desensitization   39
Obedience Training   40
Teaching Special Skills and Trick Training   43

"There are two means of refuge from the misery of life — music and cats."
— Albert Schweitzer

The animals we choose to work with are first and foremost our beloved pets and family members. It is our obligation to insure their happiness, their safety, and their health. This requires provision of proper nurturance, nutrition, socialization, preventative as well as reactive health care, recreation and physical exercise, and positive training techniques. In addition, there are areas that require attention if your pet is to be a working animal in AAT. This chapter delineates the training process you need to perform with your therapy pet to prepare it for therapy work.

The training a therapy pet needs to work in AAT requires proper socialization, touch desensitization, basic obedience, and, ideally, some special skills and trick training. It is a common misconception that AAT workshop or course training involves animal training, when in fact the AAT courses and workshops offered are specifically designed to train the human, not the pet. The pet's training is performed by the pet's owner. While workshops and courses are useful in explaining what type of training the pet requires, it is up to the owner to train the animal. This is why most AAT workshops and courses ask participants to not bring their animal to the AAT workshop or training course.

The training of a pet by the pet's owner for therapy work is really not much different than the training that any pet should receive to be a well-behaved citizen of the community. Even special skills and tricks that are helpful for a therapy pet to know to enhance AAT work are simple commands easily taught by the pet's owner. AAT pets do not require the highly structured and standardized training regime that service animals require. Training a pet for AAT work is a relatively simple process. But make no mistake, proper training for a pet that is to be a pet practitioner is vitally important.

Socialization

Any pet that is going to go out and work in the community needs to be well mannered. The best way to provide for this is to socialize the pet, that is, to expose it to a variety of stimuli starting early in the pet's life while it is still very young. The pet should meet and be petted by a number of different types of persons varying in age range, ethnicity, ability/disability, and both genders. Include those that the pet is not familiar with, that is, persons other than just family members or friends. The pet should be taken out into the community to meet and greet lots of different folks. A pet that stays at home most of the time is not going to be comfortable meeting people when away from home. The pet should be exposed to a variety of different types of clothing and accessories that people may wear or accompany, for instance, hats, backpacks, briefcases, purses, crutches, canes, walkers, wheelchairs, and so forth. The pet should become comfortable with being transported, such as riding in the car. Start by going short distances at first and then gradually extend the time and distance of the trip until the pet is very comfortable with travel.

When I get a new puppy, I spend a few minutes several times a week training my dog to get into the car and go for a ride. If the pup is still too small to get in by itself, then I gently lift it into the car. I use lots of praise and, in the beginning, some very small dog treats. My dogs travel in a crate secured in the back of the car or sometimes they sit in the back seat wearing a canine seat belt. Rusty never had a problem with riding in the car and to this day still runs to the car with exuberance when I suggest a trip. However, Dolly experienced really bad carsickness when she was a puppy. So she had to be medicated with prescription medication for motion sickness at least 1 hour before any car trip and hand carried to the car against her will. It was important that I never got angry with her at these times and that I provided as much loving assurance as possible during her carsickness episodes. I also had to carry material to clean up an almost certain mess when the medicine did not work as well as it should. At about 6 months of age, Dolly grew out of being carsick but she had a very good memory of it. So I had to continue to hand carry her to the car and give loving reassurance during the trips. By the age of 9 months, Dolly's behavior began to change and she began following Rusty to the car of her own free will, albeit without his enthusiasm. Her behavior suggested that she was feeling, "Okay, I want to go on a trip with Rusty and my mom, but I am not really excited about having to go in a moving vehicle." Finally, at 11 months of age Dolly began happily trotting to the car behind Rusty when I suggested a trip.

If you have more than one pet, such as two dogs, practice taking the dogs out separately at times so the dogs become comfortable spending time away from one another. I evaluated a handler who was shocked to see her normally confident, friendly, and outgoing Labrador Retriever act very shy and afraid during the evaluation. The dog was so frightened when just walking around the evaluation room beforehand that I chose not to begin the formal evaluation test. In a discussion with the handler, it was revealed that this was the first time this dog had ever gone anywhere without the family's other Labrador Retriever. The dog showed confidence and friendliness when out and about in the community with the family's other dog, but without the company of his familiar companion, this dog was very frightened. I recommended the handler spend time taking each dog out separately sometimes so the dogs could become comfortable with being apart from one another, and then when she thought he was ready, she could bring the dog for another evaluation.

The potential pet practitioner should be exposed to different types of places with a variety of activity and noises. Pet stores, hardware stores, and garden stores usually allow you to bring your pet inside. In the pet store, walk by the birdcages and aquariums and by any other animals so you can expose the pet to a variety of species. Make sure your pet does not upset the pet store stock however. In a hardware store and nursery, be careful not to allow the pet to consume any poisonous or hazardous material. Walk the pet around large moving equipment and loud noises, such as loud saws cutting lumber and construction equipment, while keeping a safe distance.

When Rusty was less than a year old, we would go walking in a city park that was being relandscaped by large, noisy bulldozers and big hauling trucks. I walked Rusty in the safe area of the park but only about 15 yards from the equipment. I watched him carefully to make sure he was not being stressed out by the loud noises. If he had been, I would have done the training at a further distance to start and gradually moved in closer as his comfort level allowed. I also walked Rusty several times near a construction site on the campus where I work where large, looming cranes were lifting steel beams and sections of concrete wall into place. This type of training really paid off. Rusty remains calm around large and loud vehicles including motorcycles, large trucks, buses, and speeding fire trucks and ambulances with their sirens blaring. This type of exposure is imperative for your pet if you ever want to provide animal assisted counseling services in response to a crisis, disaster, or other emergency situation.

It is important for a dog to be comfortable around other dogs. Give your puppy many opportunities to play with other friendly dogs of various sizes in the neighborhood or in a dog park to allow for adequate social interaction with other dogs. Be careful that your puppy has the necessary vaccinations before exposing them to unfamiliar dogs. It is also important that a dog be exposed at an early age to other types of animals such as cats, horses, and farm animals. Both Rusty and Dolly are comfortable around cats since they were raised around two playful cats at home. I was fortunate that this transferred to their behavior of showing only a polite, casual interest toward cats they see away from home or on therapy visits.

When Dolly was 6 months old, I received permission to take her with me to an equine therapy center where I occasionally volunteer. I made special trips out there just for the purpose of exposing her a little at a time. The first visit to the ranch was only 15 minutes long so as to not overstress Dolly. I started with a large, well trained, friendly, and calm horse that was in a small corral. I kept Dolly on a leash and we stayed outside of the corral. We started about 25 feet away, and we approached the corralled horse gradually until Dolly began to show some visible signs of discomfort, such as slowed walking, hesitation, looking away from the horse or back at me, growling, and barking. I would pet and reassure Dolly and then we would casually walk away to a distance where she acted more comfortable. We gradually approached the horse in the same way two more times and then moved on. We used the same technique with the other ranch critters: miniature horses, goats, sheep, a donkey, a mule, pigs, rabbits, chickens, and ducks. The next visit, I followed the same regime but spent a little more time with each animal. Each time we visited the ranch critters, Dolly showed fewer signs of discomfort and we could walk closer to the animal. By the fourth visit, Dolly could be led within only a few feet of each of the ranch critters with no visible signs of discomfort and showing no more than casual interest in each. Dolly is a small dog of only 22 pounds, and so I watch her carefully when she goes to the ranch with me so as to prevent injury to her. She is very comfortable with the horses and even touches noses with them. Dolly really enjoys her visits to the ranch, and I enjoy having her out there with me. The teens that receive therapy services at the ranch nicknamed her "Daring Dolly" because of her fearless nature around the large horses. We hear the occasional comment from the kids that are initially afraid to get near the horses, "If Dolly can do it, then I can," followed by their moving over close to pet the horse. During the group process portion of the therapy at the horse ranch, an adolescent seems to be comforted when they hold and pet Dolly while sharing feelings. I am glad Dolly has been socialized to go just about anywhere with me because her therapeutic skills come in very handy for a variety of AAT settings. Dolly is a very versatile therapy dog, getting along with every person and every creature she meets, with the exception of squirrels, which she chases from tree to tree in our backyard.

It is important to socialize a therapy animal in the setting in which the animal is going to work. Several practice sessions of therapy with various volunteers of different ages playing the role of a client with you working as a therapist and your pet as a pet practitioner in the actual therapy room may be very helpful in assimilating the pet into the therapeutic environment. The volunteers who pretend to be a client for you should be relatively unknown to the therapy animal. With this practice, the therapy session experience becomes familiar and comfortable to the pet.

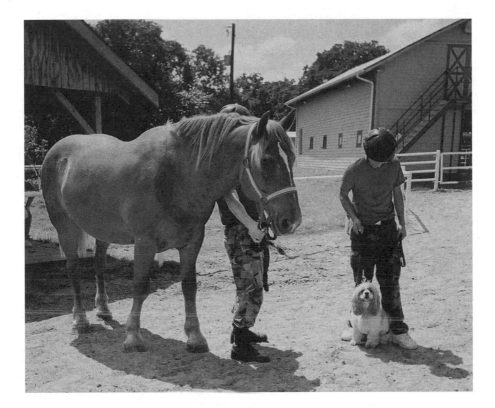

Figure 4.1 Therapy dog Dolly has been socialized and trained to work around many types of ranch and farm animals. Brave little Dolly is a role model for juveniles who are at first afraid of the big horses.

The more familiar a pet is with a particular atmosphere and routine, the more comfortable it will be in that situation while working.

Touch Desensitization

From the time the pet is very young, it should be handled gently and frequently. It is important for a young pet to become desensitized to human touch so that it may be handled by you and by unfamiliar persons. A good approach for this is to incorporate a daily massage into the pet's routine care. This gives you and the young pet some special time together for bonding and trust building while at the same time teaching the pet that it is safe to be touched by humans. Massaging your pet also has added health benefits for it.

One animal massage technique was designed specifically for touch desensitization training and was taught to me by an obedience trainer that was working with me when I was training Dolly. It is described as follows: When massaging your pet, position yourself and your pet on the floor or on a couch and make sure the pet is comfortable and well supported so it feels safe enough to relax. Make sure you have good back support yourself so you are comfortable during the exercise. Gently and slowly massage all parts of the pet's body by making small circles on the surface of the skin with the tips of your fingers. For dogs and cats, massage the mouth, the head, ears, neck, shoulders, torso, hips, legs, paws, toes, chest, stomach and tail. For the ears, start at the base of the ear and make gentle kneading motions all the way out to the tips. Some animal behaviorists have said that the quickest way to calm a dog is to rub its ears in this manner. During the pet's massage, use a simple calming word or phrase that the animal can associate with relaxing. As you massage say in a calm quiet voice, "just relax." This same phrase can come in handy at other times when you want or need the animal to relax. Even if your pet is tense the first few times you try the massage, it will gradually get used to the routine and respond more positively each time you do it. It is important for you to be relaxed while doing the pet's massage, otherwise the animal may pick up on your tension and this would prevent the pet from relaxing. I still use this massage technique with my pets, who actually come to me in the evening one at a time at their own initiation while I am watching television and position themselves in front of me in my lap waiting for their massage to begin. Frequent massage for my pets also helps to alleviate the stress that may build up in their bodies.

From the time Dolly was a puppy, she was uncomfortable with anyone touching her tail and she would pull away and sometimes even growl if you did so. Her dislike got worse as she grew older. It was going to be very important that she get over this if she were going to be a candidate as a therapy dog. Incorporating the touch desensitization massage technique with a relaxing anchor phrase, "just relax," eventually desensitized Dolly to having her tail touched by the time she was several months old. Now Dolly is comfortable with being touched all over her body, even by persons she is not familiar with. I have also used the anchor phrase, "just relax," when the veterinarian needed my dog to lie still for a procedure or when I needed to calm my dog.

Obedience Training

Every therapy animal must be well mannered, but horses and dogs require special training. Horses must be trained for riding, and dogs must be trained in basic obedience. At a minimum, a therapy dog must be able to respond to the commands of sit, down (lie down), stay in place, come when called, and walk politely on a leash. Obedience training can begin when the dog is just a few months old in a low-stress puppy class. As the dog gets older, it can take basic obedience and even advanced obedience. The dog must be able to perform obedience commands at home and away from home in the presence of many distractions. Check with your local pet store or veterinarian for an obedience-training group near you. I will warn you that some of the pet store sponsored obedience trainers have many years of dog training experience, but some have only a few months of experience. Check the background and experience of your dog trainer, and only use those who have several years of training experience and that come highly recommended by persons you trust. Group obedience training is preferable to individual obedience training because the addition of the other dogs is good for socialization of your animal and effective training around distractions. Also, I highly recommend that you work with your dog in the obedience classes, in other words, do not send your dog away to dog school to be trained by someone else. The high level of mutual communication and understanding that you and your dog form during the shared obedience training process is priceless and will serve much better when you and your dog work together as cotherapists. A good obedience trainer will teach you what you need to know to train your dog; however, my many years of training and working with dogs has provided me with some additional tips that I would like to share with you.

You will need to practice a great many times with your dog all of the commands you learn in group obedience class. Practice at home, in the park, in the pet store, and so forth, so the dog learns to generalize its training outside of the obedience class. Use only positive training methods when training your dog. Positive training methods include lots of praise and treats. Treats can be the reward of a favorite toy after the dog has completed a command and is released by you from that command, or treats can be very small food pieces that are healthy and nonfattening, given to the dog after the completion of a command. Training must be fun for your dog and for you. During a training session, never get angry or frustrated with your animal. Also, never yell at your dog or hit your dog. Use encouraging techniques. Be patient, kind, and understanding. Your dog will eventually learn if you are dedicated to working with it and you maintain a positive attitude during the training. Dogs are very intelligent and will look forward to training sessions when you make it a fun and playful experience.

When training your dog, teach it to respond to both verbal commands and hand signals. Hand signals are especially useful when you and your dog are working in a loud area or when you need to command your dog from a distance. You can design your own hand signals or have an obedience trainer teach you some common hand signals used by trainers in the field. Hand signals can be associated with any number of verbal commands, but the most common hand signals are taught for the commands of sit, down, stay, come, wait, heel, let's go, and get back (sit close to me at my side).

When you want your dog to stop what it is doing, such as barking, or you want to teach a young pup not to bite, then you should attach a command name to the word "no," such as, "no bark" or "no bite." If you simply say "no" all of the time without differentiating between behaviors, the dog may not understand what you want from it. Also, be careful to not use the same word for different intentions. For example, you should not use the word "down" for both a lie down command and to tell the dog to get off the furniture or to stop jumping up on a person. I use "down" for the lie down command and the word "off" to mean get off of something or stop jumping up on someone. You will need a correction command for obedience training, but I recommend you not use "no" as an obedience training correction command because too frequent use of the word "no" in training could dilute its usefulness when you really need it to mean other things. Instead of using the word "no" when a dog fails to fulfill a training command, use a negative vocalization sound; if the dog is supposed to be in a "stay" position and it starts to get up and walk, then you can use the negative vocalization sound that the dog comes to understand to mean "Oops, I better not do that." For example, if my dog has been told to "sit" and "stay" and she starts to get up and move without my permission, then I make a loud sound deep in my throat that sounds like "Eh, eh." From training, she has learned that this means to stop her intended behavior and remain with what she was doing before. By having "Eh, eh" as a useful and commonly used training correction sound, the use of the word "no," such as in "no bark," is reserved for meaning other more direct behavior cessation.

When practicing obedience or other types of training with your dog outside of obedience class, keep your training sessions to only 10 minutes or at the most 15 minutes with a built in break in the middle. You can have up to two short training periods per day with your pet. A minimum of one short training period per day is recommended for at least 5 days a week, though 7 days a week is better. A dog's attention span is short, and it will start to lose interest in training after just a few minutes. Positive reinforcement with food rewards, praise rewards, and interspersed playtime with the dog's favorite toy will help keep the dog's interest in training. You will have to repeat training each exercise many times before a dog learns it well enough to retain it. Some dogs learn faster than others, especially working breeds and sporting breeds. But any dog can learn obedience if you spend the time and effort necessary to train it and you make it a fun and enjoyable experience for the dog.

As you will learn in your basic obedience class, animal training requires trial and error training with you rewarding any behavior that slightly resembles the ultimate behavior goal you are striving for. For instance, when training a dog to shake hands, you first make sure the dog knows you have a treat, such as a favorite toy or a small morsel of food, in your hand so the dog is interested in what you are doing and motivated to get that treat. Then you can start with touching the dog's paw and say "shake." The dog will have no idea what you want so you will have to repeat the action. The dog will start getting excited because it wants the treat and it will eventually move its paw accidentally in its excitement, even though it may have only moved its paw ever so slightly. But you immediately reward the dog because it moved its paw. You reward the dog by giving it a morsel of food or toy to play with as soon as the desired behavior is achieved. Pair the treat reward with the phrase "good dog" and give the dog a friendly rub on the head or shoulder. Then you keep touching the paw and say, "shake" until the dog moves the paw even more. Repeat this command, dog movement, and reward-the-dog interaction until the dog starts to consistently move the paw and even starts to raise the paw from the ground. So now you get the idea, you are gradually shaping the dog's behavior until it finally completes the task that you intend for it to complete. With continued praise and reward, you gradually shape the animal's behavior in the direction you want it to go until it successfully completes the command or trick you are trying to teach it. Then you continue to reward it for the completed trick or command. When the trick or command is new to the animal, it may have forgotten it somewhat the next day. Thus, you may have to reshape the animal's behavior again until it once again successfully completes the command or trick. In my experience with my American Cocker Spaniels, it takes about 2 to 3 days of brief training sessions twice a day to be able to successfully complete a newly learned trick upon my first request without the dog having to work up to it. And it takes about 2 to 3 consecutive weeks of everyday practice, in 5- to 10-minute periods twice a day, before they thoroughly retain the newly learned command or trick. By always pairing the treat reward with praise, such as saying the words "good dog" and providing a friendly rub on the head or shoulder, the dog will eventually be willing to do the trick or command without the expectation of a treat and instead will do it for the gratitude expressed by you in the form of praise. Thereafter, only occasional practice of the trick or command with treats will be required to keep the animal's interest in maintaining the skill. Animal training is a lot of fun, but it does take time and patience. It is very rewarding for both you and your animal, so you will find it a very fulfilling accomplishment and the time it takes well-spent quality time with your animal.

When teaching a dog to perform a new command or a new trick, you may have to gently guide the dog into position the first few times to help it understand what you mean. For example, when training my dog to "sit," I put a treat in my hand in a closed fist and move my hand over the dog's head from nose to neck just inches above the head and the dog follows the treat with its nose and has to sit to keep looking at it as it passes backward. As soon as the dog sits I say, "sit." Then I immediately reward the dog with the treat and say "good dog" and pet it. Then I repeat the exercise. This is a natural way to train your dog. Sometimes you may have to gently fold the dog's legs beneath it in a sit position while saying "sit" to get the dog to perform the task. Since you need to repeat the exercise many times during training, you want to give tiny pieces of a treat so the dog does not get filled up fast. Also, train before the dog's mealtime so it is motivated to work for the treat.

Another training tip is to teach the dog commands separately and practice them with breaks in between different types of commands. For example, practice a "sit" with your dog, praising and rewarding after each successful try. Then take a brief 60-second play break and practice "down." Then a brief play break and practice "stay." Then a brief play break and practice "come." This helps the dog to learn the commands separately and not fuse them together. If you always practice "sit" then immediately tell the dog "down" it may start lying down before you tell it to because it anticipates what is coming next. Or, if you always practice "stay" and then walk away and tell your dog to "come," the dog may start breaking the "stay" prematurely because it anticipates that you will always call it to you soon after you say "stay." So, "stay" has to be practiced separately from "come" many times so the dog learns each as a separate command.

Even though you intend to enroll in obedience class with your dog, it is important to supplement your dog training education with some selective reading. A good dog-training book is *Mother Knows Best: The Natural Way to Train Your Dog* by Carol Benjamin (1985). This book teaches you to communicate with and train your dog in ways that are more natural for the dog to comprehend. The training approach is positive and nurturing as well as effective. The book discusses housebreaking, crate training, leash training, and all of the basic obedience tasks. Another basic training book I recommend is *The Canine Good Citizen: Every Dog Can Be One* by Jack and Wendy Volhard (1997). The book is designed to help you train your dog to be a well-mannered dog and to pass the Canine Good Citizen Test sponsored by the American Kennel Club. These positive training books will help you avoid making those mistakes that can make for a frustrating experience for both you and your dog. Positive training methods make the time training your dog very enjoyable and an experience that enhances the level of trust and communication between you and your canine.

Teaching Special Skills and Trick Training

It can be beneficial to teach your dog or cat some special skills and tricks that can come in handy in a therapeutic setting (Burch, 2003). In addition to basic obedience, special skills that are helpful for a therapy dog to know include:

- "Leave it." A command for the dog to ignore food or some other object on the floor
- "Take it." To gently take an object you hand to the dog

- "Drop it." To drop an object the dog is carrying
- "Hug." To be receptive to getting a hug
- "Say hello." To approach and greet someone you point to or are facing
- "Up." To jump up on top of a sturdy surface you point to
- "Off." To get off of something or jump down from a higher surface
- "Kennel." To go into a crate or kennel
- "Place." To go to a designated mat or bed and lie down and be quiet
- "Stand." To stand up on all four feet
- "Paws up." To reach up and place the front paws on a designated surface, e.g., the edge of a sturdy chair or bed
- "Heel." To walk close in at your left side and at exactly your pace
- "Wait." To wait in the same place and position until you give another command. This is especially helpful when going through doors or waiting at a street curb for traffic to pass
- "Let's go." Tells the dog to come with you
- "Release." To be released from an existing command and to relax at ease
- "Watch." To look at you and be attentive and get ready for another command
- "Get back." Tells the dog to move in close to your left side and face the direction you are facing and sit down and be quiet. This prepares the dog for when you start walking with a let's go or heel command
- "Do it." To relieve itself or go potty on command (if it needs to)

Some fun tricks to teach a therapy dog are:

- "Shake." Shake hands
- "High five." While sitting, slap its paw up in the air against your palm
- "Kiss." Give kisses on command
- "Sit pretty." Sit back on its haunches with its front paws in the air
- "Over." Roll over
- "Dead" or "Bang." Roll over on its back and play dead
- "Crawl." Crawl along the floor on its belly
- "Fetch." Fetch a ball, Frisbee, or other object
- "Catch." Catch a ball, Frisbee, or other appropriate object
- "Through." Jump through a hoop
- "Jump." Jump over an object
- "Speak." Vocalize a sound such as a bark
- "Find it." Find an object that was shown to the dog (and that the dog was allowed to smell) and then hidden for the dog to find

There are several good dog trick training books in the field, but some I have found useful are, *The Trick Is in the Training: 25 Fun Tricks to Teach Your Dog* by Stephanie Taunton and Cheryl Smith and *Dog Tricks: Step by Step* by Mary Ann Rombold Zeigenfuse and Jan Walker.

My dog Rusty just loves to train. He will train until I tire out. As a result, he knows most of the above tricks and a few more to boot. He will jump high in the air and do a 360° twist and land back on his feet. He will go either direction depending on your hand motion. If you hold a ball or Frisbee at the apex of the jump he will grasp it in the middle of his twist and come back down with it. Likewise, he is very good at catching a ball and Frisbee in the air, and he chooses to do so most of the time by

Figure 4.2 Therapy dog Rusty patiently waits for a ball to be tossed by a juvenile in a detention facility. Juveniles look forward to their time with a therapy pet.

doing a half twist in the air and catching the ball or Frisbee over his shoulder. As you can probably guess, clients who engage in play with Rusty get a big kick out of watching Rusty perform his acrobatics. This type of activity is more common for herding dogs, such as border collies, and to see a chunky fur ball like an American Cocker Spaniel perform it is very entertaining.

While a therapy cat is not required to know basic obedience commands of any kind, it can be helpful if the cat knows some special skills. Some special skills that are helpful for a therapy cat to have include:

- Walk on a leash attached to a harness
- Travel quietly in the car
- Be comfortable in a crate or kennel

Figure 4.3 Rusty launches himself to intercept a ball tossed by a juvenile in a detention facility. Juveniles are motivated to participate in therapy for the opportunity to spend time playing with a therapy pet.

- Tolerate being held and petted by unfamiliar persons
- Sit or lie quietly in a lap for prolonged periods of time
- Sit or lie quietly next to someone while being petted
- Tolerate being in a crowd of people

- Play with a toy during therapy
- Go to see another person when called
- Tolerate being hugged
- Tolerate being brushed
- Give kisses on command
- Retrieve a toy
- Get off of something on command
- Respond to the "no" command

It is also possible to teach a cat a few fun tricks if you are the patient type.

Chapter 5

Evaluation of a Pet for Therapy Work

American Kennel Club Canine Good Citizen Test   50
TDI Testing Requirements   51
Delta Society Pet Partners Evaluation   51
Pet Partners Aptitude Test   52
Pet Partners Skills Test   52
Tuskegee Behavior Test   54

"The best thing about animals is that they don't talk much."
— Thornton Wilder

An animal must successfully complete a standardized evaluation before working in a therapy setting. Dogs and cats must be at least 1 year old before they can be evaluated. Other species can be evaluated once they reach maturity, whatever age that may be for that animal. There is more than one model for evaluating the fitness of a pet for therapy work. Four well-known models are reviewed here. These models can be adapted to apply to most species; however, for standardized evaluation of a horse for therapy I refer you to the organizations NARHA (2003) and EAGALA (2003); contact information is provided in the reference section at the end of the book.

American Kennel Club Canine Good Citizen Test

The American Kennel Club (AKC) evaluation is referred to as the Canine Good Citizen Test (CGC) and can be used to evaluate dogs for good behavior and temperament. The AKC CGC was first introduced in 1989 "to ensure that our favorite companion, the dog, can be a respected member of the community" (American Kennel Club [AKC], 2003, p.1). The CGC emphasizes the importance of training a dog to be well behaved and under control at all times even if just a family pet. The CGC consists of 10 exercises. During all 10 exercises, the dog must be obedient and under control of its handler (typically its owner) as well as friendly and cooperative with the evaluator and not show aggression, shyness, or fear. The exercises are:

- Accepting a friendly stranger. The dog allows a stranger to approach its handler and shake hands with the handler.
- Sitting politely for petting. The dog sits quietly while being petted by a stranger.
- Appearance and grooming. The dog permits an examination for cleanliness and allows the evaluator to lightly brush it.
- Out for a walk (walking on a loose leash). The handler walks the dog a short distance, and the dog must be able to walk with the leash hanging loosely, requiring no significant control efforts by its handler.
- Walking through a crowd. The handler and dog walk around the room with several persons walking in close proximity.
- Sit and down on command and staying in place. The dog must respond to the handler's commands of sit, down, and stay.
- Coming when called. The dog must stay in place while the handler walks about 10 feet away and then come to the handler when called.
- Reaction to another dog. A second handler and dog walk past the handler and dog being tested, the handlers shake hands and then walk on past. The dogs must show little to no interest in one another.
- Reaction to distraction. A dog may show curious interest to a loud noise or distraction made by the evaluator but should not react with great fear or aggression.
- Supervised separation. A dog is left with a person other than its handler for a minute and should not whine, bark, or pull on the leash.

All of the tests must be performed on a leash. Owners/handlers may use praise and encouragement throughout the test and may pet the dog in between exercises. Any dog that eliminates during the test is marked as failed. A dog that growls, snaps, bites, attacks, or attempts to attack a person or another dog is not a good citizen and must be dismissed from the test.

Many therapy animal organizations utilize the AKC CGC as their evaluation and screening tool. It is my opinion that, although the AKC CGC is useful as a guide for pet owners to train their pets to be well behaved in the community, the AKC CGC by itself is not a sufficient credential for a volunteer or professional who desires to work with a pet performing AAA or AAT. A more rigorous evaluation and certification process is required to determine if a human–animal therapy team is ready to provide service to the community. Evaluation procedures designed specifically to determine the readiness and appropriateness of an animal therapy team to provide services are reviewed below, that of TDI, Delta Society, and the Tuskegee PUPS Test.

TDI Testing Requirements

The TDI testing requirements incorporate all 10 of the AKC CGC tasks plus an additional four tasks specific to TDI. Following is a complete list of TDI testing requirements (TDI, 2003):

- Accepting a friendly stranger.
- Sitting politely for petting.
- Appearance and grooming.
- Out for a walk (walking on a loose leash).
- Walking through a crowd.
- Sit and down on command/staying in place.
- Coming when called.
- Reaction to another dog.
- Reaction to distractions.
- Reaction to medical equipment. The dog is exposed to a piece of common medical equipment such as a wheelchair, crutches, a cane, or a walker to judge the dog's reactions.
- Leave it. The handler with the dog on a loose leash walks past food on the ground that is about 3 feet away, and the dog should ignore the food on command.
- Acclimation to infirmities. The dog's reaction is observed when the dog is exposed to persons walking with an uneven gait, shuffling, breathing heavily, coughing, wheezing, or other types of conditions or distractions that may be encountered on a therapy visit.
- Supervised separation.
- Say hello. The dog is tested on its willingness to visit a person and be accessible for petting.

The TDI evaluation is performed by a TDI certified evaluator. To locate a TDI evaluator near you, contact TDI or visit their website (http://www.tdi-dog.org/).

Delta Society Pet Partners Evaluation

Delta Society established its Pet Partners Program in 1990. Delta Society has a rigorous evaluation that is based on the AKC CGC but is also designed to simulate the therapeutic environment (Delta Society, 2000, 2003, 2004). There is a strong emphasis on evaluating the pet, the handler, and the interaction between the two. The Delta Society evaluation was designed to determine the fitness for handlers and their pets to receive national registration in Delta Society's Pet Partners Program. A unique aspect of Delta Society is that it certifies a variety of animals, including dogs, cats, horses, rabbits, birds, farm animals, and certain small animals (such as gerbils and hamsters). The Pet Partners Team evaluation described below is for dogs; however, it can be adapted using Delta Society guidelines to better fit other types of animals. A therapy team's evaluation must be performed by a Delta Society licensed team evaluator. When no Delta Society evaluator is available in your area, a request can be submitted to Delta Society to use an alternate yet qualified evaluator, such as a veterinarian or an animal behavior specialist. But they must still use the same guidelines as a Delta Society certified evaluator. To locate a Delta Society evaluator near you, contact Delta Society or visit their website (http://www.deltasociety.org).

The Delta Society Pet Partners Team evaluation has two parts: the aptitude test and the skills test. The evaluation takes place in one area large enough for the exercises to occur. The location must be one that the pet is unfamiliar with, and the evaluator must be someone that is not familiar to the pet being evaluated. Both the handler and the animal are being evaluated. The evaluator is looking for positive and affirming interactions between the handler and the pet during the entire evaluation. In place of the "sit," "down," and "come when called" evaluation exercises, a cat or other small animal is only required to sit quietly while being held by three different persons who are sitting down. A cat or other small animal may be carried in the arms of the handler or in a basket during the evaluation.

Pet Partners Skills Test

These 11 exercises are similar to the AKC CGC test described previously:

- Accepting a friendly stranger
- Accepting petting
- Appearance and grooming
- Out for a walk (walking on a loose leash)
- Walking through a crowd
- Reaction to distractions (loud noise)
- Sit on command
- Down on command
- Stay in place
- Come when called
- Reaction to a neutral dog

Pet Partners Aptitude Test

These 10 exercises are designed to simulate events that might occur on a therapy visit:

- Overall exam. This exercise tests for touch sensitivity, that is, will the animal tolerate being examined and touched all over?

- Exuberant and clumsy petting. Can the animal tolerate being touched using clumsy movements and by someone with a high-pitched voice?
- Restraining hug. Will the animal accept a gentle, restraining hug?
- Staggering/gesturing individual. Will the animal be calm in the presence of someone staggering and gesturing wildly?
- Angry yelling. Does the animal stay calm and remain receptive to two persons who have exchanged loud and angry words with each other?
- Bumped from behind. Can the animal recover when someone bumps into it?
- Crowded and petted by several people. Will the animal tolerate being petted by a group of people crowding in on the animal?
- Leave it. Will the animal ignore a toy placed a few feet away when commanded to do so by the dog's handler?
- Take a treat gently. When offered a treat, can the animal take the treat gently without scratching or nipping the fingers of the evaluator? It is permissible for the animal to just ignore the treat completely.
- Overall reaction. Were the overall reactions of the animal team to the complete test positive and acceptable?

There are four possible ratings a therapy team (handler and animal) may receive from the Delta Society Pet Partners Team Evaluation:

- Not suitable for therapy. A pet may receive this rating if it is aggressive, is overly fearful, or has considerable shyness or if it is considered not suitable for some other reason. These pets do not pass the evaluation, and it is recommended that they not retest.
- Not ready. A therapy team does not pass the evaluation but shows some good potential and may retest at a later date.
- Predictable. The therapy team passes the evaluation, but it is recommended that they work only in environments where activity and circumstances are consistent and predictable and where there are additional staff members to assist if necessary. An example of this would be a structured and predictable environment such as a school or a senior citizen residential facility with fairly healthy patrons and good supervision.
- Complex. The therapy team passes the evaluation and is suitable to work in environments with high and potentially unpredictable activity and with no additional staff presence required. An example of this would be a less structured and less predictable environment such as a hospital or a health care facility for the very ill.

If an animal is to work in a therapeutic environment, it is probably best that the animal be able to achieve a "complex" rating to assure that the animal has the proper temperament and training to work in a professional setting.

When Rusty was 17 months old, he was evaluated by a Delta Society evaluator for his first time. For the first 2 years of his life, Rusty was a very high-energy and very playful dog. His playful attitude during the evaluation resulted in a passing rating called "Intermediate" (now referred to as "Predictable"), as opposed to the highest possible rating he could have received, an "Advanced" rating (now referred to as "Complex"). Rusty calmed down considerably after turning 2 years old and even more when he turned 3 years of age. When he was evaluated his second time at the age of 3½ years, he received the highest possible rating of "Complex." I had Dolly evaluated for the first time when she was a little older and more mature than Rusty was his first time. Dolly was first evaluated when she was 1 month shy of turning 2 years old. She was awarded the Delta Society rating of "Complex" her very first time.

Delta Society requires attendance by handlers (without their pets) at a 1-day training workshop before the therapy team can be registered with Delta Society. Pet Partners Training workshops are lead by a Delta Society instructor. Instructors are available across the U.S. and in some foreign countries. Contact Delta Society or check the Delta Society website to locate a workshop nearest you. The team evaluation is typically held the following day after the workshop, and the evaluation itself lasts only about 30 minutes for each team. Advantages to national registration as a Pet Partners team with Delta Society include liability insurance for volunteer work, networking through postings on the Delta website, and receiving copies of the Delta Society periodical *Interactions*. Handlers only have to attend one Pet Partners Training Workshop no matter how many pets they want to get certified. Pet Partners certification for additional pets only requires the team evaluation. Delta teams must be reevaluated every 2 years. Rigorous training and evaluation requirements are reasons that a Delta Society registration is often preferred over other AAT certifications/registrations by many professionals and therapeutic facilities. The Delta Society registration process also includes a thorough health screening by the pet's veterinarian using Delta Society guidelines.

To register with Delta Society, the handler mails in the certificate of completion of the Pet Partners Workshop, the results of the team evaluation, the health report completed by the veterinarian, and a registration fee along with the appropriate Pet Partners registration forms and a photo of the handler with their pet. The handler receives from Delta Society a Pet Partners tag for the pet's collar and a laminated badge with the photo of the handler and the pet for the handler to wear. The pet's tag and the handler's badge make it easy for others to recognize the pair as a trained and credentialed AAT team. Also available from Delta Society for Pet Partners teams are professional vests and scarves for the pet to wear, further identifying it as a registered therapy animal.

Tuskegee Behavior Test

The Tuskegee Behavior Test for Selecting Therapy Dogs was developed in 1993 (Schaffer, 1993) out of a desire to offer a successful pet visitation program to patients and residents of the local Veterans Affairs Medical Center and area nursing homes. The Tuskegee screening test is called the PUPS after the School of Veterinary Medicine's Pets Uplifting People's Spirit Visitation Program. Eight stations were designed to simulate the conditions of the nursing home or hospital where the pets would be working:

- Waiting room
- Examination room
- People in the hall
- Distractions
- Obstacle course

- Noise in the hall
- Elevator simulation
- Simulated day room

The following response categories were evaluated in each of the eight simulations:

- Pet's general condition, appearance, and behavior
- Interaction between pet and handler
- Pet's reaction to other pets
- Pet's social graces, e.g., reaction to other people, obedience, and not urinating or defecating during exercises

The two acceptable responses by the dog in each of the eight simulations would be "attentive" or "playful." Unacceptable responses would be "aggressive," "submissive," or "passively submissive." A real benefit to the Tuskegee PUPS evaluation is its realistic simulations for each exercise. The PUPS can also be adapted for evaluating cats for therapy work.

As you can see, the process of becoming a therapy team with your pet requires proper training and evaluation of you and your pet by qualified trainers and evaluators. It is important to make the effort to achieve a certification credential in AAT as a quality control measure for providing this therapeutic modality. By presenting yourself and your pet as certified AAT providers, you are sending the message to your clients and colleagues that you are working within your competency area, that is, that you have met at least some minimal standard that demonstrates you have received the proper training to provide AAT services.

Chapter 6

Risk Management in Animal Assisted Counseling

Professional Disclosure and Informed Consent to Participate in AAT   59
Client Screening for AAT   59
Recognizing Stress in Therapy Animals   59
Understanding Your Pet's Communication   61
Preventing Injury and Infection during AAT   66
Preparing a Pet for a Therapy Visit   69
Ethical Considerations for AAT   70
Dangers for Animals in Elderly Residential Care Facilities   70
Dangers for Animals in Institutionally Based Residential Programs   71
Concerns for Animals in Visitation Programs   71
Concerns for Wild (Nondomesticated) Animal Programs   71

"The dog is the only being that loves you more than you love yourself."
— Fritz von Unruh

One of the best ways to minimize the risk of injury or accident while practicing AAT is to make sure one understands how to properly apply established techniques. AAT-C should only be practiced by a credentialed professional counselor or a student in training who is under proper supervision. Remember, AAT is not an independent profession but rather it is a treatment modality utilized by professionals consistent with that professional's training and practice. In addition to being a credentialed counselor or supervised counseling student, the practitioner should have some standardized training in AAT. At a minimum, the counselor and therapy pet should have certification equivalent to Delta Society Pet Partners training or TDI. In addition to obtaining an entry-level credential to practice AAT, I highly recommend you obtain additional training to enhance your professional AAT skills. The entry-level credential is necessary and sufficient for volunteer AAA service but, in my opinion, an entry-level credential is not sufficient by itself for professional AAT work. A very fine example of a more advanced AAT training curriculum is the AAT Applications Course offered by Delta Society for the animal's handler/owner (not the pet). This is a half-day workshop that covers AAT topics such as client screening, assessment, evaluation, treatment planning and goal setting, documentation, and a variety of client interventions. This training provides the therapist with the tools necessary to determine which clients may or may not benefit from AAT and how to integrate various AAT techniques into the therapy process to achieve a variety of treatment goals. Although workshops are a good device for providing brief and concentrated AAT training, I believe that comprehensive AAT training is best provided via a college or university course format, but currently this type of semester-long training course is difficult to find. But hopefully, the popularity of AAT in a counseling setting will grow to the degree that more counselor education programs will offer an AAT training course.

The benefits to formal training in AAT include not only increasing the chances for therapeutic success, but also reducing and managing risks that may be involved with this type of therapy. At a minimum, a mental health professional who engages in AAT practice should demonstrate knowledge and skill in the following areas:

1. Social skill development and obedience training for the pet
2. Therapy and activity skill training for the pet and handler
3. Establishing and maintaining a positive relationship with fellow staff
4. Assessing the appropriateness of AAT with a particular client
5. The basics of zoonoses (transmittable diseases) and risk management that include attention to both human client and animal welfare
6. Establishing therapeutic or educational goals and applying interventions
7. Assessing therapeutic progress

All counselors and counseling students practicing AAT should carry professional liability insurance and should inquire as to whether that insurance provider offers coverage for the practice of AAT. The American Counseling Association (ACA) performed a special committee review of this issue, and in 2002 established a policy that the ACA insurance underwriter would cover the practice of AAT as long as the therapist and therapy pet held certification as a Delta Society Pet Partner Team or AKC CGC or the equivalent. I served as an outside consultant for this committee during its review process.

Professional Disclosure and Informed Consent to Participate in AAT

Every practicing counselor must provide the client and/or the client's legal guardian with a professional disclosure of information statement describing the counseling service. A basic professional information statement and informed consent for services form should contain the following information: a description of the counselor and the counselor's credentials, a description of the services provided, procedures for appointments, length and number of sessions, the nature of the relationship between the therapist and client (in that it is a professional relationship and not a social one), fees/payment information, limits to confidentiality and the duty to warn, addresses and phone numbers for communication with the client, risks of therapy/ counseling, after-hours emergency information, disposition of client records in case of death of the therapist, waiver of right to child's records/information, and signature lines for the client (and/or legal guardian) and the therapist (Bernstein & Hartsell, 1998). A copy of the signed form should be given to the client and an original kept in the client's file. For AAT practice, I recommend the professional information statement and informed consent for services form include information about the therapy animal: the type of animal (dog, cat, bird, and so forth), the training and credentials of the therapy animal, the relationship of the animal to the therapist, and the types of activities a client can engage in with the therapy animal if the client chooses to do so. The consent form should also inform the client of his or her right to request that the therapy animal not be present for counseling sessions.

Client Screening for AAT

All clients should be screened before they participate in AAT for the protection of the client as well as for the pet. Clients with a tendency toward violence or history of animal abuse should not participate in AAT-C. Clients that may not understand the consequences of their actions must be carefully supervised during therapy to protect the animal from injury. A colleague of mine performs animal assisted play therapy with autistic children. On a first visit by one client, the child approached the therapy dog and in his excitement grabbed the dog's ear tightly and pulled hard. The dog let out several yelps before the therapist could get the grasp released. The dog has been a bit shy around that child ever since. Clients with specific animal phobias should not participate in therapy with an animal of which it is afraid. And a therapist utilizing AAT should always inquire about possible animal allergies of clients. The Client Screening Form for Animal Assisted Therapy was developed by the author and a copy is provided in the appendix for your convenient use.

Recognizing Stress in Therapy Animals

As a cotherapist with your pet, it is vital that you understand some of the basic premises of animal behavior. For example, when a dog is in a stressful situation, it might try to calm itself by exhibiting one of the following behaviors: turning away or averting its eyes away from the stressor, licking its lips, or yawning (Gammonley et al., 2003). These types of behaviors in a stress-inducing situation are called "calming signals" and serve as useful information for the pet's handler who would then need to reassure the animal or remove it from the stressful situation.

It is vital that a therapy pet handler be able to recognize signs of stress in a therapy pet. Some typical well-known signs of stress for dogs include (Delta Society, 2000, pp. 68–69; 2004, pp. 91–92):

- Shaking (the body)
- Panting and salivating
- Dilated pupils
- Excessive blinking
- Sweating through the pads of the feet
- Restlessness, distraction, agitation
- Lack of eye contact
- Yawning
- Excessive shedding
- Excessive vocalizing
- Licking lips
- Hiding (behind handler)
- Turning away
- Attempts to leave
- Need for repeated commands
- Inappropriate defecation or urination

Each of these stress behavior signs must be viewed in the context of the environment that they occur. For example, a dog that is hot or thirsty will also pant. The key is to know your animal and be sensitive to its moods and needs. Be objective and receptive to what your pet may be trying to tell you.

Some typical signs of stress for other animals frequently working as therapy pets include (Delta Society, 2000, pp. 68–69; 2004, pp. 91–92):

Cats

- Restlessness, distraction, agitation
- Clinging
- Unusual passivity
- Defensive vocalizations
- Excessive shedding
- Dilated pupils

Rabbits

- Body tense, with tail up
- Enlarged eyes with whites showing
- Ears laid back tightly
- Growling or squeaking noises
- Flinches when touched
- Rapid breathing
- Licking lips
- Lack of interest displayed

Birds

- Ruffled feathers
- Lack of desire to socialize
- Increased elimination
- Increased pecking
- Looking away
- Abnormal vocalization

When the signs of stress are recognized in a therapy pet, the pet's handler must take some action. An attempt to reduce the stress for the animal should be made. The handler could attempt to reassure the therapy animal. The animal could be given a break or taken home. The therapy animal may even need a vacation from therapy for a few days or weeks. If stress symptoms persist over the course of several therapy visits, the handler should reassess whether the therapy animal is appropriate for therapy work in a given environment or not appropriate for therapy at all. Also, when a therapy pet becomes too old or too ill to work, then the pet should be retired from therapy service.

One way to help an animal manage stress that comes with working in therapy is to give the animal a massage before or after a day's work. One recommended technique that is very soothing for an animal is called the Tellington Touch, developed by an internationally known horse trainer and teacher of riding instructors and horse trainers, Linda Tellington-Jones (Tellington-Jones & Taylor, 1995). The Tellington Touch technique is appropriate for all types of therapy animals.

An animal can work as a therapy pet if it has a long-term disability, but the handler must take precautions so that the disabled animal does not experience undue discomfort or stress from working with this disability. One of my favorite dogs to evaluate had only three legs, one front leg having had to be amputated as a result of being hit by a car. The dog can stand and walk by himself on three legs, but the owner typically positions himself close to the dog so the dog can lean slightly on him for balance when stopped. The handler allows a little extra time for the pet to walk at a slowed pace and for rest breaks. The dog does well on therapy visits and seems to really enjoy the clients.

My therapy cat, Snowflake, is deaf, most likely from birth. While his visual startle reflex is a bit more heightened, his audio startle reflex is nonexistent. Despite his deafness, Snowflake acts calm and comfortable as well as sociable and playful on therapy visits. Because of his hearing disability, I must take special precautions at home and on visits to insure his safety. At home, he is not allowed outside unless he is on a leash and I accompany him. On therapy visits, he primarily works indoors, but on occasional therapy visits outdoors he wears a chest harness and a leash. I make sure those he visits are aware of his disability. If your animal has a disability, when you and your pet are ready for certification, you should inform the animal evaluator of that disability before the evaluation begins so appropriate allowances may be made if necessary.

Understanding Your Pet's Communication

Most of us know our pets fairly well and can understand what their behaviors are conveying to us. But again, some of us love our animals so much that we may be in denial about what they are communicating. If we lose our objectivity about our animal's behavior, then we place our pet and our clients in jeopardy. For example, I was evaluating a therapy team one day, a teacher and her large mixed breed dog that happened to be a dog she had rescued from a shelter and had been living with her for a little over a year. She had already been taking the dog to her school and was so pleased with how the children were responding positively to the dog's presence, she had decided to start a reading practice program with her dog. She was even going to spearhead the recruitment of other volunteers to join in with their dogs. The whole venture was very exciting, and I was very pleased that she was interested in community service with her pet. She had decided that it was best to get some proper training and certification with her pet before continuing with her project so she had completed the Delta Society Pet Partners workshop the day before and now she and her pet were going to go through the Delta Society animal team evaluation.

When she and the dog came into the evaluation room, I did not see the same enthusiasm in the pet that I saw in the pet's handler. The dog acted as if he was not very interested in his surroundings or in the people in the room. The pet's owner reassured me by saying that he was just a very calm dog and everything was all right. I had been an animal evaluator for only a brief period at the time, but still my training combined with my intuition about the dog lead me to proceed with caution. The dog was very still and very quiet with an attitude of indifference. He averted his head when I approached, demonstrating dislike for my presence. I questioned the handler as to whether we should proceed because it did not seem to me that the dog really wanted to be a part of what was going on around him. Once again the owner reassured me that the dog was feeling just fine. I wrestled with the idea of terminating the evaluation but, being fairly inexperienced at the time, I felt I had not enough evidence to justify that position. The dog was not being friendly but the dog was not aggressive either. The dog had been looking toward the exit door frequently as if plotting an escape route. I empathized with the dog's seeming desire to leave and was watchful of additional signs that would support the termination of the evaluation. Then we came to the part in the evaluation where I was to hug the dog. I moved forward and leisurely extended my reach. The dog lunged at me, targeting my left hand, snarling and baring all of his teeth. I moved quickly but still felt the outside of the dog's teeth brush against the tips of my fingers as I jumped back to get out of the dog's way. After the initial lunge and snap, the dog did not pursue me further and immediately quieted back down. Fortunately, I was not bitten or injured by the dog despite the dog's clear intention of doing so to put a stop to the evaluation once and for all.

The dog's owner was shocked by the dog's behavior. I consulted with the volunteers working with me in the room, and they had observed what I had, that the dog had been uninterested and somewhat unhappy about participating in the evaluation but had not shown any signs of aggression until that moment when I began to hug it. Well, obviously the dog did not pass the evaluation and I gave the dog a "not suitable for therapy" rating. I informed the owner that she should not use the dog for therapy and should stop taking the dog to school because it was likely that someone was eventually going to get bitten by this dog. The owner erupted in tears and for the first few minutes exclaimed that she had never before seen any of that behavior in her dog and did not understand it. I sensed that this was a case where the owner was just not seeing what the dog was communicating. The owner, wanting desperately to work with this dog that she rescued and loved, saw only what she wanted to see in the dog's behavior. After a few minutes of inquiry, the owner began to acknowledge that she had seen certain similar behaviors of lack of interest and unhappiness in her dog when she took it to school but had not interpreted them to mean that the dog was uncomfortable. I conveyed two important considerations for the owner: (a) that she was not being as objective about the dog's behavior as she could be, and objectivity was extremely important for AAT work; and (b) her dog was what I refer to as a "stealth dog" — the dog gives you some clues, but no real obvious warning that it is about to attack; you can almost not see it coming unless you pay close attention and know what to look for. A "stealth dog" is a time bomb for biting someone. Because owners are typically not objective about their own pet's behavior and because some pets' negative behaviors and attitudes are not obvious to the untrained eye, it is very important that before any pet works in therapy, it be evaluated to determine if the pet is appropriate for that type of public activity. With more years of experience as an animal team evaluator since this incident, I now trust and follow my evaluator's intuitions much more quickly. I have never gotten bit during an evaluation, and since this episode, never came so close ever again.

To learn more about a dog's communication behavior, I suggest you do some reading about it. A book I recommend for this is *Dogspeak*, edited by Matthew Hoffman. Each dog has its own little behavior quirks and you probably know your dog best. However, some universal facial patterns for dogs have been described that can be helpful in interpreting your dog's mood (Hoffman, 1999). A dog's eyes that are wide open can communicate the dog is surprised or afraid. A frightened dog typically tightens its whole face, pulls its ears back, and pulls its lips down and back. A dog that is afraid may also lower its head and look away from the object that concerns it. On the other hand, a long, hard intense stare is usually a conveyed threat or warning by a dog. A slightly furrowed brow with a stare may convey intense interest, whereas a deeply furrowed brow with a stare may convey fear or extreme caution. Exaggerated eye blinking is a way a dog communicates that it is stressed out and does not want to be seen as a threat, as is a dog that averts its gaze away from another dog or person. A blank stare and extremely limp ears can communicate boredom for a dog. Narrowed or half-closed eyes typically mean the dog is happy and relaxed. A keen alert look with pricked up ears may convey a dog is feeling happy and confident. A dog that is staring but trying not to show it, like staring out of the sides of its eyes, is probably planning something, usually something playful in nature.

Schaffer (1993), a veterinarian, has classified and described six various canine postures that are helpful in interpreting a dog's communications: aggressive, fearful, submissive, passively submissive, playful, and attentive. The first four are considered negative behavior categories, whereas the last two are positive behavior categories. An "aggressive" dog will begin with its ears pointed forward and then pull the ears out and down as the aggression escalates and will pull the ears all the way back when it actually attacks. The aggressive dog's eyes are fixed and staring. Its lips are raised with the mouth open and nose wrinkled. The head is held high, and the dog's body is stiff and tense and leans forward with the weight shifted to the front. The dog's tail is raised up and over the rump and toward the back of the neck. The dog's fur may be raised over the rump and neck; this is referred to as having the hackles raised. A front leg may point at the object the dog is concerned with. The dog is typically vocalizing with a growl, snarl, and bark.

A "fearful" dog lays the ears back and down against the head and has its eyes wide open and fixed. The dog's head will be down and the mouth slightly open. The fur will be raised over the dog's neck. The dog's weight will be shifted backward on its rear legs, and its tail will be tucked under its abdomen. (Note some breeds of dogs have a naturally tucked tail all of the time that does not imply a negative expression, such as the greyhound.) The dog may tremble, urinate, or defecate. The dog may move in quick motions in an attempt to find an escape route, and it may whine.

A "submissive" dog will have the ears and eyes down. The dog's head will be lowered with the lips down and pulled back horizontally. The dog's fur will be down against a body that is leaning back with the weight shifted to the rear. The dog's tail may be wagging or hanging down or be tucked close to the body. It may whine. A "passively submissive" dog will have ears down, eyes down, lips down, hair flat, and head down. The dog will be lying on its side or back with the tail tucked close to the body. The dog may urinate.

A "playful" dog will have the ears up and the eyes will be moving. The dog's fur will be flat against a body that is leaning back with weight shifted to the rear. The dog's lips will be relaxed. A front paw may wave in the air. The tail will wag up high and fast in a broad motion. The dog may pant, bark, or whine. And finally, an "attentive" dog will have the ears up and the eyes will be moving. The dog's head will be up with lips relaxed. The dog's fur will lie flat against its body that has weight evenly distributed. The tail will be stiff and horizontal and moving slowly as aroused. And, typically the dog is not vocalizing.

What is missing from the above list of dog behavior categories is what I describe as the relaxed dog posture. A calm and relaxed dog, whether standing, sitting, or lying down, will have relaxed, soft, slightly closed eyes and relaxed body muscles, will be looking around leisurely, will be quiet with no vocalizations, may have a slow, relaxed tail wag or completely relaxed tail, and its fur will be flat against its body. The calm and relaxed dog posture is a common posture for a well-trained and experienced therapy dog, unless of course the therapy dog is engaged in active play therapy or some similar active therapeutic exercise, in which case it would look more like an attentive dog or a playful dog.

Schaffer (1993) has described four various cat postures that may help to interpret negative feline expressions: fearful, defensive aggressive, offensive aggressive, and submissive. A cat that is very "fearful" and feels somewhat trapped becomes very tense and crouches its body low against the ground. It will lay its ears flat back and down against the head, have dilated pupils, and stare intensely at the object of which it is afraid. The whiskers will point backward against the face, while the cat's tail whips back and forth briskly. The fur will be up and bristled all over the body. It may make negative vocalizations like hissing or spitting. A cat that is afraid but feels it still has options open may take a "defensive aggressive" pose. The ears will also lie flat, back, and down; the pupils will be dilated and staring intensely with whiskers pulled back against the face; and the fur will be up and bristled all over the body. But instead of crouching low, the cat arches its back up high and lowers the head. The tail will arch over the back and jerk briskly. The cat leans away from and keeps its body at a right angle to the object of which it is afraid. It may slap its front paws. The mouth will be wide open, nose curled into a snarl with teeth showing. It may hiss, growl, or spit. A cat that is intent on attack will take an "offensive aggressive" pose. The ears will be up away from its head but still point backward. The head will be held sideways and sway slowly. The eyes will be fixed on the target with constricted pupils. The whiskers will be spread out and point forward. The cat's fur will be raised in a ridge down the back midline and on her entire tail. The body will be stretched and tense with the nails extended and a front paw raised. The mouth will be open with lips curled, and it may make hissing, spitting, yowling, or growling noises. A nonaggressive yet "submissive" cat expression is one with ears flat, head down, and chin tucked. Eyes will be down with no eye contact and the pupils dilated. The eyelids will be partly or totally closed. The whiskers will lie flat against the face. The cat's fur will lie flat against a crouched body. The cat's tail will be down and thump the ground. The cat may mew or open its mouth and emit no sound. While this last cat described is not being aggressive, it is certainly not very comfortable either.

Schaffer (1993) describes two postures of positive feline expressive behaviors: friendly/relaxed and attentive/playful. A friendly/relaxed cat will have the ears up and pointed slightly forward. The head will be up with the eyes almost closed, and the cat's pupil size will vary according to the light available in the room. The cat's whiskers will be slightly fanned and point sideways. The cat's fur will lie down against a body that is stretched out and relaxed. The cat may rub against a person or touch noses. The cat's tail is stiff, motionless, and vertical. The cat may purr, meow, or murmur. A cat that is "attentive/playful" will have its head up with ears up and pointed forward. The whiskers will be spread out and point forward. The cat's eyes will be moving with dilated pupils. The fur will lie down flat against a tense body. The tail will be motionless but jerk when aroused. The tail will be down when the cat is stalking, or if the cat is playing, the tail will be up, arched, or in an inverted U-shape. The cat will either be silent or elicit teeth chattering or lip smacking when excited.

It has generally been accepted by scientists that animals experience the primary emotion of fear as an instinctual survival mechanism. But whether or not animals experience complex secondary emotions like love, sadness, grief, and so on has been much debated in scientific circles. Now new scientific technology that allows for the examination of brain chemistry and brain imaging is beginning to provide supportive evidence for the experience of complex secondary emotions in animals. New research is discovering that animals have similar neurochemical responses as humans when seeming to express affection, face stress, or experience the loss of a companion (Tangley, 2000). This objective evidence compounded with subjective observations of animal behavior strongly suggests that animals do in fact experience complex secondary emotions. In addition, some behaviorists suggest that domesticated animals, such as pet cats and dogs, have evolved to a social level of actively expressing a large variety of secondary emotions to their owners, such as a dog exhibiting a play bow to express a desire to frolic or cuddling on the couch to express affection, or a cat curling up in a lap and purring and rubbing a cheek against your hand as an expression of affection (Schultz, 2000).

While the debate goes on as to whether your dog or cat actually experiences emotions like love, happiness, sadness, grief, and so forth, I prefer to land on the side of the argument that assumes that animals do experience more complex emotions and to more meaningful levels than we currently can understand. Even if I am wrong, I see no harm in potentially erring in this direction. If the suggestion by new research is correct that animals are potentially capable of experiencing complex emotions, then the potential benefits and risks to AAT may be enhanced. Risks may be enhanced in that a therapy animal may actually take on some of the emotions of a human client it works with, such as the client's depression or anxiety; or after termination of counseling, an animal may miss a client it has interacted with on a regular basis. Benefits may be enhanced in that as we learn better to accurately interpret animal expressions, we may better understand how a therapy animal's interactions with and reactions to a human client can provide valuable information about and for that client.

Research has determined that animals have a distinct personality that is unique to each animal, that is, not species or breed specific, and is in fact manifested in much the same way as human personality. In a direct comparison of dogs and humans, it was determined that judgments of specific and uniform criteria measuring personality were found to be consistently and accurately applied for dogs, and in the same way as for humans, leading the researchers to conclude with confidence that personality differences do exist and can be measured in animals other than humans (Gosling, Kwan, & John, 2003). Seventy-eight dogs and their owners were recruited from a dog park to participate in the research. A four-factor model was used to examine the dog's personality: "neuroticism," represented by the dog's emotional reactivity; "extraversion," represented by the dog's energy; "openness" to new experience, represented by the dog's intelligence; and "agreeableness," represented by the dog's affection. This four-factor model was based on the well-accepted five-factor model used to measure personality for humans with the factor of "conscientiousness" omitted for dogs. The standardized assessment for the five-factor model, the Big Five Inventory (BFI; John & Srivastava, 1999), was used to measure the personality of the dog's owner, and a slight modification of this same instrument was used to measure the dog's personality by both the dog's owner and objective observers. The research determined that the dog's personality traits that were observed while the dog was interacting were not based on mere looks or appearance, because distinct personality traits were not found when a separate group judged the same dogs only by examining still photos of the dogs. And, the dogs' personality traits were measured consistently across time by different observers. This evidence strongly supports the concept that each animal has a unique personality that distinguishes it from animals of the same species and the same breed.

The research finding that an animal, such as a dog, can have a personality unique to that particular animal is highly relevant to the application of AAT. A therapist that is very aware of his or her pet's unique personality characteristics and how these are presented in the therapy setting can make more meaningful interpretations of human client and therapy pet interactions. This could result in additional valuable information for facilitating client recovery. Also, a therapist can make more accurate predictions of anticipated animal and human behavior in a therapy session based on an understanding of the personality traits presented by a therapy animal that is interacting with a human client. Increased ability to interpret and predict animal and human behavior in a therapy session enhances the benefits and reduces the risks of the AAT process.

Preventing Injury and Infection during AAT

Minimizing the risk of injury to the therapy animal and to the clients the animal works with is imperative. For this reason, all therapy dogs should be kept on a leash and small animals provided a small crate or basket in which to be carried. Only the trained handler should ever control the therapy pet and supervise the animal's interaction with clients. The therapy pet should never be left alone with a client or left with a staff member the pet is unfamiliar with. If there is a need to leave the pet, the pet should be properly crate trained so the animal can be safely secured in a crate and be comfortable being left alone for short periods.

A colleague of mine who was a director of a counseling clinic told me of a nightmarish incident involving an intern who brought a therapy dog to her clinic to perform AAT. The intern had attended a one-day training workshop, and she and her dog were nationally certified for volunteer work in AAA. (In my opinion, this intern had not received sufficient training to perform professional AAT.) A series of serious mistakes by the counseling intern then ensued. First, the intern brought the dog to the counseling clinic without the knowledge or permission of the clinic director or any supervisor. Second, the intern did not screen or inform clients in advance before bringing the dog nor did she properly evaluate which clients would be appropriate for AAT. Given the above errors, the clinic director informed the intern that she could not work with the dog that day when seeing her clients. The student had not brought any type of dog crate with her and did not want to cancel with her clients, plus there was no time to take the dog home and get back in time to see her first scheduled client that day. Thus, the clinic director agreed to let the intern place the dog in the director's office with the door closed so the intern could counsel her clients down the hall in a therapy room. So the situation presented was a young, playful, and inexperienced therapy dog, placed alone in an unfamiliar environment, away from the owner and not under proper supervision, and not properly confined in a dog crate. This is a condition that can likely lead to some kind of trouble. Thus, being a young and inadequately trained dog left alone without proper confinement or supervision, the dog did what many similar dogs might do in a similar situation, he looked for something to do to entertain himself. He spotted a squirrel outside the window of the director's office and began jumping at it, an exercise that resulted in destroying an entire wall of expensive window blinds before the squirrel chase was discovered. The irresponsible actions of the intern resulted in the dog being banned from the clinic. Given a similar situation, the best action would have been to simply cancel the intern's clients for the day or for the time it would take to send the intern home so the dog could be left in a safe and familiar environment, given that the intern had not brought a crate for the dog. This type of incident creates the potential for the dog to injure itself and to give a bad reputation to AAT. It is imperative that animal assisted therapists act responsibly to insure the safety of a therapy animal, the safety of clients, and the safety of facility staff and furnishings and to demonstrate the best side that AAT has to offer.

Properly trained and socialized therapy pets are highly unlikely to cause injury to a client. However, it is possible for accidents to happen. For instance, what if a client did not see the dog's leash between you and the animal and the client tripped and fell to the ground. It is important to have a well thought out plan of action in place just in case injury to a client does occur during AAT. Delta Society (2000) has a clear policy for handling injury to a client by certified Pet Partners. The animal should be safely secured as soon as possible so you can manage the situation. Do not tie the animal to furniture. This invokes nightmarish images of a chair chasing a frightened dog down a hallway that can only escalate the situation by implying the animal is out of control. The animal should, preferably, be secured safely in a crate in an office. If the person you are visiting is injured, get help for the person as quickly as possible. Get an appropriate staff person to administer or call for medical aid if necessary. Only properly trained facility staff or medical personnel should administer medical treatment of any kind, including the application of a simple bandage on a scratch. If the incident occurred in an agency or facility, the pet's handler should report the incident to the appropriate facility supervisor or administrator and all proper paperwork should be completed. The handler should also report the incident to any sponsoring AAT organization the handler belongs to, such as Delta Society. There should be no more therapy work involving the animal for the rest of the day. Animals are very sensitive to stress, and the situation calls for giving the animal the rest of the day off.

To keep the animal safe from injury, the handler must scan the environment for objects that might harm the animal, such as stray food, sharp objects, or contaminated objects on the floor. The handler must be careful that the animal does not run into any furniture or knock over objects in the room. On one visit with Rusty, Snowflake, and Dolly to the juvenile detention center where I volunteer, it was the winter holiday season and the adolescents had made cardboard fireplaces and strung yarn in the shape of Christmas trees in the individual section units of the facility. Seeing the changes to the areas that the pets had frequently visited, I supervised the adolescent residents while they slowly walked the therapy animals around so the animals could see the new obstacles in the room. Even given such precautions, during a ball fetch exercise that day Rusty got briefly tangled in a yarn Christmas tree, and once Snowflake the cat tried to jump on top of a flimsy cardboard fireplace mantle that brought the whole structure tumbling down. No person or animal came near to being injured that day, and it would have been difficult for that to happen given my assessment of the lack of danger presented by the objects; but the incident demonstrates the importance of being aware of the working environment and to keep it safe.

Sometimes danger to the therapy animal can be invisible. Rusty frequently accompanies me to my office at the university where I work. On one occasion, we had been there about 10 minutes when I noticed his usually light pink and brown freckled stomach was a fiery cherry red and extremely warm to the touch. I immediately rushed him to my veterinarian, who diagnosed and treated him for an unidentified allergic reaction. Rusty recovered quickly and I took him to the university office again the next day. Again, shortly after our arrival his stomach turned fiery red. This second time the veterinarian suggested that it was likely something at the office that Rusty was reacting to. I called the administrative staff and reported the vet's suggestion. Being animal lovers and Rusty fans, the staff began to examine what Rusty might have been reacting to in the office suite. The discussion revealed that all of the staff had been suffering with respiratory problems for several days that they had thought was just a bad cold being passed around. It was further discovered that the head administrative assistant had gone to the hospital for emergency treatment of a severe asthma attack. Convinced something was terribly wrong with the office environment, the staff contacted the environmental management office on campus, reporting Rusty's reactions and their own illnesses. The environmental office was hesitant to take the case seriously but the staff insisted that based on the dog's reactions, something was seriously amiss. Environmental management investigated and discovered that a new member of the custodial staff had recently cleaned the carpet in the office suite but had inadvertently used the pure concentrated form of a cleaner instead of diluting it as instructed on the ingredient container. In its concentrated form, the cleaner was dangerously toxic. After the office suite was treated to neutralize the toxins, the administrative staff's respiratory ailments cleared up and Rusty had no reactions while at the office. Rusty was credited with being a bit of a hero for this incident.

Unfortunately, there was a second, similar incident that occurred several months later during a therapy visit to a juvenile detention center. This detention center is divided into sections with about 5 to 10 juveniles in each section. Each of the juveniles in the section has a private room that opens into a shared, larger meeting area. My therapy team (me, trained graduate students, and my three therapy animals) conducts weekly group animal therapy visits to three sections dedicated to the long-term, residential postadjudication program; two sections of boys and one section of girls. During one visit with my dog Rusty and my cat Snowflake, a trained assistant and I noticed after about 10 minutes of arriving in one section that Snowflake's ears were turning a dark, cherry red. We watched him and Rusty closely. Then the cat's nose and paws became dark red and he began to have difficulty breathing and Rusty's stomach turned red. A rushed visit to the vet followed with treatment for Snowflake and Rusty for an allergic reaction. I reported the incident to the facility staff and clarified it was only in the last section we visited that day. The therapeutic programs coordinator reported back to me that an investigation of that section revealed that residents and staff had been suffering from some type of respiratory problems thought to have been a cold of some type being passed around. It was felt that the allergic reaction by the therapy animals in combination with the respiratory problems of residents and staff suggested a possible environmental problem. An investigation by environmental management staff ensued that narrowed the possible causes to either mildew caused from a recent plumbing problem in that section or to a misuse of concentrated cleaning materials. The section was thoroughly cleaned to neutralize the problem. However, on a subsequent visit to that section, both the cat and dog had a strong allergic reaction and the visit was quickly ended. These allergic reactions subsided on their own several minutes after leaving the facility. Finally, after several cleanings, it was safe again to visit with Rusty and Snowflake in that section. Many types of chemical agents, including a variety of common cleaning materials, are toxic to animals. It is very important that a counselor working with a therapy pet be aware of possible toxic agents that must be avoided for the safety of the therapy animal.

Zoonoses are diseases that can be exchanged between people and other animals (Delta Society, 2000). The risk of a therapy pet infecting someone that it works with can be minimized by the owner keeping the pet on routine vaccinations and keeping the pet parasite free, that is, no fleas, ticks, worms, and so forth. Also, the pet should never work if it is ill or has an open wound. At the work site, a designated location should be established for the pet to relieve itself, and all feces should be removed immediately following defecation and properly disposed of. Clients should wash their hands before and after visiting with a therapy pet as germs can be spread from person to person via the animal's fur. If no sink is available for hand washing, then antibacterial hand wipes can be used, albeit these are not as thorough or effective as hand washing for killing germs.

Preparing a Pet for a Therapy Visit

When working with a therapy animal, the therapist must make sure the animal is clean and well groomed. Dogs and cats should also have their nails trimmed and filed smooth before a therapy visit. A therapy animal kit should be carried at all times or maintained at the location of the therapy facility. The kit should include waste bags for disposing of dog excrement and paper towels and a stain and odor remover in case an accident happens indoors. The cleaner should be safe for animals, kill bacteria, and not discolor carpet or flooring. The local pet store is a good source for this. The pet should only drink bottled water or water brought from home and served in a dish you have brought. Toys, chews, and treats should be included in the kit so if a client wants to offer the pet a treat it is one that is healthy for the animal. A small, very soft bristle grooming brush can be included for clients to safely brush the pet. A spare leash and collar are necessary in case the current one wears out. The leash and collar for therapy visits should not be made of metal but rather of leather, cloth, or nylon. The leash should not be more than 6 feet in length. No choke collars or pinch collars can be used during therapy. Buckled neck collars, chest harnesses, or head halters are permissible. Also have available a pet first aid kit for handling small emergencies if the pet becomes ill or gets injured. Your local veterinarian can recommend some good contents for this first aid kit, but this usually entails some bandages, antiseptic, and something to stop bleeding as well as something to counteract a severe allergic reaction. It is also useful to include in the therapy kit a lint brush for participants to remove animal hair from their clothing after the visit. Also useful are antibacterial hand wipes or gel for participants to clean their hands with, if soap and a sink are not handy, before and after visiting with the therapy animal.

Ethical Considerations for AAT

The practice of AAT is growing throughout the world. Because the therapy involves animals that are highly dependent upon humans for protection and care, some ethical concerns arise regarding the potential exploitation of these creatures.

> Questions have arisen over the past few years about the ethics of using animals in some or all therapy programs. While some animal protection groups encourage programs involving animal visitations or animal-assisted therapy, others view this use of animals as yet another form of exploitation.... However, people who participate in animal assistance programs are more often than not aware of animal welfare and animal rights, and many either support animal protection activities or consider themselves to be sensitive to those issues.
> (Iannuzzi & Rowan, 1991, p. 154)

In an attempt to clarify issues regarding potential exploitation or abuse of animals in animal assistance programs, a survey was conducted by two researchers with an assortment of individuals involved in AAT programs across the U.S. The surveyors reported that although most AAT programs had a relatively benign impact on the animals, some troubling cases were uncovered. Following is a brief description of some of the troubling cases as reported by the authors of the survey research for the following AAT programs: elderly residential care, institutionally based residential programs, visitation programs, and wild animal programs (Iannuzzi & Rowan, 1991).

Dangers for Animals in Elderly Residential Care Facilities

At one elderly residential care facility, animals suffered from excessive feeding and too little exercise, with some animals dying prematurely as a result of congestive heart failure. Some dogs were left to roam outside a facility and were killed by cars.

At another facility, one dog froze to death when left outside on a winter's day. An animal at another facility strangled to death when left tied on a leash unattended.

Dangers for Animals in Institutionally Based Residential Programs

For animals at residential programs, fatigue of the therapy animal was found to be a concern if the animal was not allowed enough time to rest. At prisons, animals ran the risk of abuse with some incidents where even the guards abused therapy dogs when they were in the kennel. Some incidents of birds being killed and eaten in a prison facility were also reported. Providing adequate supervision of therapy animals for their protection in a long-term residential facility was found to be of great concern.

Concerns for Animals in Visitation Programs

Visitation programs are the most widespread type of AAT program. Visitations were stressful for the visiting animals, and the ability to cope and manage the stress varied greatly from animal to animal. A lack of ability to control the atmosphere and availability of water was found to be problematic in visitation programs. The combination of heat and dehydration was stressful and in some cases lead to exhaustion of the animal.

Concerns for Wild (Nondomesticated) Animal Programs

The survey researchers uncovered several concerns regarding dolphin swim programs. Dolphin swim programs have been used as possible assistance for autistic children. Dolphins are very social animals, and isolation from other wild dolphins can be very stressful as can confinement in a pool without unlimited access to their natural habitat. Dolphins fed by humans lost the ability to hunt and feed for themselves. Dolphins have very sensitive hearing, and loud environments may create stress for them. Captive dolphins, especially those exposed to many human beings, show enlarged adrenal glands. Thus, it is clear that dolphin swim programs are a potential danger to the dolphin.

Based on the above cases reported by Iannuzzi and Rowan (1991), it is clear that ethical concerns for the use of therapy animals are warranted, and the need for clear, established, ethical guidelines for the use of therapy animals would be helpful to the field. A therapist who utilizes a therapy animal should follow basic guidelines for animal protection and welfare. It is best that only domesticated animals and not wild animals be incorporated into therapy programs (an exception being wildlife rehabilitation and release programs that are under the supervision of a licensed wildlife rehabilitator). The therapy animal should always be adequately supervised for the pet's safety and provided sufficient rest and proper care and nutrition. And, the handler of the therapy animal should be properly trained and educated in animal welfare and risk management.

Chapter 7

Animal Assisted Counseling Techniques

Animals as a Surrogate for Therapeutic Touch   74
Animal Assisted Rapport Building   75
Animal Assisted Psychosocial Goals and Techniques   79
Animal Facilitated Life Stage Development   85
A Typical Animal Assisted Counseling Session   89
Introducing the Pet Practitioner   90
Animal Assisted Basic Relational Techniques   91
Accessing Feelings through the Use of AAT   93
Animal Assisted Family History Gathering   99
Animal Assisted Interventions and Clinical Diagnoses 101
Animal Assisted Metaphor   102
Animal Assisted Play Therapy   106
Play Therapy Yard   109
Animal Assisted Group Play Therapy   109
Equine Assisted Counseling   110
The Therapeutic Zoo   120
Termination Issues in AAT-C   123
Documentation and AAT   124
Program Evaluation and AAT   125

"I think dogs are the most amazing creatures; they give unconditional love. For me they are the role model for being alive."

— Gilda Radner

AAT is a therapeutic modality with goals that are consistent with all of the basic counseling theoretical orientations. It is considered an adjunct to therapy in that it encourages and facilitates client motivation and participation, enhances the client–therapist relationship, stimulates client focus and attention to task, and reinforces positive client change. AAT can be integrated with any style of counseling practice, be it directive or nondirective. It offers a variety of techniques that are flexible enough to be applied in individual, group, or family therapy formats.

Questions I am asked frequently by therapists exploring the possible incorporation of AAT into their own counseling practice are, "What do you do with the animal in the therapy room?" or "What does the animal do as part of the therapy?" These questions will be answered in this chapter. Yet, one important therapeutic aspect of a pet practitioner can be its presence in the therapy room. The pet can contribute significantly to an atmosphere of cozy comfort and lessen the negative impact for the client of being in an unfamiliar environment. A pet practitioner is a therapeutic agent of warm and cuddly feelings. In AAT-C, I have observed clients pet and snuggle with an animal in a therapy room and report that the animal makes them feel safer and more secure. With AAT-C, the client seems to warm up to the therapist faster because the client observes a positive relationship between the therapy animal and the therapist. Clients also report that petting the animal is soothing and comforting. I have observed clients become more expressive in therapy and search for personal insights more deeply when the therapy animal is present to interact with as compared with when it is not. The presence of the therapy animal may soothe the client's pain to allow the client to explore their issues and concerns longer and more deeply. For those who may argue that an animal in a therapy session may impair the therapeutic process because a client needs to feel the full extent of their pain in order to recover from it, I reply that I do not perceive that the therapy pet interferes with the therapeutic process, but instead temporarily soothes the client's pain just enough to allow the client to examine their pain-inducing issues more closely.

Even with the number of benefits the presence of a therapy animal can offer, it is important to note that it is not just the mere presence of the therapy animal in the room that contributes to client change. Therapist's orchestrated interactions between the client and the therapy animal as well as between the client and the therapist are a vital component to the success of therapy that incorporates the use of a therapy animal. AAT is not magic, but it can be an integral and powerful contribution to therapeutic progress.

Animals as a Surrogate for Therapeutic Touch

A therapy animal may work well as a surrogate for therapeutic touch. For the most part, it is prohibitive for a human therapist to touch a client because of a real or perceived danger of client exploitation. And yet, there are some times during a therapy session when a client could greatly benefit from the nurturance that appropriate unconditional, genuine, and caring physical contact can offer. This is another instance where an affectionate therapy animal can be very beneficial. Clients can hug, pet, and appropriately touch a therapy animal when the need or desire may arise without fear of landing in a compromising position. The advantage of hugging or petting a live animal over that of hugging a toy is that the animal responds in kind with affectionate behaviors that reinforce the therapeutic benefits of the touch.

When I take a therapy pet with me to the juvenile detention facility for animal assisted visitation or counseling, the adolescents initiate touch with the therapy pet as soon as we enter their section. And the juveniles continue to reach out and pet, touch, and hug the therapy animal during the duration of the counseling session or the visitation time. There is obviously something about touching or petting an animal in nurturing ways that is enjoyable to most humans. When a client is in special need of nurturance, therapeutic touch with an animal can provide comfort for the client.

On some days at the juvenile facility when a juvenile is emotionally distraught, staff may seek out a counselor with a therapy animal for a few moments of nurturing companionship to help console the adolescent. For example, one day a really young juvenile was admitted to the detention facility, he was 10 years old but his size and expression made him seem even younger. He was pretty scared to be in the facility on his first day. A program counselor sought me out and brought the young man to meet Rusty and visit him for a few minutes to help soothe the child's nerves. As is common with this intervention, the child managed a small smile, brighter eyes, softer face, and slower breathing as he knelt down and pet Rusty on the head and scratched behind his ears. Seeing and petting a friendly dog in an otherwise scary place may help a client to feel a bit safer.

On another day, the juveniles who were more advanced in the rehabilitation program had returned from a field trip to a local Holocaust museum. One of the senior adolescents was especially distraught over the experience. Rusty and I had stopped by his section to drop off another adolescent we had been counseling. Rusty immediately sensed the overwhelming sadness in the senior juvenile and walked over to the young man while slowly wagging his tail. He was a large, husky 17-year-old fellow who typically presented a strong, quiet presence, but on this day he was crying. Rusty gingerly put his head on the knee of this kid and stared up at him with his big brown eyes. The kid reached down and scratched Rusty's ear with one hand while he held his head with his other hand and continued to cry. I stood by quietly. After a few brief moments, the young man began drying his tears and looked down at Rusty who was still looking up at him while his ears were being scratched. The kid simply said, "Thanks, Rusty" and looked over at me a few feet away and said thanks to me. We left while the young man continued to dry his tears. A therapy animal can extend a silent kindness to help soothe a saddened soul.

Animal Assisted Rapport Building

Rapport is defined as "a close or sympathetic relationship; agreement; harmony" (Agnes, 2002, p. 1188) and as "a relationship, especially one of mutual trust or affinity" (Houghton Mifflin, 2001, p. 694). The quality of the therapeutic relationship is thought of as a key to a successful therapy experience for the client. Thus, building and maintaining rapport with a client by a counselor is vital for effective counseling. Following are some real-life examples shared with me by various counselors of how animal assisted rapport building facilitated a therapeutic process.

The Intuitive House Cat

Flower is a black and white house cat that stays in a renovated, old, southern-style mansion that is used as an office suite by a handful of counselors in Denton, Texas. One of the counselors, Dr. Anetta Ramsey, specializes in helping clients with eating disorders. Soon after a client enters Dr. Ramsey's office, Flower can be heard meowing at the door. She always shows up at the beginning of the session. The counselor asks the clients if they would like Flower to join them and the answer is almost always yes. According to Dr. Ramsey, Flower has a keen sense of which clients to visit, she only invites herself to those sessions of clients who like cats or are not allergic to them. How the cat seems to know this no one can figure out, but it constantly amazes the clients and counselor alike. On those days when Flower is a little tardy in attending the session, some clients request that Flower attend and the session is slightly delayed until Flower is retrieved. The counselor reports that her clients find comfort in holding the cat during therapy. The clients say that holding Flower helps them feel safe and helps them to better get in touch with their feelings.

The Irresistible Puppy

Several years ago, play therapist Nancy Innis was working with a young girl who was a selective mute. The child had chosen not to speak to anyone in her life, including her parents. After several sessions of seemingly no progress, the play therapist was running out of ideas. On a whim the counselor decided to bring in her new Boston Terrier puppy to the session to see if the girl would show any interest. The child immediately responded verbally to the puppy and very soon thereafter responded verbally to the therapist. The child began to show steady progress in therapy with the puppy present and eventually overcame her choice to be mute. Nancy was convinced that the child and puppy interactions lead to greater rapport between the child and the human therapist allowing for progress to occur. Convinced of the therapeutic benefits of AAT, Nancy Innis has for many years now practiced AAT as a school counselor in Arlington, Texas, with her Boston Terrier therapy dogs.

The Fuzzy Bunny

A counselor relayed this story to me at a workshop I was leading. She was working with a young child who had severe depression. The child was unresponsive to the techniques the counselor had usually found very effective with this age of client. However, she had never before worked with a child with this deep a level of depression. The counselor had recently acquired a light brown dwarf bunny as a pet. The bunny's name was Fuzzy. Fuzzy began going to work with the counselor to visit with this child. In the first session with the bunny, the child responded with a brightened mood as she held and petted the rabbit. With a brighter mood, the child responded much better to the counselor. Fuzzy became a regular part of therapy sessions, and the child made steady progress in therapy. As a result of the success with this child, the counselor began receiving numerous referrals from parents with similarly depressed children. The therapist claimed that Fuzzy was an integral part of the progress made in therapy by each of these children.

The Purposeful Poodle

Denette Mann, a private practitioner in Dallas, Texas, was working with a five-year-old boy who was engaged in group play therapy with two other boys his own age. The other two boys were engaged in an activity that had this one boy feeling left out. He felt rejected and chose to hide under a table across the room. Rosie, a lap-sized, white therapy Poodle, had been resting on her bed in the play therapy room observing the boys play. She followed the dejected boy with her eyes as he disappeared under the table. Rosie got up and leisurely strolled over to the table to see what the boy under the table was doing. She stopped just at the edge of the table, sat down, looked at the boy, and wagged her tail. A few long seconds passed before a small hand reached out from under the table to lightly pet Rosie's head. Rosie responded with an accelerated tail wag. After a few more seconds, an elbow became visible as the boy pet Rosie a little more vigorously. The shoulder was soon sticking out followed by both arms that engulfed Rosie with a hug. The boy then spent a moment giving Rosie a good petting. Rosie was up on all four paws wagging her tail and enjoying the rubdown immensely. The young boy confidently made his way back over to the other boys, followed close behind by Rosie, and asserted himself nicely into the play. The three boys played well together the remainder of the session with Rosie looking on.

The Friendly, Furry Face

My dog Rusty and I had been volunteering our services for individual AAT and group AAA at a juvenile detention facility for about 6 months when we were called upon to spend some one-on-one time with a young man aged 15 years that we will call Larry. Larry had a reading difficulty and a speech problem resulting from low self-esteem and poor self-concept. In conversation with adults, he would not make eye contact and he mumbled in a very low and oftentimes inaudible voice. Larry had been observed in detention as having great difficulty relating well with peers and authority. He had been very resistant to counseling and was easily prodded by his peers into fights. He came from a very abusive home and had a quick temper and hypersensitive nature. He did have a positive interest in animals and missed his own dog while he was in confinement. Sensing an opportunity, the therapeutic programs coordinator referred Larry to me for AAT. Rusty and I saw Larry once a week for 1 hour. During that time, he played with and petted Rusty for about 10 minutes, practiced reading a book aloud for 20 minutes, was counseled for 20 minutes, and played with and petted Rusty for 10 more minutes. While Larry practiced his reading and participated in counseling, Rusty slept with his head resting on Larry's leg while Larry petted him. Larry often verbalized how Rusty helped him be less anxious while practicing his reading and talking about painful things in counseling. Larry said he felt more comfortable with me as a counselor because he could see what a positive relationship I had with Rusty. After a few sessions, Larry often said goodbye to Rusty with an "I love you, Rusty" added. Larry responded very well to this type of therapy. After only 6 weeks, his reading skills had greatly improved, and when conversing with others, he could make good eye contact and speak in clear and audible tones. Larry credited Rusty with his motivation to attend and work hard in weekly therapy sessions. It is important to note that while Larry had difficulty trusting and liking people, he did love animals and thus it was easier for him and comforting for him to spend therapeutic time with Rusty.

Rusty is a very affectionate Cocker Spaniel with a very friendly, furry face. His spotted, red on white coloring gives him a nonthreatening appearance. When you add a scarf around his neck, those red freckles on his face give him a canine "Howdy Doody" appearance. His friendly and outgoing personality, affectionate nature, and really cute appearance attract a lot of people to him for petting, which he just loves.

One day Rusty and I were walking Larry back to his room when we passed an interview room with the top half of the wall made of glass. Inside were two female probation officers trying to communicate with a belligerent looking juvenile girl we will call Stacy. As we passed, one of the officers came out to greet us. She introduced herself to me as Larry's probation officer and said she had heard many good things about Rusty the therapy dog and wanted to meet him. I asked Larry to introduce Rusty to his officer and he did so with beaming pride, a big smile, and in clear and coherent speech. While we were conversing, the other probation officer had been called out of the interview room to take a phone call, leaving the young juvenile female alone in the room with the door open. A few moments passed as Larry, his probation officer, and I were conversing when the three of us looked down at Rusty to see that he had made eye contact with Stacy through the doorway into the room where she was still sitting. Stacy's face had changed since I had first seen her through the glass only a few moments before. Initially the muscles in her face were tight, her forehead deeply furrowed, her lips frowned, and her eyes angry. But now, her face was different as she looked back at Rusty. Her eyes were soft and had a longing look. Her frown had slipped into a slight smile, and her forehead was more relaxed and smooth. She looked very much like she wanted to pet Rusty who was actively wagging his tail in an expression of wanting to greet her. The probation officer and I made eye contact in recognition that something very special was taking place between Stacy and Rusty. The officer asked Stacy if she would like to pet Rusty, and without hesitation she gave a nod and moved from the small room down to the floor in the doorway. Rusty accelerated the speed of his tail wag that caused his whole body to wag with it and crawled into her lap and snuggled up against her chest. Stacy put her arms around Rusty and began to cry. As the heavy teardrops hit Rusty's curly coat, he pushed his head up to her shoulder and nuzzled his nose against her neck as if to say, "It's okay, I am here for you." With Rusty snuggled against her body Stacy began to sob heavily. Rusty continued to snuggle with Stacy as her tears of anger and fear poured out of her. The rest of us stood quietly for these few precious moments while Rusty provided therapeutic affection to Stacy. When Stacy's tears began to slow, I made a few simple reflections about how Rusty cares about her and knows she is having a hard time. Stacy dried her tears on her shirtsleeve, and she and the probation officer resumed their interview while Rusty and I escorted Larry back to his room.

After Rusty and I were back in the car ready to leave for home, I allowed myself to release my feelings and as my eyes teared up I told Rusty what a very, very good dog he was. My heart was full of joy and compassion and once again it was affirmed to me that my choice to work with Rusty as a partner in therapy was indeed a very good one. I received a phone call a few days later from the therapeutic programs coordinator who told me that the two probation officers were saying glowing things about AAT. They said that after just a few moments of empathy exchange with Rusty, Stacy had become cooperative with the officers. The belligerent and resistant attitude she had only moments before her visit with Rusty had disappeared after her visit with Rusty. Sometimes, it takes a friendly, furry animal face to help people who are frightened of other people feel safer.

Animal Assisted Psychosocial Goals and Techniques

Delta Society offers a half-day course called AAT Applications I for professionals seeking information on how to incorporate AAT techniques into their practice. I highly recommend the course and am myself a Delta Society certified instructor for the course. The text for the course does a nice job of delineating AAT goals and techniques in the following four domains of human growth and development: physical, speech and communication, cognitive, and psychosocial. Delta Society presents a number of psychosocial goals that can be achieved utilizing a variety of AAT techniques (Gammonley et al., 2000, pp. 43–47; 2003, p. 38); these include:

Common Animal Assisted Psychosocial Treatment Goals

- Improve social skills
- Brighten affect and mood
- Provide pleasure and affection
- Improve memory and recall
- Address grief and loss
- Improve self-esteem and self-worth
- Improve reality orientation
- Improve cooperation
- Improve problem-solving ability
- Improve concentration and attention
- Decrease manipulative behaviors
- Improve ability to express feelings
- Reduce general anxiety
- Reduce abusive behavior
- Improve ability to trust
- Learn about appropriate touch

Common Animal Assisted Counseling Techniques

- Give and receive affection with an animal (pet or hold the animal)
- Learn gentle ways to handle an animal
- Learn to communicate with an animal
- Learn about how animals learn
- Observe and discuss animals' response to human behavior (immediate consequences)
- Generalize animal behavior to human circumstances
- Brush the animal
- Learn about proper care, feeding, and grooming of an animal
- Engage in play with the animal
- Talk to the animal
- Talk about the animal

- Learn and repeat information about the animal and other animals
- Share animal stories
- Ask the animal to do tricks or commands it knows
- Teach the animal a new trick or command
- Follow a sequence of instructions with an animal
- Learn to feed and care for an animal
- Take the animal for a supervised walk
- Introduce the animal to others
- Recall information about the animal
- Recall information about client's own pets, past and present
- Discuss how an animal might feel in certain situations
- Learn about animal behavior
- Predict or forecast animal behavior
- Develop a cooperative plan to accomplish something with the animal

The animal assisted techniques listed above can be incorporated into counseling sessions to help meet a variety of psychosocial treatment goals. For example, to work toward the goal of improving a client's social skills, the client can practice interacting with a therapy dog by sharing nurturing touch, playing together, and teaching the pet commands or tricks. The client can describe or demonstrate the accomplishments to someone else or teach another person these same skills. Self-esteem can be enhanced by the successful accomplishment of a difficult task with a therapy animal, such as cleaning a horse's hooves or teaching a dog simple tricks or complex agility commands. Compassion and gentleness can be taught and reinforced in a client who must learn to enter a pasture with a posture and attitude that instills a sense of trust in a horse the client must approach and successfully halter. A client's sense of self worth can be enhanced by a therapy animal that desires to interact or play with a client. Clients who work together in animal facilitated team activities, such as dog obedience or horsemanship, must practice good communication and cooperation in order to achieve efficacy with the animal activity. Reducing general anxiety in a client can be accomplished through petting and hugging a therapy cat. Improved reality orientation can be achieved through brushing a pet or asking a pet to do a trick or command. Concentration can be improved in a client learning and repeating animal information. Motivation to attend and participate in counseling is potentially enhanced by a client's desire to interact with a therapy animal. The positive benefits to be gained from therapy can be more immediate when a therapy pet is involved, especially to a client who may have initial resistance to therapy that can likely be reduced by a desire to be with the therapy pet.

A therapist who wants to reinforce the importance of proper communication in getting oneself understood might invite a client to ask a pet to do a trick. The pet's response to the client can be entertaining for the client but also affirm or refine the client's skill at communication. I frequently use this approach with the juveniles that I work with at detention. I am left-handed and have trained my dogs to respond to verbal commands in conjunction with left-hand signals. Most of the juveniles are right-handed. So when they give a right-hand signal to Rusty and he does not respond I work with the juvenile to teach how specific and clear communication must be to get oneself heard and understood. When the juvenile uses a different word with my dogs than what I trained them with, and the dogs do not respond, once again we discuss the importance of how clear and concise messages must be conveyed so that the message one intends is the message that is received. If you ask Dolly or Rusty to "lay," which is a word they are not familiar with, they will stare blankly at you. On the other hand, if you ask the dogs to "down" then they plop down to the ground and lie there until released. We process the exercise to relate the lesson to real-life experiences involving different communication approaches a client can use to convey messages in a way that might serve a better purpose for the client. Sometimes this involves not only being clear in one's communication, but also discovering the best way to actually be heard depending on whom one is speaking to.

My dogs are most familiar with my vocal tone, speed, and accent. Some of the juveniles speak very differently from me, such as at a faster or slower speed, more or less clearly, more or less loudly, or with a different accent. Thus, sometimes the dogs do not respond to the verbal requests of the juveniles as well or as quickly as they do for me. I will watch a juvenile struggle to get Rusty to do a trick. Rusty will try and understand the juvenile and may even attempt a few different things he knows in hopes he will hit on the right one. The juvenile may get frustrated easily and give up. This happens very quickly in this population, after only about two or three tries. This makes for a great opportunity to teach and reinforce patience and frustration tolerance. I encourage the juvenile to stay with the dog and keep practicing. I may even share a few suggestions to help. The juvenile is motivated to keep trying because it is obvious that this adolescent really wants to experience the sense of self-efficacy that comes with successfully completing the command or trick with the dog. After several more tries, success is achieved and we process what the juvenile did to finally achieve that success. The juvenile is smiling with a sense of accomplishment and relays his or her understanding about the event with great interest and pride. I will often see that same juvenile carefully instructing a second juvenile who may be struggling as the first juvenile did. The second juvenile is motivated to be receptive to the instruction from this peer, as opposed to being closed-minded and mouthing off, because this adolescent is motivated to complete the exercise with the dog. Thus, a previous attitude of coercion, manipulation, or "one-upmanship" that is common with this population is replaced with a sense of mutual cooperation being built between the juveniles because of their desire to interact positively with the dog.

AAT can contribute to a decrease in a variety of antisocial behaviors. Juveniles in the detention postadjudication program I participate in are not allowed to participate in animal assisted social activity if they misbehave a certain amount. A misbehaving juvenile "goes off program" for a while, meaning they are not currently earning points toward release from the facility. To "get back on program," the adolescent must demonstrate proper behavior for a designated time period, and then they can also once again participate in recreational types of activity such as animal assisted social visits. I have had reported to me and have observed myself on numerous occasions juveniles making conscious decisions to correct behavior or remind a peer to correct behavior so they could spend time with the animals. Social workers, counselors, and probation officers at the facility have all reported to me how sad juveniles were when they found out their behavior was going to prevent them from participating in AAT or AAA and that the juveniles worked hard to correct the situation so they could once again interact with the therapy dogs, cats, or horses that are involved with the juvenile rehabilitation program. Thus, AAT is a powerful motivational force for engaging and maintaining engagement of an at-risk youth in rehabilitative therapy.

The concept of animal assisted rehabilitation is so effective that simple information about animals can reinforce good behavior maintenance or encourage behavior correction. One day, I brought to the detention facility an article for each adolescent on the history of the various dog breeds classified as "pit bull." The kids had been asking for an article on this topic for some time and were excited for me to get around to this variety of dog breeds when bringing articles about animals each week. When it was time for me to bring information about "pit bull" type dogs, one particular juvenile was not allowed to have the article because he was "off program" and standard procedure prohibited him from receiving it. His disappointment was profound. Sensing an opportunity for reinforcing rehabilitation, I shared the juvenile's disappointment about not getting the article with the adolescent's caseworker at the facility. So the caseworker made a deal with the juvenile, he would keep the article for the adolescent and give it to him as soon as he "got back on program." The adolescent verbalized he would start immediately with his behavior correction. He worked really hard and was "back on program" within a day, and he was as happy as he could be about the article he got to have and read. On my next weekly visit, he told me all he had learned about the dogs from the article in great detail. He was quite proud of himself for learning all of that information and verbalized that he was maintaining his good behavior because he missed playing with the pets when I visited and he wanted to keep getting the information articles about different dogs. He then made a request for a dog breed he wanted me to bring information on when I could. I made a special effort to bring that information the next week to reinforce the good progress the juvenile was making in the program.

Many of these adolescents in detention come from homes that have a "pit bull" type of dog as a pet, or tragically a family member had chosen to fight these dogs. But, sometimes the kids are just intrigued by a stereotypical reputation that "pit bull" dogs have as being the toughest, meanest dog of them all. I use the opportunity of sharing information about "pit bull" dogs with the juveniles in detention as an opportunity to reeducate the adolescents about the cruelty of dog fighting and also about the positive characteristics that these dogs have that should be nurtured.

There are several dog breeds that are often referred to as "bully breeds." Primarily these include the American Pit Bull Terrier (also called a Pit Bull), the American Staffordshire Terrier, the Bull Terrier, the Staffordshire Bull Terrier, Miniature Bull Terrier, and the American Bulldog (Christie, 2002). The dog breeds typically classified as "bully dogs" vary in personality characteristics, some more friendly than others, some more affectionate than others, but all in all, most of these "bully breed" dogs when appropriately trained, properly socialized around people and animals, and raised by a loving family make affectionate and well-behaved companions (Coile, 1998). In fact, the 1999 winner of the prestigious Delta Society national special service award *Beyond Limits* was the animal therapy team of owner Linda Bates with her American Pit Bull Terrier named Rowdy who enriched the lives of the people they visited in a California psychiatric hospital (National American Pit Bull Terrier Association [NAPBTA], 2000).

There have been several dogs associated with the "bully" variety that have achieved positive notoriety in the U.S. Sharing stories of positive accomplishments by a breed of dog that has a really bad reputation helps to overcome the bad rap that the breed has and place into perspective how any dog from any breed can achieve good and sometimes wonderful feats, despite any reputation the breed might have. This metaphor may also instill hope in juveniles who wish to overcome a somewhat bad reputation they have developed for themselves. Below is a list of some well-accomplished "bully" dogs that I share with my juvenile clients (Deneen, 2002; Orey, 2002; Thornton, 2002):

- The well-known commercial image of a dog sitting next to an RCA gramophone in 1900 and later a television was a dog named Nipper, a mutt that was part Bull Terrier with a trace of Fox Terrier.
- A well-known department store named Target featured for several years in the early 2000s in its advertisements and on gift certificates a white Bull Terrier with a red bull's eye.
- A well-known beer company named Budweiser debuted a television commercial on its Bud Light product during the 1987 Super Bowl that starred a Bull Terrier they called Spuds Mackenzie. The commercial ran until 1989, and during the period the commercial ran, the popularity of the breed experienced a large rise.
- A dog who starred in the popular 1930s "Our Gang" comedies was Pete, an American Staffordshire Terrier.
- A Bull Terrier appeared in the 1996 Disney movie *Babe*.
- A Bull Terrier appeared in the 1963 original version of the movie *The Incredible Journey* and an American Bulldog starred in the 1993 remake of the film.
- Prominent people who have owned Bull Terriers include the famous World War II General George S. Patton, famous actress Dolores del Rio, famous author John Steinbeck, and former U.S. President Woodrow Wilson.
- Famous actors Humphrey Bogart and Lauren Bacall owned a "pit bull" type dog named Harvey.
- The famous author and teacher Helen Keller (who was both blind and deaf since early childhood) owned an American Pit Bull Terrier.
- An American Staffordshire Terrier mix named Popsicle, left for dead after a pit fighting past, achieved fame in 1998 as a narcotics detection dog because of his tremendous nose and resilient spirit.
- A Bull Terrier named Lady Amanda was inducted into the Purina Animal Hall of Fame in 1987 for saving her sleeping female owner by leaping at and pinning an intruder up against a wall until the police arrived.
- A Pit Bull named Weela was recognized as a Ken-L Ration Dog Hero in 1993 for her bravery in saving 30 people, 29 dogs, 13 horses, and a cat during heavy floods in Southern California.
- An American Pit Bull Terrier mix named Buddy was a stray puppy found on the carport and adopted by a family that he later saved from a devastating house fire in their Florida home in the year 2000.
- An American Staffordshire Terrier named Norton saved his owner's life when he went for help after she collapsed from a deadly allergic reaction in 1997. He was later inducted into the Purina Animal Heroes Hall of Fame in 1999.
- An American Staffordshire Terrier named Cheyenne was an abandoned, abused, and mange-covered 4-month-old puppy in California who was going to be put to death simply because of her breed, a "pit bull." The dog was rescued by her current owner who had a life-threatening illness. The dog was instrumental in the owner's recovery, providing emotional support and physical assistance, such as licking the owner's forehead when she was feverish and retrieving household items needed by the disabled owner. Cheyenne's nurturing abilities encouraged

her owner to share the dog's gifts of healing with others. Cheyenne now works as a therapy dog in a hospital. With her owner, she visits patients in recovery along with a second "bully" dog adopted into the family, an American Pit Bull Terrier named Dakota.

Hearing or reading about accomplished dogs can inspire an individual to achieve. One can easily assume that, "If a dog can be a contribution to society, then why can't I?"

There is no doubt that as a group, "bully dogs" have been unfairly stereotyped as bad dogs. Any dog that is trained to be aggressive or is not properly trained to be a good citizen, and therefore is undisciplined and unruly, is potentially a dangerous dog. Even a badly behaving Chihuahua can inflict a painful bite. However, a small, badly behaving dog does relatively little damage, whereas a strong and powerful badly behaving dog can maim and kill. Initially, it is not the dog's fault if it is a danger to society; rather it is the owner's fault. All dogs should receive proper socialization, nurturance, and training to be good companions and to be well-behaved citizens in a community. On a rare occasion, a dog may be born with something neurologically wrong with it and successful social training is not possible. But normally, dogs are genetically wired to be intelligent and social creatures that desire companionship and respond well to socialization and obedience training (Alderton, 2000b). Helping adolescents realize the damage that can be done by bigoted stereotyping of animals is a helpful tool for teaching fairness in judgment and proper management of the responsibility that comes with pet ownership.

During AAT-C, clients frequently tell stories about their own pet or a former pet. And to emphasize how facilitative a therapy pet can be for stimulating conversation about a client's pet, I would like to point out that in my experience with my therapy pets, about 90% of the people that engage with me while I am accompanied by a pet, whether a stranger on the street or a client I am working with in therapy, initiate a discussion, without any query from me, about his or her own pet or a pet of a family member or friend. If it is a former pet, opportunity to discuss grief and loss issues is presented. If it is a current pet and the client is confined in a facility that separates the owner from the pet such as a hospital, nursing home, or detention facility, opportunity is presented for the client to process how much the client misses the pet. If it is a current pet waiting at home, the discussion usually centers on the special feelings a client has for the pet and the personal needs the pet fills in the client's life. Each of these is a significant relationship issue that can stimulate client exploration and sharing of very deep emotions. The significance of a client–pet relationship or a client's loss of a pet is too often overlooked by a therapist. Much can be discovered about a client by exploring client–pet relationships. And, opportunity to heal bereavement from pet loss can contribute to greater well-being for a client. Also, discussion about client–pet relationships or feelings a client has or had for a pet leads easily into exploration about relationships with people.

There are a number of additional activities that can be useful in AAT (Delta Society, 1999):

- Gain knowledge about animals
- Learn humane animal care
- Develop motor and physical skill through human–animal interactions
- Learn animal training
- Practice appropriate discipline and correction

- Incorporate an attitude of kindness and compassion
- Learn about nurturance
- Practice loyalty and responsibility
- Experience human–animal bonding
- Learn responsible pet ownership
- Learn AAT and AAA training and activities

As mentioned earlier, I bring information about animals to share with the juveniles in detention, and this has become a very popular activity among these adolescents. They very much look forward to receiving handouts or copies of articles that describe information about dog and cat breeds or that tell interesting and true animal stories. If I forget to bring an article or could not because the photocopy machine was broken, the juveniles' disappointment is apparent. A good source for dog stories is the American Kennel Club's *AKC Gazette*. *Dog Fancy* and *Cat Fancy* magazines are also full of good animal stories. My veterinarian saves his old issues and gives them to me for my counseling work. Dog and cat breed information can be obtained from Alderton's *Cats* or *Dogs* or from Coile's *Encyclopedia of Dog Breeds*. A source for stories on AAT is the Delta Society magazine *Interactions*. Also, at the local pet store, I find entire magazine volumes dedicated to one specific dog breed that contain a history of the breed and some really good true stories about dogs of that breed achieving some type of fame, notoriety, or act of heroism. It is possible that accomplished dogs portrayed in true stories serve as surrogate positive role models.

It is important that articles that are shared with clients be appropriate for the population. For instance, for juveniles in a detention center, all animal related material must be screened for curse words. Even the "b" word that typically refers to a female dog is not allowed in materials handed to the juveniles as a precaution against misuse of the word by the juveniles in the facility. No addresses or contact information or advertisements are allowed in the materials to be shared with juveniles in the facility. All reading material must be age appropriate and serve a positive educational or therapeutic purpose. Also, no staples or paper clips should be used to hold multiple pages together as these can be used as instruments of harm toward self or others. Having the pages three-hole punched before distributing them makes it easy for the juveniles to store the information in their notebooks of collected educational material.

Animal Facilitated Life Stage Development

Therapeutic work involving a therapy animal may facilitate an individual's progression through primary stages of psychosocial development.

> Within the first series of life stages, the primary goals that need to be achieved pertain to a child's needs to feel loved and to develop a sense of industry and competence. In a practical sense, the animal's presence in therapy … may assist a child in learning to trust. Furthermore, the animal may help the clinician demonstrate to the child that he is worth loving. Unfortunately, for some children, their reservoirs of life successes are limited and they feel incompetent. This sense of incompetence may be acted out aggressively toward others

or internally against oneself. A therapist may utilize an animal to help a child see value in life.

(Fine, 2000b, p. 190)

It is important to consider that the various core conditions required for a person to adequately assimilate one or more stages of development might be aided by social interaction with a therapist working in conjunction with a therapy pet. Below is a developmental model for psychosocial development proposed by prominent psychologist Erik Erikson in 1968 (Kolander, Ballard, & Chandler, 2005, p. 30). Let us examine Erikson's model in conjunction with suggested animal assisted therapeutic interventions to facilitate life skill development. For purposes of discussion we will hypothetically assume that for some reason in a child or person's life there might have been some impairment in the development of a particular stage or stages of normal psychosocial development or there was a desire to expand upon a current normal level of development.

Erikson's Stages of Psychosocial Development

If the life task is mastered, a positive quality is incorporated into the personality. If the task during each stage is not mastered, the ego is damaged because a negative quality is incorporated into it.

- Trust vs. distrust (0–1 year of age) learning to trust caregivers to meet one's needs or develop distrust if needs are not met.
- Autonomy vs. shame and doubt (1–2 years of age) gain control over eliminative functions and learn to feed oneself; learn to play alone and explore the world and develop some degree of independence; or, if too restricted by caregivers, develop a sense of shame and doubt about one's abilities.
- Initiative vs. guilt (3–5 years of age) as intellectual and motor skills develop, one explores the environment and experiences many new things and assumes more responsibility for initiating and carrying out plans; or caregivers who do not accept the child's own initiative instill a feeling of guilt over labeled misbehavior.
- Industry vs. inferiority (6–11 years of age) learning to meet the demands of life, such as home and school, and develop a strong sense of self-worth through accomplishment and interaction with others; or, without the proper support and encouragement, one begins to feel inferior in relation to others.
- Identity vs. role confusion (12–19 years of age) develop a strong sense of self; or become confused about one's identity and roles in life.
- Intimacy vs. isolation (20s and 30s *for males only; and 12–19 years of age for females. Intimacy develops in conjunction with identity in females and intimacy development follows identity development in males.*[*]) develop close relationships with others; or become isolated from meaningful relationships with others.

---

[*] The italicized comments above, which represent Erikson's acknowledgement of gender differences in development, do not appear in Erikson's traditional presentation of the psychosocial life-cycle stages. Although Erikson acknowledged female differences in some of his writings, he typically only presented the male model as the standard for development, thereby showing some gender bias regarding normal psychosocial development.

- Generativity vs. stagnation (40s and 50s) assume responsible, adult roles in the community and teach and care for the next generation; or become impoverished, self-centered, or stagnant.
- Integrity vs. despair (60 years and over) evaluate one's life and accept oneself for who one is; or despair because one cannot determine the meaning of one's life.

The first stage of psychosocial development proposed by Erikson, that of trust versus distrust, requires the experience of a relationship with a caregiver or care provider in which a child can trust that the provider will not harm the child and will in fact insure the safety and welfare of the child. This would typically be the child's parents. However, the child may not have had nurturing parents or may have had an abusive experience with an adult or older child thus potentially impairing the development of trust for the client. This early developmental impairment may cause psychosocial difficulty for the client at any time or throughout the client's life. A counselor may be able to help a client to repair early childhood impairment through a therapeutic process. A counselor is trained in basic relational skills that assist the therapist to convey empathy to the client and to facilitate a trusting relationship. Even so, an impaired client may have difficulty trusting the therapist's presentation given that some individual in the client's life was neglectful or betrayed trust. Thus, any additional information that may reinforce the client's ability to observe and experience trust with a therapist can be most beneficial. When a client observes the trust conveyed between a therapist and the therapist's pet this provides the client with strong evidence that a therapist might be trustworthy. Furthermore, a counselor can teach a client what an appropriate nurturing and loving interaction looks like by demonstrating that type of interaction with the therapy pet. Additionally, the client experiences the unconditional and genuine affection offered by a therapy pet to the client showing the client that he or she is in fact lovable. Finally, a client can take initial risks in expressing trust, love, and affection in the safe environment of the therapy room by interacting with the therapy pet, giving and receiving nurturance and affection, and developing a trusting relationship with the pet and transferring that trust to the pet's handler, the therapist.

The second of Erikson's stages, autonomy versus shame and doubt, describes the developmental process whereby the child either develops the necessary confidence and courage to explore the world or instead is inhibited by self-imposed shame regarding one's perceived inadequacies and doubt about one's abilities. Progression toward proper development in this stage or rehabilitation regarding impairment of this stage may be facilitated with AAT. Interactions with a therapy pet can offer a client opportunity to demonstrate competency, for example, the client may teach a therapy pet a trick or train the animal in basic commands.

The third stage of Erikson's model for psychosocial development, that of initiative versus guilt, implies that the child either receives support and encouragement for the behaviors they initiate on their own or they feel guilty because their initiative is labeled as misbehavior. A child can easily become discouraged without proper support and encouragement regarding their choices about behavior. This discouragement can play a dominant role in determining the client's healthy versus poor behavior choices throughout life. Opportunity to initiate productive behaviors with rewarding effects can be offered through the care of animals. Choosing to participate in the daily care of an animal through feeding, grooming, training, and cleaning its bedding offers positive evidence for the client that he or she can make good choices and participate in productive and rewarding behaviors.

The fourth stage in Erikson's model for psychosocial development is industry versus inferiority. In this stage, the client must develop a sense that they are a worthwhile person who can successfully interact with others and accomplish things of importance. An example of animal assisted facilitation or rehabilitation of the life tasks in this stage is assisting a client to teach a therapy animal some advanced skills that can result in rewards for the client and the animal. This might include obedience training or agility training for a dog and participation in competitive dog trials or riding skills with a horse and competitive riding competitions. Some of the horses and dogs trained by the client can have been rescued by the humane society or other rescue groups and need training for adoption. Thus, the client's sense of self-worth is further reinforced by accomplishing a task for self and by doing something valuable for someone else, the animal and the animal's future adopted family.

The fifth stage of psychosocial development proposed by Erikson is identity versus role confusion. A client must develop a sense of self in this stage; failure to do so can result in confusion and a lack of direction in life. Providing a client with opportunities to participate in animal assisted interventions can lead to greater life direction. For instance, vocational skills can be developed regarding dog or horse exercising, training, and grooming, plus veterinary technical skills can be acquired, as well as knowledge and experience in animal boarding and kenneling, and so forth. In addition, assisting a client to team with a pet and get training and certification so they can visit patients in a nursing home or hospital can demonstrate for the client the benefits of integrating the role of community service provider into their identity development. This may eventually lead to a profession directly or indirectly related to human services or other types of benevolence.

The sixth stage in Erikson's model of psychosocial development is intimacy versus isolation. A therapist might encourage a client who is lonely or isolated to get and care for a pet. The pet can provide good companionship for that client. In addition, walking a pet out in the community stimulates social interaction for a client with others who may want to engage with the client's pet, talk about the client's pet, or discuss their own pet with the client. This introduction may lead to the establishment of acquaintances or friendships that offer opportunity for additional social interactions.

Generativity versus stagnation is the seventh of Erikson's stages for psychosocial development. An individual can find personal and financial fulfillment through the practice of animal related professional activities, hobbies, or community service. Perhaps if you are reading this book, you are considering incorporating animals into your professional practice. Many clients are attracted to the idea of working with a therapist who partners with a therapy animal, thus AAT may increase your client base. Furthermore, some therapeutic goals might be more easily accomplished with a client with the assistance of a therapy animal, thus enhancing the efficacy of your practice with particular clients. In addition, you may be sought out for contract work by other agencies such as schools, hospitals, prisons, or detention centers for training faculty or staff in animal assisted therapeutic techniques or in providing AAT. Thus, working with animals can foster the professional development and satisfaction of an individual, including yourself.

The final stage of psychosocial development described by Erikson is integrity versus despair. AAT is a common practice with elderly clients. Therapy animal visitations can increase the social interaction and brighten the mood of an elderly client. In addition, the therapist's animal may encourage the client to discuss pets they have had in their life, thus initiating a life review process for the elderly client. This life review can reinforce for clients the many interesting experiences and productive accomplishments the client has had throughout their life and reassure clients that their life has been a meaningful one. An elderly client may be somewhat isolated or may no longer have anyone to care for. Suggesting the client get a pet to care for, such as in the client's own home or maybe a resident therapy dog or cat in a senior care facility, can give the client chances to experience being important and meaningful to another living being.

This brief presentation on how AAT can facilitate normal psychosocial development or rehabilitate impaired psychosocial development for a client is meant to demonstrate just a few ways a therapist incorporating animal assisted therapeutic interventions into a counseling practice may assist a client at any stage of life. Many different types of animal assisted or animal related interventions or activities might be incorporated into a therapeutic practice to assist a variety of clients with a variety of concerns.

A Typical Animal Assisted Counseling Session

As mentioned previously in this chapter, AAT is an adjunct tool that may be used by a therapist during a typical individual or group counseling session. A nondirective therapist may simply introduce the therapy pet to the client and explain that petting or playing with the pet during a session is a standing invitation during any point of the client's session. A more directive therapist may build in a few minutes at the beginning or end of the counseling session, or both, specifically as a time dedicated for the client to interact with the therapy pet, but also invite the client to interact with the pet during the session by petting or holding it. Also, a directive therapist may actually structure interventions for the client aided by interaction with the pet, all done with the permission of the client. This might include any number of activities or interventions, for example, helping the client to feel more comfortable in the therapeutic environment by facilitating a response to the client's request for the therapy dog to perform certain tricks, or relieving tension by having the therapy dog catch a ball tossed by a client, or guiding a therapy dog to snuggle with a client who is sad, or placing a cat in a client's lap to soothe the client's anxiety, and so forth.

It is quite acceptable for a therapist to pet a therapy animal that seeks affection from the therapist during a therapy session. This nurturing interaction provides useful information to the client about the positive and trusting relationship between the therapist and the pet and may help the client feel more comfortable with the therapist after observing such kind and gentle behavior. Also, the client may be encouraged to interact with the pet simply by observing the therapist's and pet's nurturing interaction.

In a group therapy setting, the same approaches, nondirective or directive, can be incorporated depending on the therapeutic style of the therapist, the nature of the group, and the goals for that particular group therapy. Again, the therapist may direct specific, structured interventions between the pet and the clients or simply have the therapy pet in the therapy room for when the clients might choose to interact with the pet. A unique aspect of AAT group therapy is how group members' interactions with the pet might reflect the formation of cohesion and role development among group members. Some group members may ignore the pet altogether while other group members may focus a great deal on the therapy pet. There may even be some competition among group members vying for the pet's attention. The addition of a therapy pet in a group therapy session requires the group leader to be aware of the potential dynamics stimulated by the pet's presence and assimilate this information to better understand the group. The group leader may sometimes reflect this information back to the group, when appropriate, to assist the group members' self and other awareness.

A colleague of mine who is a counselor at an equine counseling program recently had a graduate class studying group counseling visit her facility to learn more about group equine assisted counseling. As part of the visit, she had the class participate in a couple of actual equine assisted interventions; such as, in pairs, approach one of the horses loose in an arena and halter it; and, as one group, get a specific horse to move between two orange cones on the ground that were about 10 feet apart without touching or bribing the horse or talking out loud to one another in the group. After each exercise, she processed the experience with the group class. Several individual and group dynamics were shared by participants that exemplified enhanced self and other awareness. For instance, one student shared that she was aware of some performance anxiety because the other classmates knew she had some previous experience with horses and they were looking to her for information and leadership. She was very nervous about messing up because she wanted to get it "right." The therapist asked her how this need for perfection played out in other aspects of her life. Self-insight was gained as the student integrated a new perspective regarding the pressure she puts on herself, a pressure caused by not allowing room in her life for any mistakes.

Having introduced the topic of "a typical AAT-C session" I would like to point out that there really is no "typical" session. The manifestation of animal assisted individual or group therapy depends very much on (a) the therapist's preferred style of therapy, (b) the clients' needs and wants, and (c) the therapy animal's abilities. There is no "cookbook" for performing AAT. The therapy animal is basically an assistant to the human therapist. Though therapy animals are referred to as pet practitioners and cotherapists, they are under the direction and guidance of the human therapist and assist in facilitating counseling sessions. The human therapist has to decide if, when, and how a therapy animal may fit into a counseling session or sessions to facilitate clients' recovery. AAT intervention strategies are provided as ideas for a therapist who might choose to incorporate AAT into counseling practice at certain times with certain clients.

Introducing the Pet Practitioner

A counselor that utilizes pets in the therapeutic process must disclose this information to clients in advance of their attendance at an AAT session. Thus, if clients do not wish to have a therapy animal present in the session, the counselor has ample time and opportunity to make arrangements for the therapy pet to be secured in the pet's crate in a corner of the counselor's therapy room or in another room altogether or left home that day. The therapy pet should always be secured in a safe and comfortable place when not engaged in a therapy session. For clients who do wish to work with the therapy pet, the first introduction to the pet should be made outside of the therapy room if possible, such as in a waiting area, with plenty of personal space between the client and the animal. After introductions with the pet, the therapist then may invite the client and the pet to meet and greet one another. The therapist has the responsibility to make sure therapy pets, especially the therapy dog, understand not to jump up on clients in their enthusiasm of meeting them. Experienced and well-trained therapy dogs will meet and greet with all four paws on the floor. It is okay if the therapy pet rolls over on its back for a tummy rub as is common practice by therapy dogs because this is nonthreatening behavior and very cute to boot. After everyone has had a chance to meet for the first time and seems to be okay with the relationship, then the therapy team can proceed into the therapy room for a counseling session.

Animal Assisted Basic Relational Techniques

There are four basic listening responses every effective counselor utilizes in a helping relationship to convey empathy and facilitate a therapeutic relationship; these are reflection, paraphrase, clarification, and summarization. Reflection is the counselor responding to the feelings expressed by the client. A counselor will reflect these feelings to the client by rephrasing the affective part of a client's message. The intended purpose of reflection is to assist the client: to be more expressive, to be more aware of feelings, to acknowledge and manage feelings, and to accurately discriminate between feelings (Cormier & Nurius, 2003). Paraphrase is the counselor responding to the content expressed by the client. A counselor will accurately rephrase the content of the client's message in the counselor's own words. The intended purpose of paraphrase is to assist the client to focus on the content of the client's message and to highlight content when attention to client feelings is not appropriate (Cormier & Nurius, 2003). Clarification is the counselor requesting more information from the client. Clarification frequently takes the form of a counselor asking the client a question. The most effective therapeutic questions are open-ended questions that allow for comprehensive answers by the client and usually begin with how, what, when, where, or why. The intended purpose for clarification is to encourage more client elaboration, to check the accuracy of what the therapist heard the client say, and to clear up vague or confusing messages (Cormier & Nurius, 2003). Summarization involves the therapist joining together two or more paraphrases or reflections that sum up the client's messages partway through the session or sum up the client's messages at the end of a session. The intended purpose of summarization is to tie together multiple elements of client messages, to identify common themes or patterns presented by clients, to interrupt excessive rambling by a client, and to review client progress (Cormier & Nurius, 2003).

In an AAT-C session, it can be very therapeutic to reflect, paraphrase, clarify, and summarize the behaviors and expressions of the therapy pet, the client, and the interactions between them. The therapist must be astutely in tune with the therapy pet to be able to observe and oftentimes acknowledge even the most subtle reactions of the pet for therapeutic purposes. Most dogs demonstrate a keen intuition in their relations with others. The therapy pet's interactions with and reactions to the client can provide a therapist with additional information about what is going on with that client. Even more important is the client's interactions with and reactions to the pet; these can provide extremely useful information about the client's emotional state, attitude, and relational style and ability.

To draw a clearer picture of what some animal assisted relational responses may look like, I have provided a few examples from my own experience. In the past, with a particular client or another, I reflected, "When you got very quiet, Rusty walked over and placed his head on your knee and looked up at you and your eyes filled with tears." Or, "A moment ago you seemed a little anxious and your voice was fast and high-pitched. Now as you sit there stroking Rusty's fur, you seem quieter and more introspective." Some sample paraphrases I have used are, "When you began to focus inward I saw you look over at Dolly sleeping on the floor, you took a deep breath, and then you shared something painful in your life." Or, "Each time, as you begin to talk about your father, you start scratching Rusty's ears a little more vigorously." Some sample clarifications I have used are, "There are certain times during the session that Dolly walks over to you looks up at you and wags her tail, this seems to make you smile. What are you experiencing?" Or, "Rusty was a bit wiggly when you first arrived and you seemed a bit anxious, but now as you sit there rubbing his ears you seem calmer and he seems calmer as you both have slowed down your breathing and you both seem more relaxed as he rests next to you. How do you experience yourself differently now as compared to when the session first began?" Or, "When you talk about your mother you cuddle with Rusty, when you talk about your father you pick up the ball and roll it back and forth with Rusty. How is your relationship with your mother different than your relationship with your father?" Some sample summarizations I have used are, "You have spoken a great deal today about how important it is for you to regain your father's confidence in you, that you are not sure he realizes how hard you have been working on your issues and how much you have changed. You have reached out to pet Rusty a lot in the session mostly during the times you talked about your father. This is a deeply emotional issue for you." Or, "You have shared today how you have been putting off dealing with some family issues in your life, and it is getting to the point you feel you can no longer avoid these issues. But you are unsure as to how to begin to address them. You said you did not realize how much you had been negatively affected emotionally by avoiding the issues until you noticed in yourself during the session how much comfort you got from sitting close to Rusty and petting him. You realized you have really been stressing out and not wanting to acknowledge it."

The intent of the above examples is to demonstrate how occasionally including useful information during a session about the client and therapy animal interactions can provide additional information that may benefit the client. These animal assisted relational statements are not meant to take the focus off of the client, but rather meant to further the client's self-understanding and reinforce the client's introspective process. These animal assisted relational statements are also designed to communicate to the client that you are very aware of what is going on in relationship to the client in a session and the inclusive empathy conveyance may increase the client's confidence in your therapeutic ability. You may recall what it was like for you when you took your first basic counseling techniques course and you had to learn not only how to properly reflect, paraphrase, clarify, and summarize, but when it was most appropriate to do so for the maximum therapeutic benefit. It is equally true for animal assisted reflection, paraphrase, clarification, and summarization; timing is very important. Incorporate animal assisted relational techniques when they can specifically enhance the therapeutic process for the client. Animal assisted relational techniques should be used strategically during a session so as to retain their potential benefit.

Accessing Feelings through the Use of AAT

Sometimes it is difficult for a client to get in touch with or express feelings. Having an animal present can often help a client with this. Techniques to facilitate emotional expression can be very subtle or very direct. One direct technique is to ask the client a question from a therapy animal's perspective. For instance, "Dogs have a keen sense and oftentimes know people better than other people do. So, if this dog could talk, what would he say about you?" or "If this dog could talk, how would he say you are feeling?" And, "If this dog were your best friend, what would he know about you?" or "If this dog were your best friend, what would he know about you that nobody else would know?"

One subtle technique for accessing clients' feelings is to have the client briefly focus on the animal and try to empathize with it. For instance, when a client is scratching Rusty's ear and Rusty is relaxed, eyes closed or drooping, slowed breathing, and so forth, I will ask the client to observe and describe Rusty's emotional state and guess how he might be feeling right then. We will discuss what has to happen for Rusty for him to feel safe, relaxed, and content and what would interfere with that state. Likewise, I proceed to have clients relate the same types of condition in their life where they feel safe and relaxed and when they do not, and so forth. So the client–animal interaction serves as a lead to initiate expression of feelings that the client may be struggling to recognize or to share.

I have learned from previous experience that Rusty is sensitive to the internal state of the client, and if the client is anxious, nervous, or angry, Rusty becomes a little unsettled and wiggles a lot or gets up, walks around, and lies down several times. This has made for a great opportunity to suggest the client focus inward and become more aware of what feelings are inside of the client and what impact these feelings may have even though the client may try to hide the feelings from self or others. When a client is sad, Rusty seems to know this intuitively, and he gravitates toward the client and puts his head in the client's lap or against the client's knee in a snuggle-like pose. This has elicited client tears on many occasions.

One day I was doing a brief demonstration of AAT for a colleague's doctoral counseling practicum course. A student in the class volunteered to be the client, and she and Rusty and I sat on the floor as there were no comfortable chairs or couches for Rusty to get up on to be next to the client in the classroom. With the whole class looking on, I invited the student to interact with Rusty by petting him if she wanted to while we talked about how her day and her week were going. I instructed Rusty to lie down next to her, and she sat there stroking the fur on his back while she talked. The volunteer talked about fairly superficial things regarding her day and her week. After a couple of moments, Rusty got up, walked in a tight circle, nuzzled her hand, and lay back down again, and the client resumed talking and stroking his back. Rusty did this several more times when I reflected his behavior to the client and asked her what she thought about it. She had been sharing very surface level information up to that point, but after my inquiry she said she felt that Rusty acted unsettled and was so probably because she was unsettled. With encouragement from me, she continued to explain that she in fact was very stressed out and frustrated about some issues in her life and felt a lot of inner turmoil. I invited her to share that which she felt comfortable sharing in a group environment, and she began to express some of her personal problems. As she talked, she shifted her voice and body tone while becoming more inner reflective. I noticed her hand, which had been stroking Rusty's back, slowly move up his neck and begin gently rubbing his ears. She seemed to be petting him without thinking much about him; she was focused on herself while conveying her personal concerns. As she talked on, she continued to rub his ears, and Rusty slowly rolled over onto his side and lay quietly with his eyes drooping. The client was very intent and focused on telling her story while gently rubbing Rusty's ears. Rusty lay quietly snuggled next to her and began to drift off to sleep. At the conclusion of this approximately 30-minute demonstration, I asked the volunteer client how she experienced the session. She said that she was nervous about being in front of the class and at the same time very anxious about issues in her life. She had been putting off things and trying not to deal with them or even think about them. She felt that Rusty could sense her anxiety and so he felt unsettled around her. She further conveyed that when she did acknowledge to herself that she had to face and talk about her concerns, she began to sense some internal relief and that is when Rusty settled down. She felt that she and Rusty were very in tune with one another and he was at first a source of providing self-awareness for her and then later in the session a source of affirmation and soothing comfort for her. She felt that by observing Rusty's unsettled behavior she was gently confronted with having to face her issues instead of running away from them because she too felt very unsettled. Her unsettled feeling was mirrored by Rusty's unsettled behavior. Then as she began to acknowledge her issues and express them, Rusty settled down, and that affirmed for her that she was releasing some anxiety by expressing herself. Rusty then served as a source of soothing comfort for her as she rubbed his soft, warm ears and observed his relaxed, slowed, easy breathing as she shared her uncomfortable personal issues. She went on to say that if this had been a more private counseling session she would have put her arms around Rusty and cried for a bit. Even so, she said she felt better after spending just a few minutes engaged in AAT as part of the class demonstration. Thus, in just one short classroom exhibition, Rusty assisted in demonstrating how a therapy dog can assist a human therapist to provide greater self-awareness for a client, encourage client expression, and contribute to the client's experience of some relief.

I have observed an interesting and consistent phenomenon between Rusty and the clients he works with. At the beginning of the session, the client mostly strokes Rusty's back. As the client gets deeper into personal issues, the client's hand moves up to rubbing Rusty's neck and shoulders. And, when the client is talking about the most intense personal issues or is in touch with emotional pain, the client rubs Rusty's ears starting at the tips and then moving to rubbing the base of the ear where it connects to the head. Rusty progressively relaxes both his posture and his demeanor through this touch process moving from friendly and calm to relaxed and then deeply relaxed. This relaxing touch progression happens without any direction from me. I do not know why it happens, but I can speculate. Back stroking or patting a dog may be a more superficial acquaintance interaction that helps the client and Rusty get to know one another. Rubbing Rusty's neck and shoulders is a more soothing activity that helps both the client and Rusty relax. And, finally, rubbing Rusty's ears initiates a strong relaxation response in Rusty that is further soothing and comforting for the client and makes it somewhat easier for the client to share painful issues, introspect, and gain personal insights. Many behavior specialists recommend rubbing a dog's ears to relax a dog, especially at the base where the ear meets the head. I find it interesting that clients intuitively interact with Rusty via touch in a progressively comforting manner that soothes and relaxes the dog and then likewise soothes and comforts the client. There seems to be a natural pacing and matching process of human and animal emotional and behavioral energy levels that does not require conscious awareness to occur. Therapeutic reflection of observations of when this does occur can be very facilitative of insight and growth in a client.

Deb Bond, a very talented and insightful equine assisted counselor in Keller, Texas, often points out to a client how a nervous horse is responding to the nervous energy generated from within a client. Or a horse that is acting stubbornly is likely responding to a client's attempts to bully the horse. She teaches her clients the importance of looking within themselves to become aware of any negative emotional energy they are projecting and to modify that energy to project a more positive energy resulting in the presentation of a more positive and friendly posture. This counseling technique assists a client to learn to be more aware of negative internal emotional states, to learn the importance of resolving issues that give rise to such states, and to learn to modify a destructive or counterproductive internal negative emotional state to a more positive and constructive emotional state. Ms. Bond shared a story with me about a young adolescent who was taking part in group equine assisted counseling with her therapy team. The young man was working with a therapy horse named Tom, a sorrel and white paint. Tom is known to be irritable and moody sometimes. But today, when working with this young man, the horse Tom was especially cantankerous. Tom even resorted to attempts at nipping and kicking each time the young man approached him. Tom did not react this way when any of the other adolescents in the group approached him, but he seemed to be very uncomfortable with this lone young man. The young man responded with disappointment, frustration, and declarations that "Tom does not like me." One of the counselors worked with the young man and asked him why he thought it was that Tom did not seem to like him. The boy thought it through and said, "Because I do not like myself." The young man had previously been diagnosed with bipolar tendencies, and he did not like how his condition made him so different from other adolescents; he really did not like himself because of it. In a group process at the end of that session, each adolescent was asked if there were one thing they could change about the attitude or behavior they had that would make it easier to relate to the horse they had worked with that day, what would it be. This young man shared, "I would change being bipolar." The other adolescents in the group were all appropriately responsive and supportive of this young man. No one else shared his same condition, but they displayed positive empathy toward the young man and expressed acceptance of him as he was. It was apparent from his reaction that this was very healing for the young man. And interestingly enough, at the next equine therapy session the following week, the young man seemed different. He was calmer and more confident. Something inside him had made a shift. And, guess what? He and the horse Tom got along just fine after that. It is apparent that animals have a keen sense about humans and can even read emotions and behaviors that are buried beneath the client's defenses.

A friend of mine and a private practitioner in Plano, Texas, Dr. Sara Harper, relayed a story to me about how her blond Labrador Retriever therapy dog Brie really got one family's attention regarding the family's dysfunctional communication.

As I remember the story, the therapy session began when family members were greeted merrily by the friendly therapy dog and all was cordial. Then the family members raised their voices and started in on one another with blame and accusation. The dog eventually tired of it and went to the corner of the room and lay down on her bed. The family's mutual word barrage continued and escalated loudly. Just then Brie got off of her bed, walked to the center of the therapy room, and regurgitated. Everyone stopped talking instantaneously. Before the therapist could share the apology posed on the tip of her tongue, the family members became concerned for the dog and began to direct kind and nurturing words and pats toward Brie. All family members spontaneously began to discuss how they felt they had made the dog sick with their angry words in the therapy room. Recognizing this as a metaphor for how they were treating one another, the family focused the remainder of the session on how they were hurting each other with their words and behavior and how they needed to get better. The session became very productive, and the therapist had great success with this family as the things learned in the therapy session generalized to the home. The family members were always nurturing of Brie in continuing therapy sessions and were careful to keep their communications healthy for fear of upsetting Brie. In speaking with me about this story, Dr. Harper conveyed that she was not sure if Brie threw up because she coincidentally had an upset stomach or if the family's extremely dysfunctional interaction had actually made her ill. Brie had not become ill before in sessions and has not since, but she also has not experienced such poor behavior from clients as she had from this particular family. A therapy dog vomiting in a therapy session is not supposed to be a therapeutic intervention and should be avoided if possible, but sometimes accidents do happen. It is difficult to tell why Brie threw up since she cannot tell us, but the incident served to help one family become more aware and motivated them to work and grow together. Therapy dog Brie remains a good barometer of anger for clients as she still does gracefully exit the therapy session when voices are raised, making it difficult for clients to deny their anger. Dr. Harper is well known in North Texas for her AAT work that has been featured in the *Dallas Morning News* (McKenzie, 2003). In addition to Brie, she also works with two Tonkinese cats, Katherine and Elliot. Along with animal assisted individual and family counseling, Dr. Harper combines biofeedback therapy with pet therapy to assist patients to recover from a variety of conditions. Adult as well as child clients are calmed when they pet one of the therapy cats that are more than willing to sit and purr in a client's lap while the client learns and practices the therapy skills taught by Dr. Harper. And children who might not otherwise want to come for therapy instead look forward to playing a brief game of soccer in the waiting room with Brie, who is very adept at kicking a tennis ball back and forth. Dr. Harper has used animal assisted biofeedback therapy to effectively treat clients to recover from stroke, attention deficit disorder, anxiety, grief and anger issues, and other concerns.

DePrekel and Welsch (2000b) have designed a structured activity that can be used in an individual or group format to assist with the recognition and expression of affect. It consists of providing the client with a simple line drawing of a dog or horse on a sheet of paper and asking the client to color the various body parts based on the following schema. Colors represent the following feelings: blue=sad, red=angry, orange=happy, green=confused, yellow=scared, and purple=curious. The body parts represent the following topics: tail=friends, head=family, ears=school(work), feet=myself, body=love, and neck= (left blank to be filled in by client). The resulting discussion about the client's end product can initiate the sharing of important issues and the feelings surrounding them.

I prefer a slightly different format for using animal illustrations for accessing client feelings. I ask clients to choose their own colors and label what feelings each represents within them. Likewise, I ask the client to label the animal's body parts to represent significant areas in the client's life. (See the illustrations of a dog, a cat, a horse, a rabbit, and a parrot along with accompanying exercise instructions provided in the appendix for your convenient use.)

Another helpful exercise to access feelings is to provide the client with a picture of a dog or a cat posed in different expressive positions, for example, an angry dog barking with hackles up or a fearful dog with its tail tucked and ears back. After exploring together what the animal in the picture might be feeling, the therapist can guide the client in a discussion about how the client may feel. Also, the client and therapist can discuss how animals typically show how they feel. But in contrast, sometimes humans express how they feel and sometimes they hide their feelings. The therapist may inquire when and under what circumstances the client hides feelings and when the client shows feelings genuinely. (See the illustrations of a dog and cat in expressive poses along with accompanying exercise instructions provided in the appendix for your convenient use.)

Sometimes it is easier to stimulate a conversation for clients to talk about themselves when clients have something to compare how they see themselves. The therapist can provide a photo or picture of certain dog breeds with accompanying descriptions of common characteristics for that breed. The client can pick one or more dogs out to represent shared characteristics of how they see themselves and the dog as similar. For example, if I were to compare myself with one of the dog breeds characterized below, I would have to say that I am most like a Great Dane. You can also have a client describe a breed or characteristics of different breeds that they would aspire to be more like to check out the self-acceptance level of the client. For example, I am pretty happy being a Great Dane, but, not being completely satisfied with myself, I would prefer to be more like an American Cocker Spaniel except with better protection ability and fewer grooming requirements, like that of a German Shepherd. I guess in my ideal world, this would make me something like a spaniel-shepherd. You can also have the client pick out which family members share certain characteristics with certain dog breeds or a combination of dog breeds. This stimulates a discussion around family dynamics and potential family misunderstandings and conflicts. A therapist can also use this exercise in a team-building workshop to help participants describe their perceptions of self and of the colleagues they work with in an effort to build a greater understanding of how one is perceived and how this impacts working relationships. This is also a good exercise to inquire as to what type of dog characteristics clients see themselves as having in different situations, such as home versus work, or with friends versus with family or a spouse. It would be interesting to discover that the client is more like one dog at home and a different dog at work and so forth. This exercise explores the potential dichotomies within the client's life. The exercise should be introduced with the idea that no dog breed is a bad dog breed; every dog breed has its own unique characteristics that make it special. Following is a sample list of just a few contrasting dog breed characteristics acquired from Coile (1998) that can be useful for initiating such an exercise (Coile thoroughly describes over 150 breeds in her text):

- American Cocker Spaniel. Considered a medium-sized dog. Average weight 24 to 28 pounds. Average height 13.5 to 15.5 inches. Watchdog ability high but protection ability very low. Medium energy level. Extremely friendly and playful. Easy to train. Very high affection level. Grooming requirements very high. This dog is cheerful, amiable, sweet, sensitive, willing to please, and responsive to its family's wishes. It is also inquisitive and loves outings in the country, but is equally at home in the city and happily walks on a leash for its exercise. (pp. 30–31)

- American Staffordshire Terrier ("pit bull" type dog). Considered a large dog. Average weight 57 to 67 pounds. Average height 17 to 19 inches. Watchdog ability and protection ability very high. Medium energy level. Not very friendly. Low training ability. Medium affection level. Low grooming requirements. Sweet, trustworthy, docile, and playful with its family. Friendly toward strangers as long as its owner is present. Generally good with children. Aggressive toward other dogs — especially those that challenge. It is stubborn, tenacious, and fearless. Loves its owner's fond attention. (pp. 146–147)

- Bloodhound. Considered a very large dog. Average weight 90 to 110 pounds. Average height 23 to 27 inches. Watchdog ability high. Protection ability low. Energy level medium. Friendliness high. Affection level very high. Playfulness very low. Grooming requirements very low. Ease of training very low. This dog is gentle and placid, has calm manners, and is extremely trustworthy around children. It is also tough, stubborn, and independent. A great tracker used for hunting and search and rescue. (pp. 64–65)

- Border Collie. Considered a medium-sized dog. Average weight 30 to 45 pounds. Average height 18 to 23 inches. Watchdog ability high. Protection ability medium. Energy level very high. Friendliness medium. Playfulness high. Training ability very high. Affection level medium. Grooming requirements medium. A bundle of energy. One of the most intelligent and obedient breeds. Needs lots and lots of exercise. It is a dependable and loyal companion. (pp. 288–289)

- Bulldog. Considered a medium-sized dog. Average weight 40 to 50 pounds. Average height 12 to 15 inches. Watchdog ability very low and protection ability low. Energy level very low. Friendliness high (but not toward other dogs). Playfulness high. Training ability low. Affection level very high. Grooming requirements low. This is a jovial, comical, docile, and mellow dog. It is willing to please although it does have a stubborn streak. (pp. 246–247)

- Chihuahua. Considered a very small dog. Average weight 6 pounds or less. Average height 6 to 9 inches. Watchdog ability very high but protection ability very low. Very high energy level. Not very friendly or playful. Not easy to train. Not very affectionate. Low grooming requirements. A saucy dog with intense devotion to a single person. May try to be protective but is not very effective. Often temperamental and may bark a lot. (pp. 204–205)

- Dachshund. Considered a small dog. Average weight 16 to 22 pounds. Average height 8 to 9 inches. Extremely high watchdog ability, extremely low protection ability, high energy level, somewhat friendly and playful, but hard to train. Affection level medium. Grooming requirements low. Bold, curious, and likes adventure. Likes to track and sniff things out. Is independent but likes to join in on family activities. Reserved with strangers and may bark a lot. (pp. 68–69)

- German Shepherd. Considered a large dog. Average weight 75 to 95 pounds. Average height 22 to 26 inches. Extremely high watchdog and protection ability. Somewhat friendly (but aggressive toward other dogs). Very playful. Medium energy level. Easy to train. Affection level medium. Grooming requirements low. Very intelligent with great ability as a working dog. Very devoted and faithful to its owner but suspicious toward strangers. May try to be domineering. (pp. 298–299)

- Golden Retriever. Considered a large dog. Average weight 55 to 75 pounds. Average height 21.5 to 24 inches. Watchdog ability medium. Protection ability low. Energy level medium. Extremely friendly, playful, and affectionate. Very easy to train. Medium grooming requirements. This dog is friendly, devoted, and obedient. Needs lots of exercise and active nature outings. Is overly exuberant, boisterous, and enthusiastic about everything. Is eager to please and enjoys learning new things. (pp. 16–17)

- Great Dane. Considered a very large dog. Average weight 100 to 120 pounds. Average height 28 to 32 inches. Watchdog ability high. Protection ability medium. Low energy level. High friendliness and very playful. Easy to train. High affection level. Low grooming requirements. This dog is gentle, loving, easygoing, and sensitive. Generally good with children and friendly toward other dogs. It is a powerful dog (and can be hard to handle if not properly trained), but it is very responsive to training. This dog makes a pleasant and well-mannered family dog. (pp. 116–117)

- Poodle (Miniature). Considered small dog. Average weight 12 to 18 pounds. Average height 10 to 15 inches. Energy level, friendliness, and affection level are high. Playfulness is very high. Watchdog ability and ease of training are very high. Protection ability is very low. Grooming requirements are very high. This is a lively and playful dog that is eager to please, responsive, smart, and obedient. (pp. 264–265)

- Yorkshire Terrier. Considered a small dog. Average weight 7 pounds or less. Average height 8 to 9 inches. Watchdog ability is very high. Protection ability is very low. Energy level medium. Somewhat friendly toward strangers but not too friendly with other pets. Playfulness is high but affection medium. Training ability is low and grooming requirements are high. This dog seems oblivious to its small size. It is eager for adventure and trouble. It stays very busy and is quite inquisitive. This dog is bold and stubborn and can be aggressive to strange dogs and small animals. (pp. 236–237)

Animal Assisted Family History Gathering

Many clients own a pet and consider their pet a close family member that they spend a lot of time with and from which they receive emotional support. With a therapy animal present in a session, it seems natural for a therapist to inquire as to whether the client has a pet. This type of discussion can easily segue into a discussion about the client's support system and how well they are utilizing personal resources.

AAT-C can be useful for gathering family histories or facilitating the client's creation of a family tree. The family tree exercise in counseling involves having the client list all significant persons in the client's life, most predominantly relatives, and describing various remembrances the client has had about them, positive and negative influences (direct or indirect) these persons have had upon the client, and any significant mental health issues or other pertinent history of these persons. The exercise is useful for helping clients understand the social influences that have impacted their own growth and development.

One type of common family tree exercise used in counseling is the client's construction of a genogram. "The genogram is a pictorial representation of the client's family tree. It quickly shows a family's history by depicting current and past relationships…. The genogram is therapeutic when a client's main concerns are family problems because the client gains insight into the issue by describing them to the helper as the genogram is constructed" (Young, 2005, p. 210). Young (2005) describes basic reasons to consider using the genogram, including the client and therapist gaining a greater understanding of:

- Cultural and ethnic influences
- Strengths and weaknesses in relationships
- Intermarriage and generational influences
- Family disturbances including addictions, divorce, and mental illness
- Sex and gender role expectations
- Economic and emotional support and resources
- Repeated patterns in the client's relationships
- Effects of birth order and sibling rivalry
- Family values and behaviors including dysfunctional patterns
- Problem relationships
- Family traumas, such as suicides, deaths, and abuse

When the therapy animal has a pedigree with some type of registry, such as American Kennel Club for dogs, sharing the animal's family ancestry is a fun way to introduce the client's own family tree exercise. When the animal's family ancestry is unknown, then the counselor can use a history of the breed of the animal. For a history of individual dog breeds, the text *Encyclopedia of Dog Breeds* by Coile is a good resource, and for a history of individual cat breeds, I recommend *Cats* by Fogle. Even if the therapy animal's particular breed history is unknown, an exploration of the history of the animal's evolutionary rise can serve as a substitute.

As an example breed history, let us briefly examine the evolution of the American Cocker Spaniel as described by Hart (1968). Spaniels are mentioned in literature written as early as 1386 and referred to by Chaucer as "spaynel." By the 15th century, spaniels were being used to flush game birds. The recognized country of origin of this hunting dog, Spain, gives it its name, and Spanish spaniels were commonly used by sporting aristocrats. The spaniel became popular in many European countries with similar hunting terrain and aspirations, especially England. Spaniels began to be bred for specific purposes, which began to divide the breed into three categories: flushing spaniels, which found and flushed the game birds; water spaniels, which retrieved; and setting spaniels, which crouched and set and pointed. From the flushing type of Spanish spaniel came the field spaniel followed by the Norfolk and Springer Spaniel. And from the Springer was developed the English Cocker Spaniel. "These 'cocker' or 'cocking' spaniels, used primarily in the hunting of woodcock, snipe, and other lowland birds, were bred down in size to be handy, hardy, and easily cared for" (p. 11). Early Cocker Spaniels in both England and America looked pretty much the same; but in 1882, the American Spaniel Club was organized and the English and American cockers began to diverge in type. The American cocker was bred to have a more distinctive head and a shorter and stockier body.

Alderton (2000a) describes a brief history of the species of the domestic dog. All dogs, wolves, jackals, and foxes are members of the Canidae family and can be traced back some 30 million years. Today there are 13 genera and 37 recognized species spread all over the world. It is thought that all modern domestic dogs are descended from the Gray Wolf. Wolves and domestic dogs share the same social, territorial, hunting, and guarding instincts. The socialization of the domestic dog is thought to have begun over 12,000 years ago, probably in the Northern Hemisphere when wolves were in greater number and spread over a wider territory than they are today. There are now more than 300 different breeds of domestic dog.

Cheetahs, panthers, ocelots, wild cats, and cats are all part of the Felidae family. There are a number of wild cats spread over the world, but it is thought that all domestic cats are descended from the African Wild Cat (Alderton, 2000b). The domestic cat has had a varied history.

> During the 9,000 years or so since the domestication of the cat began in the Middle East, these remarkable creatures have provided a mixed reception. Although worshiped in ancient Egypt, and treasured in the Far East, they suffered undeserved persecution in Europe during the early Christian era because of their associations with the old pagan religions. However, the role of cats in destroying the rats that carried the Black Death across Europe regained them some status.
>
> (Alderton, 2000b, p. 6)

Animal Assisted Interventions and Clinical Diagnoses

There is no comprehensive scientific resource that delineates how specific animal assisted therapeutic interventions can be applied to clients with a particular clinical diagnosis. However, DePrekel and Welsch (2000a) have described in their unpublished workbook, *Animal-Assisted Therapeutic Interventions (based on DSM IV)*, over 14 clinical disorders that they believe AAT can be effective with. The workbook also includes information on specific AAT goals, interventions, precautions, and contraindications. The diagnoses they address are based on the *Diagnostic and Statistical Manual for Mental Disorders, 4th edition* published by the American Psychiatric Association and include General Anxiety Disorder, Attention-Deficit/Hyperactivity Disorder, Bipolar Disorder, Borderline Personality Disorder, Conduct Disorder, Eating Disorders, Major Depressive Disorder, Narcissistic Personality Disorder, Obsessive-Compulsive Disorder, Oppositional Defiant Disorder, Posttraumatic Stress Disorder, Reactive Attachment Disorder of Infancy or Early Childhood, Separation Anxiety Disorder, and Substance Related Disorders. Verifying the accuracy of the information in the DePrekel and Welsch text would make an interesting research project. Many of the interventions are recommended for more than one of the diagnoses. A common contraindication for participation is a history of animal abuse. A few examples of the recommended diagnosis-based interventions by DePrekel and Welsch (2000a) are listed below:

Generalized Anxiety Disorder

- Slow breathing exercise with an animal
- Walk an animal to the tempo of relaxing music

Attention-Deficit/Hyperactivity Disorder

- Identify parts of an animal
- Participate in dog exercising and agility activities

Bipolar Disorder

- Compare own behavior with the turtle and the finch
- Journal about how learning from animals helps to understand self

Borderline Personality Disorder

- Substitute self-destructive behaviors with productive animal care behaviors
- Work one-on-one with an animal to form an attachment

Conduct Disorder

- Study herd behavior of horses
- Engage in proper play or other interaction with animals

Major Depressive Disorder

- Groom an animal and discuss need for daily self-care
- Learn riding and horsemanship skills to build competence

Oppositional Defiant Disorder

- Train in basic dog obedience
- Play with and exercise an animal

Posttraumatic Stress Disorder

- Hold or pet an animal while talking about own trauma
- Observe and discuss flight or fright responses in animals

Animal Assisted Metaphor

Animal assisted interventions such as animal images, stories, and metaphors used as symbols paralleling the client's experience can be very beneficial for facilitating client insight and growth. Metaphor has been defined as "a thing regarded as representative or symbolic of something else" (Jewell & Abate, 2001, p. 1074) and as "a figure of speech containing an implied comparison, in which a word or phrase ordinarily and primarily used for one thing is applied to another" (Guralnik, 1980, p. 893). Metaphors can work like distraction methods getting around client defenses and resistance. The client relates to the image or metaphor but finds it less threatening to consider because it is presented about someone or something else.

Milton Erickson used imagery and metaphor to speak with the client's "unconscious mind" (Bandler & Grinder, 1975; Zeig & Munion, 1999). When Milton

Erickson refers to speaking with "the unconscious part of the mind," he is referring to the mute or nondominant hemisphere. The left side of the brain, considered the dominant hemisphere for functioning in most humans, synthesizes language whereas the nondominant right side of the brain synthesizes space. The left hemisphere perceives detail, and the right hemisphere perceives form. The left hemisphere codes linguistic descriptions and the right hemisphere codes sensory input in terms of images. Thus, if one wants to surpass the defenses established by the logic and language of the dominant left hemisphere, this is best done through the use of imagery or symbolic metaphor processed by the nondominant, right hemisphere.

The success of the use of animal-related metaphor in therapy is based on the idea that even though the imagery and metaphor briefly shift the focus to the animal, the client will still tend to process the animal's experience or animal's story through the client's own perspective, which is formed around the client's own life experience. It is my belief that this side door technique of having the client imagine what the animal's experience is like helps to tap more deeply into suppressed and even repressed client feelings and experiences. Animal assisted metaphorical intervention sidesteps the client's barricaded self-awareness and gains access where it is typically limited when using more directive inquiry. Animal assisted metaphors must be brief and utilized somewhat sparingly so the client does not tire of them. These techniques are most powerful when the client and the therapy animal have established a positive relationship because then the client will relate more strongly with animal related stories and metaphors. Following is an example of a therapeutic metaphorical animal story I developed and used effectively in therapy.

"A failure to communicate" - (a metaphor designed to emphasize the value of education, discipline, and communication). Let me tell you a story about a friend and his dog, an 8-month old German shepherd. My friend would get very frustrated when his dog did not understand him. When they went walking the owner would get tangled up in the leash, or he would go on one side of a telephone pole and the dog would go on the other side. Sometimes he would almost trip on the leash and fall down. The dog pulled on the leash most of the time and would drag him down the street. Back at the house, when he would give the dog a treat he would get his fingers nipped by the dog's haste to get the treat because the dog had poor manners. When my friend wanted to add something to the dog's food bowl while he was eating, the dog growled at him and he was afraid he would bite him. He resisted the idea of obedience training for the dog because he did not think it was the right thing to do to a dog. He would say it was unnatural and thus not fair to the dog. Finally, out of desperation, he decided to go see what obedience training was all about. The obedience trainer started by explaining that, "Owners and their dogs need to develop a form of communication between one another. Without the ability to communicate, there could be no mutual understanding or cooperation. If you and your dog had a shared language, you would get along much better and like each other's company a great deal more. In addition, you and your dog could go more places together. You are frustrated because your dog does not behave the way you want him to. But dogs do not naturally know the English language. They have to be taught. In fact they can learn some simple words in any language. I have a friend in Seoul, Korea, whose dog is actually bilingual, responding to commands in Korean and English. So people with their dogs

need to go to school for several weeks to learn a shared language, called obedience training. It is positively rewarding for the dog and the trainer; whenever your dog understands you, give him lots of praise and reward him with petting, a food treat, or toy treat. Learning can be fun for both you and your dog. In addition, watch your dog's body language. He has no words to express his feelings, but he can say a lot with his tail up and tense that tells you he is alert to something, or his tail tucked between his legs to demonstrate he is afraid or cautious, or his tail can be relaxed and wagging sharing that he is calm and friendly. He can say a lot with his ears that will be perked up when he is alert, drawn back when he is afraid or cautious, or relaxed when he is calm and friendly. So not only does your dog need to learn your English language obedience commands, but you need to learn his 'dog speak' so he can communicate with you. It is a shared venture of learning and training to benefit your relationship and what you can get from it." Well my friend fell in love with the obedience training and not only do he and his dog now have a shared language of understanding and cooperation, they enjoy going just about everywhere together. My friend is so proud of his dog and his relationship with his best furry friend. Sometimes you just have to figure out how to communicate to have a better relationship with someone. And if you cannot figure it out by yourself, going to school or getting counseling are good places to get the information and guidance you need to be successful.

There are several symbols, images, and messages presented in the above metaphor. It is likely that the client will self-select those symbols, images, and messages that are most meaningful for the client. Several phrases in the above animal metaphor story that the client might key in on are "would get very frustrated," "did not understand," "get tangled up," "trip and fall down," or "drag him down." These phrases symbolize how things are not going very well in the client's life. The next few phrases could symbolically represent the client's life fears: "would get his fingers nipped," "growled at him," "afraid he would bite him." The next phrases might symbolically address the client's potential resistance to change: "he did not think it was the right thing to do," and "it was unnatural," and "not fair." The following phrases could stimulate a client's openness to gain insight or initiate change: "need to develop a form of communication," "mutual understanding and cooperation," "shared language," "get along much better," "like each other's company," and "go more places." The next set of phrases are designed to construct the change goals and process into perceptively achievable steps so the client feels less overwhelmed: "have to be taught," "simple words," "go to school," "positively rewarding," "praise and reward," "learning can be fun," "shared adventure of learning," and "benefit your relationship." And finally, the last set of phrases are designed to reflect the positive outcome likely to occur from the client achieving the change goals: "shared language," "understand each other," "go … everywhere together," and "proud of his dog." It is possible that the dog in the story is a symbolic representation of one aspect of the client's self or represents some other significant person in the client's life.

Following is another example of a metaphor I developed and have used effectively in counseling with clients.

"Shedding the old to make room for the new" - *(a metaphor designed to emphasize a need for change).* My Cocker Spaniel Rusty has a lot of fur. His coat is very

thick and wavy. But his coat changes when it needs to, with the changing of the seasons. For instance, in the winter his coat becomes thicker to keep him warm when the weather is cold, and in the summer his coat becomes thinner to help keep him cooler in the heat. He changes his coat when the need arises. His thinner summer coat has to be shed before his thicker winter coat can grow in, and vice versa. His coat changes naturally, but sometimes the change works much better for him when he gets help. If he gets brushed and combed regularly, then his coat stays smooth and soft. If grooming is neglected, then his hair can become so tangled that combing it takes a great amount of effort that can sometimes be uncomfortable for the dog. Sometimes in order to get a smooth coat again a piece of tangled fur has to be trimmed out. The trimmed piece of hair leaves space for a healthier coat to grow in its place. Thus, regular attention to grooming, especially during the more drastic seasonal changes, makes his coat healthier and more functional. But no matter what, sometimes tangles happen. And when they do, we deal with them in the best way we can so his coat becomes soft and smooth once more.

The above animal metaphor story is also designed with key symbolic phrases to facilitate client insight and initiate the change process. The phrases, "has a lot of fur," and "very thick and wavy," might represent the complexities of the client's issues. The next phrases may serve as encouragement for the client's desire and ability to change along with reinforcing the idea of seeking help with the process: "He changes … when the need arises," "has to be shed," "can grow," "change naturally," "combed out," "trimmed a little bit," and "works much better for him when he gets help." The following phrases may represent the client's fears: "neglected," "so tangled," and "very painful." And finally these last phrases may represent expected outcomes for change and thus motivate the client: "space for a healthier coat to grow," "healthier and more functional," "deal with them in the best way," and "becomes soft and smooth."

It is easy to create an animal assisted metaphorical story. Think of the basic elements you want to convey to your client and think about animal behavior or situations that would reflect those elements and string them into a story for your client. Be careful to include metaphors that are appropriate for your client's unique needs, for example, the part in the above "shedding" metaphor about trimming out a tangle may not be appropriate for a client that self mutilates, but may send a message for someone else to change a negative behavior or to distance oneself from negative influences. Metaphors do not require interpretation by the therapist. In fact, they work best when the interpretation is left solely to the client so greater personalization can occur. Sometimes I have a client ask me what the story means. I simply tell them, "It is just a story that may have meaning for you. Think about it over time if you like, and if you want we can discuss what it means for you." When using the animal metaphor story, I have had clients respond immediately with personal insights. But sometimes a client would seem to dismiss the story only to come back in a later session with some meaningful insights the story stimulated for them.

I hesitate to describe a structure for the development of a metaphorical story because construction is highly dependent on a counselor's particular understanding about the unique needs of a specific client. However, I have found to be helpful the placement of certain common symbolic elements in the therapeutic metaphorical stories I tell to clients. These are (a) phrases that can convey empathy and understanding for the client's problems or concerns, (b) phrases that may address a client's fears, (c) phrases that may address a client's hopes, (d) phrases that may address a client's resistance to change, (e) phrases designed to instill encouragement and motivation to change, and (f) phrases that symbolize possible positive outcomes from instigating the change process. My current skills at therapeutic, metaphorical storytelling evolved from my childhood experiences of listening to various family members who were very adept and entertaining storytellers. And, I always appreciated that many of those stories had embedded in them some meaningful life lesson that I could relate to.

Animal Assisted Play Therapy

There are different approaches to play therapy, some that are more nondirective as in Person-Centered Play Therapy (Landreth, 2002), and others that are more directive as in Adlerian Play Therapy (Kottman, 2003). Either way, play therapy and AAT-C are a natural fit, especially with dogs. Most dogs have a natural desire to play so will feel right at home with a child playing in a therapy room. The typical play therapy room requires some alterations to incorporate AAT-C. Even though the therapist will always be in the room with the animal, accidents can still happen. Very small toys that can be swallowed by a dog are a choking hazard and should be replaced with slightly larger objects. Sharp objects should also be removed as well as heavy tools that could hurt the therapy pet if used against it, for instance a metal hammer. All products in the animal assisted play therapy room should be nontoxic if eaten, including paint, markers, clay, and so forth.

An item that is good to add to an animal assisted play therapy room is a pet bed or mattress large enough for the pet and a small child to lie down on together. It should have a removable cover for cleaning. Among the standard play therapy toys should be an assortment of toys with animal themes such as dog and cat puppets, cat and dog face masks, cat and dog action figures and dolls, and so forth. There should also be toys for the pet to play with and for the pet and the child to play with together. All of the pet's toys should be grouped together on a shelf low enough for the child and the pet to reach. A small, soft-bristled grooming brush is a good item to have among the pet's toys in case the child wishes to brush the pet's fur. Good dog toys for a game of fetch in play therapy include a rubber ball (rubber can be cleaned easier than a tennis ball) and a soft nylon cloth Frisbee (only if there is enough safe space to fetch and catch the Frisbee). The rubber ball should be textured and not be smooth or have a slick surface because these types of balls, especially handballs, can slip past the tongue and get stuck in a large dog's throat and choke it quickly. The ball should be large enough not to slip down the dog's throat but small enough for the dog to grasp. A nice alternative to the rubber ball is a sponge ball that is covered with tough canvas or nylon material, found in the toy section of any large department store, especially the ones that sell swimming pool toys. This type of ball will not hurt if it hits anyone and is very durable. It can also be washed easily. Tug-of-war toys should be avoided in AAT due to the high risk of a child getting a finger pinched by a dog trying to get a better grip.

A double safety dog leash should be included in animal assisted play. A double safety dog leash can be made by attaching a 3- to 4-foot leash to a 6-foot leash and attaching the 6-foot leash to the dog. If the child wants to walk the dog around the room, down the hall, or outside, then the child holds onto the shorter lead and the therapist holds onto the longer lead that actually controls the dog. This procedure protects the dog from a child that may try to jerk it around on the leash and protects the child from a large dog that may move around and tangle the child in the leash if it is not guided by the therapist. Another safety technique is to attach the leash the client holds to a chest harness on the dog and attach the leash the therapist holds to the dog's neck collar. If the client tugs on the leash attached to the chest harness, it is less likely to cause discomfort for the dog than if the client was tugging on a leash attached to the dog's neck collar.

If the therapy pet is a cat, then the pet's toys should include those types that make for a good game of chase, such as feathers tied to a string. When working with a therapy cat, precautions should be taken to make sure the sand tray or sandbox of a play therapy room is covered at all times that a play session is not going on. The therapy cat will prefer to use its own litter box, hidden in a discrete place in the counseling facility; however, sand can be a tempting place to relieve itself. I have never heard of one single instance where a therapy cat relieved itself in a therapy sand tray or box, but why throw caution to the wind? Keep the sand tray covered in between play sessions with a therapy cat.

Before therapy begins, a brief orientation about the therapy pet should be provided to the child and the child's parent or guardian. This gives the child the opportunity to meet and learn about the pet outside of the play therapy room. The child will feel more comfortable with initiating interactions with the pet during play therapy if the therapist explains beforehand the types of activities the child can do with the pet if the child wants to at some time. Example activities that can be presented to the child might be pet the animal, play with toys with the pet, brush the pet, talk to or about the pet, hug or lay down with the pet, ask the pet to do tricks, walk the pet. Emphasize that a choice to interact or not interact with the pet is entirely up to the child. If the child prefers not to interact with the therapy pet, the therapist can place the dog in a down stay on its bed or mattress. This leaves the way open for the child to still initiate interaction with the therapy pet during a session if the child desires to. The pet's portable crate should also have a special place in the play therapy room in case the therapist needs to crate the pet for the comfort of the child or if the pet gets tired and needs a break or a nap in the crate.

As the child interacts with the therapy pet, the therapist may need to utilize a limit-setting technique when necessary, for the protection of the pet. For instance, "Rusty the dog is not for hitting," or "Rusty the dog is not for painting," and so forth. Any activity that in the therapist's judgment causes stress, discomfort, or danger for the therapy pet should not be allowed. A child should not be allowed to hit a pet or shoot a pet with a type of gun that projects objects, like a dart gun. There are some play therapists that believe a child should not point a toy gun at the therapist and pretend to shoot the therapist, "The therapist is not for shooting." These same therapists may feel that pointing a toy gun and pretending to shoot the therapy pet is not acceptable. While I am not willing to immerse myself in the "pretending to shoot the toy gun at the human or pet therapist" debate, I will recommend that a therapist use his or her own judgment given the circumstances. A common and fun trick that many dogs do well is "play dead." Again, this trick can be avoided if a therapist judges it as not appropriate given the child and the circumstances.

If a child does accidentally or purposefully pour paint onto a therapy animal, a therapist should treat the incident in the same way the therapist would if the child

Figure 7.1 Therapy dog Rusty snuggles next to a child in an animal assisted play therapy session with a graduate student counselor: A self-worth enhancing exercise for the child.

Figure 7.2 Rusty interacts with a child during puppet play in an animal assisted play therapy session: A relational enhancement exercise for the child.

had poured paint onto another child. Together the therapist and child would wipe the animal's fur as clean as possible and as soon as possible so the paint does not get in the pet's eyes or licked off by the pet and so the paint does not get further spattered. The paint should be nontoxic if ingested in case the pet does lick at it and water soluble so it washes out when you bathe the pet thoroughly when you get home. If a therapy animal will tolerate being dressed up by the child without being stressed out, then this can be allowed. If the pet shies away from being dressed up, then the therapist can simply reflect that the pet is not so sure about being dressed up or that the pet must not want to be dressed up, or something similar.

During an animal assisted play therapy session, it is very acceptable for the therapist to pet the therapy animal when the therapy animal seeks out affection from the therapist. This modeling behavior reinforces for the child that it is okay to pet the therapy animal if the client chooses to do so, and it also reassures the client somewhat that the therapist must be an okay person if the pet likes the therapist and likewise the therapist treats the pet nicely.

Play Therapy Yard

An exciting concept for animal assisted play therapy is a play therapy yard. If you can create a small outside area near your counseling office, then a play yard can be used for more rambunctious play with a therapy dog. A play yard would allow greater variety of activity for AAT, such as appropriate space for walking or running with the dog, to play a game of fetch, to take the dog through agility obstacles, and so forth. A play yard could incorporate many other aspects of nature therapy as well. You can add a small, shallow pond with fish and water plants and add a small waterfall. You can have feeders to attract neighborhood birds. You can plant a butterfly garden with plants to attract butterflies for laying their eggs, such as dill and fennel, and native nectar flowers for feeding the butterflies. A complete life cycle butterfly garden is a unique opportunity to teach the cycle of life and instill hope and faith in the wonder of nature. A word of warning, place the bird feeders on the opposite side of the yard as the egg-laying plants that attract butterflies to give the poor caterpillars a fighting chance of survival from the birds who find them a scrumptious delicacy. Once a caterpillar builds and submerses itself into its chrysalis it can be taken inside to a butterfly hatchery for safekeeping until it is time for the butterfly to emerge and be set free. As I write this piece, I am sitting out in my sunroom that looks out into my backyard and am watching a bright red, male cardinal feed two of its juveniles who have not yet learned to feed themselves. This is a common occurrence in my backyard that I have developed into a small "bird-scaped" sanctuary and water garden. And yet each time I see this parental act of nature, I am deeply moved by it. Observations of nature help keep me grounded, reassured, and realistic. The therapeutic benefits of the observation of nature by clients are potentially vast.

Animal Assisted Group Play Therapy

Reichert (1994) presented a model for animal assisted group play therapy for sexually abused girls aged 9 to 13 years. The pet therapist in the intervention was a 4-year-old part-Dachshund named Buster.

> The purpose of utilizing a pet in therapy was to build a bridge to ease tension and anxiety. The children had an option of disclosing their abuse into the pet's ear or to tell the group. Further the pet was used for playing, touching, and projecting their feelings. It was also effective as a means of gathering family histories and stories. The children would tell about their experiences with pets as well.
>
> (Reichert, 1994, p. 58)

Reichert utilized a variety of techniques. Nondirective play as well as some structured exercise were utilized to assist the clients to increase an awareness of their feelings and to openly share their feelings. These exercises were often very creative, such as making a collage that represented feelings the child expresses on the outside versus feelings she has on the inside. Clients were encouraged to tell their sexual abuse stories, and some chose puppets for this outlet. Puppet Theater was a useful medium for the therapist to convey metaphorical, therapeutic stories. Relaxation and guided imagery exercises were lead by the therapist to help each child find a "safe place" in their mind. Empowerment exercises were incorporated to strengthen the girls' inner resources that included Puppet Theater activity as well as collage making. Throughout the sessions, the therapy dog was present. Sometimes the children would "hold the pet in order to ease tension, reflect anxiety, or for support" (Reichert, 1994, p. 60).

Equine Assisted Counseling

I have been fortunate to be able to volunteer periodically at Rocky Top Therapy Center in Keller, Texas, in their trademarked equine assisted counseling program named *Right* TRAIL. This program is directed by a very talented therapy team with in-depth expertise and many years of experience with equine assisted counseling: Deb Bond, program director and head counselor; Jennifer Steinmetz, challenge course expert; and Ken Burrill, all-around horseman. This is a 24 contact hour program typically offered in a format of one 3-hour session per week over 8 weeks. It is a nice integration of instruction and participation in equine experiential activities, cowboy challenge course games and activities, and group therapy process. The purpose of the program is to build group cohesion, create a sense of community, develop a safe environment to express self and be vulnerable to learn, introduce problem solving, and develop communication skills. Approximately 6 to 10 children/adolescents participate in each group, ranging in age from 9 to 16. Some common needs of participants include self-esteem enhancement, conduct or behavior remediation, academic development, social skill development, and grief resolution. Therapy horses are marvelous tools for facilitating growth and development in children in each of these life skill areas.

The social behavior of horses is the same as humans with a few exceptions: horses are honest, they typically do not come with a lot of emotional baggage, and they do not invest energy in "looking good" and in trying to be something they are not. "Horses can increase our awareness of our thoughts, words, and actions.... Horses instinctively mirror our attitude, emotion, and behavior without allowing baggage to interfere. This occurs anytime a human interacts with a horse" (*Right* TRAIL, 2001, p. 1).

The basic lesson plan for the *Right* TRAIL program is easily adapted and modified to fit the needs of the population seeking assistance. Some of the equine assisted experiential activities of this program include (*Right* TRAIL, 2002):

- Discuss horse safety
- Discuss a horse's body language
- Choose a horse to work with
- Learn how to develop a relationship with a horse
- Lead a horse with a lead rope
- Learn about the gas pedal and brake on a horse
- Get a horse to move in a corral without touching it
- Learn to halter a horse
- Learn to tie a quick release safety knot
- Learn to groom a horse
- Learn an emergency dismount and horse safety while mounted
- Walk in rhythm with a horse
- Horse and rider role play without the horse (one participant wears a bridle and reins while the other attempts to communicate to them only using the reins and not talking)
- Learn to walk-on, halt, and turn mounted bareback on a horse
- Learn to saddle and bridle a horse
- Practice riding with saddle and bridle on a horse
- Ride around a simple obstacle course
- Learn to trot, canter, and gallop on a horse

The equine assisted activities are interspersed with a number and variety of challenge games and activities. An early activity asks each participant to take on a self-chosen ranch name that reflects a positive attribute for that person. Sometimes other participants can help someone come up with a name, if assistance was requested. Example names might be "Happy Hector" or "Dynamic Deb." The first group of juveniles from Denton County detention that attended Rocky Top recommended my ranch name. They call me "Changemaker Chandler" since I was instrumental in connecting this detention facility with Rocky Top and paid for the first groups to receive services via a research and service grant I had received. The kids gave my therapy dog Dolly her ranch name because she is so fearless, comfortable, and relaxed around the big horses; they call her "Daring Dolly."

A ropes course is undertaken at Rocky Top for team building and communication enhancement. Also, participants lead a blindfolded partner around obstacles for trust building. A life values auction aids in clarifying personal values. The group makes a rope together for cohesion building and personalization of the experience. While making the rope, participants are asked to reflect upon and share in turn what positive things they want in their life and send that energy into the rope. There is no limit to what thoughts and emotions I have heard projected into a rope by juveniles from detention: courage, hope, strength, happiness, positive attitude, wisdom, appreciation for animals and nature, love and appreciation for family members, and so forth. Each juvenile can take as many turns as they want to put good energy into the rope. The rope is put away and saved until group process on the last day of therapy. Then, on the last day, while reflecting upon and sharing their entire experience, participants cut pieces of the rope to keep as a remembrance of the Rocky Top Ranch.

Figure 7.3 A juvenile from a detention facility exercises trust and courage while experiencing the benefits of caring for and grooming a horse.

All equine assisted activities and challenge games and activities are processed in depth in a group therapy format at the end of each session to assist participants in relating personal insights to their own life. The skill of the group process leaders is key to the success of the program for the participants. A final activity is a fun hot dog roast around a ranch campfire.

I have personally observed the positive impact of the Rocky Top Therapy Ranch *Right* TRAIL program on male and female juveniles in a postadjudication program from a residential detention center in Denton County, Texas. The administrators of the detention center were so pleased with the results of the first two groups that my grant financed to receive therapy at Rocky Top that for the following year the detention center budgeted funds to take all postadjudication detention boys and girls (about 30 adolescents) through the equine assisted counseling program at Rocky Top Therapy Center. As a result of participation in this program, I observed these highly troubled, at-risk teens reduce and eliminate manipulative behaviors, overcome fears, display courage, develop and practice stress management and anxiety reduction skills, become less self-focused and more other-focused, increase communication skills, support each other, help each other, and look out for and encourage one another. The therapeutic programs coordinator at the juvenile detention center was most pleased that the equine program paralleled the rehabilitative focus of the

Figure 7.4 Before learning to ride with a saddle, juveniles from a detention facility learn to be sensitive to the horse's movement when the horse walks: An empathy building exercise.

postadjudication program, and the equine program gave the added benefit of using and practicing important lessons and skills with the horses and each other. The motivation to develop and practice these lessons and skills was enhanced by the adolescents' desire to be with and ride the horses. Because the Keller Independent School District believes in the value of this program, it contracted with the Rocky Top Therapy Center for a number of years to take at-risk school children through the *Right* TRAIL program.

To demonstrate how equine assisted counseling can benefit juveniles from a detention center, let us examine just a few pages out of my field notebook of observations I made for six girls from the detention center that participated in eight 3-hour sessions of equine assisted counseling at the Rocky Top Therapy Center. The first set of notes describes the girls working with a horse that they had not worked with before and trying to get the horse to follow them around a corral with only a rope loosely draped around the horse's neck. The horse had no halter, bridle, or saddle. The purpose of the exercise was to learn how to build a trusting relationship of

Figure 7.5 Juveniles from a detention facility learn how to work together as a group to get a horse to walk between two orange rubber cones without talking out loud to one another or touching the horse or bribing the horse with food: A potent lesson in communication, cooperation, and team-building.

mutual cooperation through the use of appropriate body language, the right attitude, and careful communication. The names of the girls have been changed to protect their identity.

At the Right Trail Corral. None of the horses were haltered. They were loose in the corral. Each pair of girls was given a rope and asked to go relate to their horse with speech and body language to get the horse to follow them around the corral. Each pair of girls draped the rope around their horse's neck and tried to get the horse to follow them. Kay and Sherry, who can be quite stubborn, based on their prior history at the detention facility, tried pulling and pushing the horse named Oscar, who of course did not move. These two girls had a body language that was not inviting to follow. This pair eventually succeeded when they began talking nicely to the horse and became more gentle and inviting with soothing speech and relaxed body language, as a result of coaching from the group leaders. They were the last pair to succeed of the three groups. But they eventually did get Oscar to walk with them a little toward the end. Janie and Denise started out with gentle and calm speech and inviting body language with the horse named Stick, and he followed them all over the corral. They were the most successful of the three groups. Jackie and Heather had initial success with their horse named Dude. But a yard worker accidentally left a gate open to a small grassy lawn, and Dude slipped in there and got spooked when the group leaders herded him back into the corral.

Now Dude was not so calm anymore. Jackie and Heather could not get near him without him running away; so they had to ask for help. With coaching from the group leaders, they were reminded that they needed to read the horse's needs and reassure his safety. When Jackie and Heather slowed down and talked gently to the horse for a time while petting him, he allowed them to lead him around again. Group process centered on being aware of the body language of the horse and what it is saying it needs or what it is feeling and how to respond to the needs and feelings of a horse to foster a relationship with it. Also, discussion was about what messages the girls were sending to the horse through speech and body language that may cause resistance to participation versus invitation to participation. Although much frustration was exhibited during the exercise, the girls did not give up and kept trying because of their desire to be successful with the horse. The attitude of the girls was very positive at the end of the session.

On another day, two of the adolescents were especially challenged by a particularly stubborn horse, and the girls really had to exercise some frustration tolerance. It was a powerful lesson that might not otherwise have been accomplished were it not for the adolescents' strong desire to spend time with their therapy horse.

At the Right Trail Barn and Therapy Pasture. The horses were to be gathered from the pasture and brought to the barn to be groomed and saddled by the girls. The horse Oscar was reluctant to come in from the pasture, but Kay and Sherry finally got him haltered when he paused to drink some water from a water bucket. Even after they got him haltered, he steadfastly refused to move. They requested assistance from a group leader who reminded them about how to get him moving by having one person wave an arm behind the horse while the other led. They finally got Oscar to the barn where he refused to lift his hooves for the girls to clean them. After many attempts by both Sherry and Kay, Kay had to walk away from Oscar and sit down for a few minutes and collect her emotions before going back and trying again to get him to lift his hoof for cleaning. She finally won him over with gentle speech and rubbing his neck. Each hoof after that came up easier. Kay and Sherry were persistent and patient with him, even though they were the last to get their horse saddled up this day.

Following is an excerpt from my field notes that describes some of the emotional and social benefits to be gained from learning to ride a horse.

At the Practice Arena. The girls practiced riding with saddles and bridles independently again today. Denise did very well with the riding today on Stick. She is looking very comfortable up on her horse. This is a continuing progression from the early part of yesterday's session. She has progressed nicely in the last 2 days with her comfort level with riding. Janie is riding very well today on Stick. Her only expressed frustration was wanting the horse to go faster. After a few instructions from a group leader, she tried the instructions to trot and had good success. Her response was "This is so cool!" Thus, her frustration turned into confidence and satisfaction. Janie is still relating well to all members of the group. Heather got her horse Dude to start galloping today, but then Heather got scared and forgot how to stop her horse. While the horse was galloping, Heather repeatedly shouted, "Whoa!" and tried to pull the reins, but she was also tensing her legs from fear of falling off and this only encouraged the horse to keep going. Heather's eyes grew very big while the horse was galloping. The horse finally came to a halt when it reached the far end of the arena. A group leader went down to the end of the arena on a horse to check on Heather, who was still in the saddle. The group leader led Heather's horse back to the near end of the arena and gave Heather the choice of continuing to ride or taking a break. Heather decided to dismount and collect herself because she was a bit shaken. Once off the horse, she began smiling and laughing with one of her peers, Sherry. When Heather was asked about the laughter, she said it was relief and humor about her situation. When Sherry was asked about the laughter, she said she wanted to laugh when she first saw Heather's horse was galloping away but quickly realized Heather was afraid. So she waited until Heather was safe on the ground and she saw Heather smiling before she laughed, and then she laughed with Heather and not at her. This was a big step for Sherry because she has struggled in the detention center with her tendency to laugh at other people's pain. When it was her partner's turn, Heather did lead a horse for her partner, Jackie, who was the only one still requiring a leader today because of her fear of riding independently. By her willingness to lead the horse for her partner, Heather was reengaging quickly with the horse that had frightened her. When her partner was done, and everyone else had also finished, the group leader asked Heather if she wanted to remount and try again. Heather said yes. Then the group leaders, staff, and other girls gave her feedback and encouragement. Heather mounted the horse, but the horse was a bit reluctant to be reined back out into the arena since it sensed the day of work was over. But with instruction from the group leader, Heather became appropriately assertive and got the horse to follow her directions. Heather took very good control of the horse and even got him to respond to a command to "back up," which is somewhat difficult. She did great assertive communication with the horse. We were all so proud of her we applauded. Jackie was so inspired by Heather's courage and success that she decided to ride on her own for the first time without her horse being lead by a rope by her partner. Jackie was doing better today with being calmer, but she was not assertive with the horse, and he just kept going to the gate wanting to leave. After instruction and persistent encouragement from the group leader, Jackie finally got assertive with her horse and had a good response from him. Her confidence shot really high after that. Sherry did better today with her behavior. She did not ride up on anyone today and looked very nice on her mount. She was relaxed and took it nice and slow around the arena. When off the horse and watching her partner, she was friendly with staff and watched her partner with interest. Her behavior was very acceptable. She has come a long way with improvements in her social skills. Kay did well today also. She also learned to trot the horse today, as did Janie, and looked great except for her tendency to lean forward in the saddle a little too much on the trot. Her partner Sherry noticed this and was about to suggest it to Kay when a group leader beat her to it and Sherry simply nodded her head in agreement. It was obvious Sherry just wanted Kay to be helped but had no investment in bossing Kay or showing off, which had been typical Sherry-like behaviors before she started the equine therapy. The girls led the horses back to the barn. They removed the tack from the horses and returned everything to the tack room and their riding helmets to the helmet room (they are never allowed on a horse without a helmet). The girls then led the horses to the therapy pasture where they released them. All of the therapy horses decided to roll in the grass today right after being released, and the girls watched and laughed at this, a couple verbalizing, "Oh, how cool!" They had not seen their horses do this before today. It was a nice way to close out the day. Today was the first day we got a little break from the heat. The past 5 days of sessions have been miserably hot, which lends even greater credit to the girls who have been willing to come back each day in the heat and participate fully in the program.

This last set of field notes of observations on the girls describes the last day of therapy. The juveniles had a final opportunity to ride, and afterward, they shared how much participation in the equine assisted counseling program had meant to them.

At the Practice Arena. I was pleased that both Heather and Jackie chose to ride Dude today even though he gave Heather a scare yesterday. Both had smooth, independent riding experiences today. Janie and Denise also did very well. Kay and Sherry had good experiences as well. Sherry trotted her horse today but was careful not to impede anyone else or get too close to anyone. Her actions were very considerate of others today, a big change for her.
On the Grass by the Pavilion. A group leader took the riders in a line, and they rode outside of the arena onto the grassy, treed area near the pavilion on the hill. This was not a fenced area. All of the riders did very well. The horse Dude was a little troublesome as he wanted to graze instead of walk, but with corrections from his rider the horse went along. The riders rode back to the Right Trail barn.

At the Right Trail Barn and Pasture. The horses' tack was put away, and each pair of girls walked their horse back to the pasture. They spent a few moments saying a final goodbye to their horses before releasing them to pasture. The girls all had tears coming back from the pasture.
At the Tree House. The girls had tears when processing their day and how hard it was to say goodbye to their horses and to the group leaders. The girls thanked me for helping make the experience possible for them and thanked the detention staff for being so supportive and trusting to allow them to come out to the Rocky Top ranch. The girls were very sincere and emotional when conveying their remarks. The group leaders passed out the rope the girls had made in an earlier session, and they each made a wish as they cut a piece to keep. They mostly wished for success through the detention program as well as in life after they had completed the detention program and they also wished for happiness. Some also wished to be able to come back to Rocky Top to visit the horses and staff. The girls were asked to name one thing new they had learned about themselves from the Rocky Top experience. Denise said, "I learned that I could cry. Before, I had to make myself cry." Kay expressed, "I discovered I was a good person who people could respect." Janie said, "I found out I could have a positive relationship with more than one person." Heather said, "I learned I am a very brave person." Jackie, said "I discovered I have a sensitive side as well as a strong side." Sherry said, "I learned that I have good

in me and can do good things and have positive relationships with people." The group leaders passed out certificates to the girls with photos on them of the girls with their horse.

At the Pavilion. We all sat under the pavilion and drank a soda, compliments of the group leaders. Jackie came up with a spur of the moment idea for the girls to march for the group leaders as a way to say thanks and to honor their total experience at Rocky Top.

In the Parking Lot. The girls demonstrated their graduation marching steps they learned and practiced at the detention center. It was meant as a gesture of honor and gratitude for the Rocky Top therapy staff, and these group leaders did in fact feel honored. Permission was given to exchange hugs. The girls loaded up in the van and drove away.

It was clear from this experience that the adolescent girls were greatly impacted in positive ways from the equine assisted counseling.

One week I was volunteering at Rocky Top with a group of adolescent boys who the therapy staff had sent to the pasture to halter and bring in some horses — a task that none of these young men had ever done before. The one young fellow I was accompanying approached his horse with a gentle attitude, and the horse stayed in one place for him as he made several vain attempts to get the halter on. The horse was very patient with him as he once even put the halter on backwards. The young man got more and more frustrated with his failed attempts and soon said, "Okay, I give up," in an attempt to get someone to rescue him. I simply replied, "Giving up is not an option. The horse is being very patient with you. Take a deep breath and keep trying. And, you might look across the pasture at some of your peers to see how the halters look on their horses' heads to help you have a mental picture of what you might need to do." He took a deep breath, smiled, and kept working at it because he wanted to head to the barn like his peers were doing and be able to spend time grooming and riding the horse. In another setting, this young man was prone to quit on himself, to give up quickly. But, with an opportunity as unique as this one, he was motivated to give extra effort. This is one of the many reasons equine assisted therapy can contribute to the efficacy of a juvenile rehabilitation program, that is, it increases the juveniles' desire to persevere with a complex task. The young man did succeed with haltering his horse a few tries later and lead his horse to the barn. He was quick to point out his success to staff at the barn and was all smiles as he told his story about not giving up on himself. He was proud that he had overcome his temptation to quit and recognized this as an important accomplishment for himself. Multiple incidents usually occur for each of these juveniles to boost self-confidence and strengthen their self-concept during just one 3-hour therapy session. And, for the several groups of juvenile boys and girls from the postadjudication program I have observed complete this 24 contact hour equine assisted counseling program, I have never seen any of them be uncooperative, belligerent, disrespectful, or choose not to participate or follow directions during the equine therapy. Most negative actions and attitudes that these kids may have chosen to exhibit while in the juvenile detention facility are not exhibited during equine assisted therapy. And, such behaviors that may have existed at the juvenile facility before equine therapy are typically significantly diminished following the equine therapy. I firmly believe that, for most of these at-risk juveniles, equine assisted therapy helps them to grow up a bit, to mature toward responsible adult character.

Figure 7.6 Juveniles from a detention facility give their full attention to a lesson on responsible horsemanship: Horsemanship lessons lead to discussions related to the development of life management skills and how to make better life choices.

An early part of the equine assisted counseling program involves the staff telling the boys to retrieve a specific group of horses from the pasture. After the group of boys had retrieved these horses from the pasture and taken them to the barn, they were instructed to release them into a small corral. Now, with a small group of therapy horses in the corral, each boy was further instructed to spend time with each horse in the corral and decide which horse they wanted to partner up with for the remainder of the therapy program. Each was further instructed to keep their choice to themselves until instructed to share their choice in the group process so that choices would not be influenced by one another. The horses vary in size and personality, so it is always informative to see which juvenile picks which horse.

In this group of six boys from detention, there was one fellow we will call Sam who was much smaller than the other boys. Instead of choosing one of the full-sized horses to work with, he requested to be able to work with a small mule named Mable that was watching the group from a nearby corral. Of the several groups of adolescent boys and girls from detention that I have observed in the therapy program at Rocky Top, this is the first time one of the adolescents has requested to work with a mule instead of with a horse. The mule had been used before with smaller children from a local school, so the therapy staff agreed to let Sam work with her. It was fascinating to watch Sam as he lead Mable around the corral where the bigger horses were. The bigger horses would approach Mable to bother her, and Sam would try to make himself as big as he could by standing tall, strutting with big steps, raising his shoulders, and moving his arms out away from his body, and he would shoo the bigger horses away. When Sam is back at the juvenile facility and he is feeling intimidated or bullied by the bigger fellows, he takes on this same posture. Thus, with Mable, Sam was transferring that same behavior into his relationship with the small mule, except in this case he was acting as the mule's protector from the bigger horses. Sam had quickly transferred his issues of being small and maybe feeling somewhat inadequate onto the mule. He was obviously trying to work with these personal issues through his relationship with Mable, and whether or not he was conscious of doing so is uncertain and not really necessary one way or the other; the opportunity to face and work on the issues was the important thing. The therapy staff felt that this experience with Mable would be very therapeutic for Sam but also recognized that in some ways working with a small mule does not challenge Sam to overcome the hesitation he may have to establish a trusting and positive relationship with someone or something much bigger than himself. Thus, one ultimate goal was to eventually move Sam to working with one of the bigger horses. In fact, this was accomplished by the midpoint of therapy when Sam agreed to mount a sorrel and white paint horse and soon achieved confident competence in horsemanship.

The juveniles tend to choose to partner with a therapy horse that is best for them whether they realize it or not. For instance, in an earlier group, the two most stubborn and cantankerous girls ended up choosing to work with the most stubborn and cantankerous horse. The therapy horses each have different and distinct personalities that become obvious only after you have a chance to spend some time with them. Some horses have more difficulty trusting new riders and are not very cooperative at first. Some horses are stubborn on some days not wanting to be haltered or ridden. Some are very friendly from the onset, but a bit mischievous, trying to steal hats off of heads or nibbling at hair. Some of the horses tend to try and boss the other horses around. Whatever horse the juvenile chooses, the desire to develop and maintain a positive relationship with a powerful being with an independent mind of its own is a very difficult yet important life lesson for a juvenile. Trying this first between a troubled juvenile and an adult, one is likely met with great resistance from the juvenile. Trying it between a troubled juvenile and a horse first, one is met with motivation to participate and to succeed from the juvenile. Undoubtedly, there are some therapeutic tasks that are more easily and quickly accomplished and better integrated with the assistance of a therapy horse.

The Therapeutic Zoo

An AAT program that involves interaction with farm animals, exotic animals, and sometimes even wild animals is the Companionable Zoo program (Katcher & Wilkins, 2002). A sample list of animals found in one particular program includes chinchilla, canary, dove, gecko, miniature goat, guinea pig, hamster, hedgehog, miniature horse, iguana, parakeet, pot-bellied pig, and rabbit. Another program actually

Figure 7.7 Juveniles from a detention facility get a saddle lesson from an equine therapist: A lesson in preparation and attention to detail.

has a pasture of buffalo. There are currently no guidelines for the choice of animals for this type of program. However, it is recommended that typically only domestically bred animals should be used, and no wild animals should be involved unless a licensed wildlife rehabilitator is on staff. The Companionable Zoo program is typically designed to provide therapeutic education for children who have attention deficit with hyperactivity or who have a conduct disorder. The children in the zoo program are held responsible for the care of the animals while learning about nature. The Companionable Zoo program "is an evolving product of therapeutic education that takes place at the junction between people, animals, and nature" (Katcher & Wilkins, 2002, p. 2). The program uses the care of animals and contact with nature to help children, and sometimes adults, learn the rules of society.

> The Companionable Zoo is a moral therapy. The ways that animals are treated and the rules governing human–animal interactions are metaphors for how the children should be treated. Children learn about human morality by reflecting upon the moral principles inherent in the treatment of animals. Without an ethic of human–animal interaction, there is no therapy in the larger sense. In thinking through the animal care guidelines, the Zoo staff should see that they, as well as the actions that they imply, define the staff's humanity and signal how the children in their care will be treated.
>
> (Katcher & Wilkins, 2002, pp. 102–103)

Figure 7.8 The ultimate motivation for participation in equine assisted counseling, riding tall in the saddle: Achieving competency in riding skills boosts self-confidence.

Some of the therapeutic and learning goals of a Companionable Zoo program include (Katcher & Wilkins, 2002):

- Modulate arousal to the demands of the task
- Experience sustained attention and comfort in a learning environment
- Take responsibility for a meaningful task
- Master fear and build confidence
- Learn skills and build competence
- Train in self-directed and other-directed speech
- Receive social skill training
- Train for positive attributions and expectations
- Train in social perspective-taking and empathic skills
- Increase engagement with reading and writing tasks
- Increase ability to work cooperatively at learning tasks

The preferred design of a therapeutic zoo program is to provide natural habitat or pasture for a variety of animals. Gardens and fishponds are encouraged. Additional activities can include supervised trips to the woods or wilderness areas. Empirical studies of the therapeutic zoo intervention:

suggest that children, especially children who find it difficult to learn in a regular school setting, are more responsive to learning tasks as well as less symptomatic when they are participating in the care of animals and engaged in nature study.

(Katcher, 2000a, p. 174)

Termination Issues in AAT-C

Termination of counseling services may occur for several reasons. Perhaps the client has completed therapy goals and no new goals have been established. Maybe the client wishes to take a vacation from therapy for a while. Perhaps the number of counseling sessions has been limited based on insurance reimbursements or agency policy. Or maybe new therapeutic client goals require a skill outside the competency area of the existing practitioner, so a referral is required.

There are standard steps to take in the termination process in counseling to promote effective and ethical practice (Cormier & Nurius, 2003). When the termination time approaches, it is important to prepare the client in advance before the last session arrives. The therapist should initiate a discussion with the client about terminating the therapy process several weeks ahead of time. The discussion should address the client's feelings about termination. Address the positive changes the client has made and give the client credit for the progress achieved. Assist the client in exploring how positive changes will be maintained and how to avoid sabotaging progress. Determine if the client desires a follow-up session to check on how they are doing. Provide the client with names of referral resources if the client wishes to continue therapy with another counselor or needs other types of services in the community.

It is likely that a client who has worked with a therapy animal will have established a strong relationship with that animal. Thus, in the termination process, the counselor needs to facilitate discussion regarding the client's feelings about having worked with the animal and about no longer having contact with the animal. Provide opportunity for the client to say goodbye to the therapy animal. Sometimes, when appropriate, the therapist can provide the client with a small token of remembrance of the therapy animal to help bring some closure to the relationship. For instance, when the juveniles complete the program at juvenile detention, they are given a color collage photocopy of photographs of my therapy animals Rusty, Dolly, and Snowflake with whom they had weekly contact. And when the juveniles complete the equine assisted therapy program at Rocky Top Therapy Ranch, they are given a certificate of completion with a photograph of themselves riding the therapy horse they partnered with for the past several weeks.

When working in the dimension of "end of life care" for the terminally ill, the client may request assistance in saying goodbye to the persons in the client's life who are important to the client. Sometimes the counselor and the therapy animal are included in this group of significant others. Thus, the counselor must be aware of offering an opportunity for the client to achieve some emotional closure on the therapeutic relationship with the counselor and the counselor's pet practitioner. When working with the terminally ill, sometimes other persons involved in providing care for the patient also become attached to the therapy animal. Thus, remember friends, family members, and medical staff when the life of the patient nears an end and allow time for these significant persons in the patient's life to say goodbye to you and the therapy pet.

Documentation and AAT

Counselors are required to complete thorough and comprehensive session reports for each client with whom they work. A popular model for documenting each counseling session is the four-part SOAP plan that includes a description of: 1) the client's subjective presentation, 2) the counselor's objective observations and other facts about the client, 3) the counselor's assessment and conceptualization of the client, and 4) the counselor's action plan for the client (Cameron & turtle-song, 2002). At a minimum, I recommend that the counselor include in every counseling session report the following information:

- Name of the client (more thorough descriptive information about the client can be recorded on the client intake and initial interview form)
- Date, time, and location of the therapy session
- Name of the counselor or counselors providing the therapy
- Type of therapy (individual, couples, group, family, and so forth)
- Any relevant diagnosis and ongoing presenting problem of the client
- Current functional status of the client (including assessment of any crisis state)
- Client's presentation during the session of issues and concerns
- Counselor's conceptualization of the client's presented issues and concerns
- Counselor's goals and plans for the client in the session
- Interventions utilized by the counselor during the session
- Assessment of the outcome of applied interventions
- Counselor's discussion of any progress (or lack of progress) observed in the client
- Any recommendations made to the client for homework or referral

If this is a termination session, then a termination summary report should also be completed that overviews the client's presenting problems, status, any observed progress across all sessions, the client's status at time of termination, the reason for termination, and recommendations or referrals made to the client at termination. If any standardized assessment instruments were used as part of the therapy process, then a brief session report should be written for inclusion in the client's file that interprets the results of the assessment.

When incorporating a therapy animal into the counseling process, the counselor must be sure to include relevant information about the therapy animal in the counseling session report. The name of the animal, its species and breed, and its credentials should be included. Describe in the session report specific decisions to include the therapy animal in the counseling session and discuss in detail what client–therapy animal interactions took place and what animal assisted interventions were utilized during the session. Finally, the counselor should discuss in the session report his or her assessment of the outcome of the client–therapy animal interactions and interventions. The information regarding client–therapy animal interactions and interventions can be interwoven into the counselor's typical session report; thus including information relative to AAT requires little additional effort on the part of the counselor.

Program Evaluation and AAT

An important consideration for validating the incorporation of AAT into counseling is evaluating the success of therapeutic intervention. Counseling program evaluation can be accomplished through qualitative or quantitative measures (Heppner, Kivlighan, & Wampold, 1999; Marshall & Rossman, 1999). Quantitative results are preferable over qualitative measures for obtaining measurable and replicable results. Sometimes it is difficult to achieve statistical significance in counseling research because in counseling interventions there is typically a small number of subjects involved and some of the statistical variance analyses, such as analysis of variance (ANOVA), analysis of covariance (ANCOVA), or multivariate analysis of variance (MANOVA), lend themselves better to a large sample size to achieve statistical significance when only two data collection points are used, such as with the commonly utilized pretest versus post-test design.

In counseling research, it is better to consider utilizing statistical strategies that are more appropriate for small sample research (Hoyle, 1999). Due to small subject samples typical of research studies in counseling, it is important to analyze clinical significance, or effect size, and not just statistical significance (Kramer & Rosenthal, 1999; Thompson, 2002). Analysis of effect size may produce clinical significance even if statistical significance is not found. Also, a researcher applying a simple pretest versus post-test comparison loses much information about potential client change with this type of two data collection points design. A greater likelihood of measuring change is possible with an intensive design, also referred to as a repeated measures design, for data collection and analysis. The intensive design is a linear, individual growth trajectory model and provides more information for analysis, such as individual growth and individual differences in growth across time, as compared to measuring individual change with simple observations limited to two time points as in the pretest versus post-test design (Maxwell, 1998; Willett, 1989, 1994). However, a repeated measures design does not provide significant benefit over a pretest versus post-test design unless at least five to six data points can be obtained (Kraemer & Thiemann, 1989).

Gathering client data across time requires taking repeated periodic measures of the client's behavior. This is not always plausible if the researcher is using lengthy assessment tools or the assessments must be gathered from others who might observe the client, such as parents or teachers. Videotaping multiple sessions with the client's permission and having independent, trained judges view and rate the tapes for certain behaviors is one way to accomplish repeated measures, but achieving high inter-rater reliability is often difficult. Another way to gather client data on multiple occasions is to use a quantified client session form with a scale for measuring client change. One example of a session-to-session measure of client change is the Animal Assisted Therapy — Psychosocial Session Form that was developed by the author (a copy is provided in the appendix for your convenient use).

It is difficult to find measures for change that work well with AAT, and the development of such an instrument would make a good research project. Following are just a few suggestions of some instruments that can be used effectively in measuring change with children and adolescent clients. The Child Behavior Checklist (Achenbach, 1991; published by ASEBA) includes a parent report form, a teacher report form, and a youth self-report form. It measures a variety of prosocial and antisocial behaviors. The Behavioral Assessment System for Children (Reynolds & Kamphaus, 1992; published by the American Guidance Service) is another useful instrument for measuring children's social behaviors with report forms that can be gathered from the parents and teachers. The Intermediate Attitudes scale (Ascione, 1989) measures a child's or adolescent's humane attitude toward animals and can reflect change across a brief time period using a pre- and postassessment design. The Symptom Checklist 90 — Revised (published by Pearson Assessments; forms available for adolescents as well as adults) provides an overall picture of functionality and dysfunctionality in several important areas, including health concerns, fears and phobias, anxiety and depression, hostility, and interpersonal sensitivity. Simple instruments that can be effective in measuring change in adults include the Beck Depression Inventory II and the Beck Anxiety Inventory (published by The Psychological Corporation). These can be useful tools to assess progress with adult clients as they are brief to administer and score and may be an efficient and effective pre- and postassessment. None of these instruments is directly related to AAT except for the Intermediate Attitudes scale.

There are numerous social and psychological assessment measures available that may be appropriate for assessment of client progress depending on a particular therapeutic focus. A useful resource for finding assessment measures includes *Buros Mental Measurements Yearbook* (available at your local college or university library or from Buros Institute of Mental Measurements over the internet at the following website: http://www.unl.edu/buros). Also, some publishers of popular psychological assessment instruments are listed below:

- American Guidance Service, website: http://www.agsnet.com/, telephone: 1-800-328-2560
- ASEBA (Achenbach System of Empirically Based Assessment), website: http://www.aseba.org/index.html, telephone: 1-802-264-6432
- Consulting Psychologists Press, website: http://www.cpp.com, telephone: 1-800-624-1765
- Harcourt Assessment (formerly The Psychological Corporation), website: http://www.HarcourtAssessment.com, telephone: 1-800-211-8378
- Pearson Assessments (formerly NCS Assessments), website: http://www.pearsonassessments.com, telephone: 1-800-627-7271 ext. 3225
- Psychological Assessment Products, website: http://www.PSYCHCORP.com, telephone: 1-800-211-8378
- Psychological Assessment Resources, website: http://www.parinc.com, telephone: 1-800-331-8378

Chapter 8

Sensitivity to Cultural Differences and Populations with Special Needs

Cultural Differences in Attitudes about Animals 129

AAT-C with Elderly Clients 130

AAT-C with Hospitalized and Hospice Clients 132

AAT-C with Clients in Prisons or Detention Centers 133

Residential AAT Programs in Prisons 134

Juvenile Detention Programs with AAT 135

"The outside of a horse is good for the inside of a man."

— Winston Churchill

The clients you provide services for may have a different opinion about animals than you do. Thus, it is important to be sensitive to varying attitudes about animals by clients that might be a result of differences in cultural background or prior experiences. A client may have a family history that considers pets to be outside animals only and may not feel comfortable with an animal indoors. A client may be afraid of large dogs, having only limited exposure to them as aggressive guard dogs or unfortunate victims of organized dog fighting. A client may originate from a country that does not generally view animals as pets but rather as food or as laborers. A client may not have had many or any opportunities to be around certain types of animals, especially farm animals or horses, therefore they might be uncomfortable around them. Or, a client may have once had a bad or overly sad experience with a pet and thus may find it difficult to be around a similar type pet. Thus, to be better prepared for the initial session with a client, it is important for the therapist to include in the client screening process for AAT inquiry about the client's previous exposure to or attitude about animals or pets (see the Client Screening Form for Animal Assisted Therapy provided in Appendix B).

To minimize anticipatory anxiety or discomfort about interacting with a therapy animal, the therapist should provide clients with an explanation for the animal's purpose and expected types of interactions the pet may engage in with the client. A description of potential benefits to be gained by working with a therapy animal can be described to the client. Clarification as to how and when a client can typically engage with a therapy animal can also be described. Also, a therapist can initiate some animal behaviors at a distance from the client to help the client warm up to the idea of being around the therapy animal. A common technique I use to demonstrate that the therapy pet is not a threat is to ask one of my therapy dogs to do a trick or series of tricks for the client. This usually gets the client smiling or laughing and helps to relieve the initial fear or distrust the client had toward the animal. Then, I invite the client to ask the dog to repeat one of the tricks at the client's request. This almost always results in the client moving in much closer to the dog and speaking to it. Once the dog has performed the trick for the client and is happily wagging its tail afterward in anticipation of a treat or pet on the head, the once uncertain client then may even reach out and pet the dog. This slow initiation technique is very useful with clients in whom you sense an uneasiness about being around the therapy animal, especially small children.

Always respect a client's desire to not work with a therapy animal. Provide a safe and comfortable place for the therapy animal to rest during the counseling session with that client. One possibility is to place the therapy pet in a crate the animal is familiar with in a corner of the therapy room away from the client or in another, nearby room. Occasionally invite the client to spend time with the therapy pet without pressuring or coercing the client to do so. If the client does choose to spend time with the therapy pet, let the client set the distance parameters for the client's own comfort level.

In my volunteer therapy work at a juvenile facility, I have experienced about 1 in every 10 of the adolescents is afraid of being around the therapy dogs the first time they meet them. This ratio is high due to the fact that many of these juveniles come from a severely dysfunctional home, and it is not uncommon for highly dysfunctional families to also have a dysfunctional relationship with a dog or not have a dog at all. Adolescents afraid of the therapy dogs have typically had or known dogs that were not properly socialized and trained and therefore the dogs were unruly or aggressive. Or, sometimes, the dogs they have known were trained to be aggressive as guard dogs or fighting dogs. Either way, the adolescents afraid of dogs usually have had a negative or absent history with them. This will seem like an exaggerated claim, but in every instance over the past 4 years that I have been performing AAT with these kids at the juvenile detention center, all adolescents that were originally afraid of the therapy dogs overcame their fears and apprehension over a period of several sessions and engaged in frequent touching and playing with the dogs. In addition, these adolescents commonly described their ability to overcome their fears with pride as they shared their animal therapy experiences with counselors, caseworkers, and family members. At the graduation ceremony, held when the juvenile is ultimately released from custody after having completed the residential rehabilitation program, the adolescents often seek me out to introduce me and the therapy dog with me to family members, and the family members comment on how remarkable it is that their child overcame their strong fear of dogs and how proud they are of their child for this accomplishment. In addition, these adolescents comment on how their work with the therapy dog has helped them be less anxious around other dogs that they could now more objectively judge as presenting no threat to them. I believe the original fear of the therapy dogs subsided quickly with these adolescents because they had multiple opportunities to observe from a comfortable distance all of the other adolescents interacting with the dogs in a fun and playful manner. They could then slowly move toward or away from the animals at their choosing to test their sense of safety and comfort until they could remain close to and interact with the therapy dogs without being inhibited by their fear. They were motivated to try to move closer because they saw how much fun the other kids were having and they wanted to experience the same enjoyment. Motivation to participate is key to any desensitization therapy, as is having a sense of control over the situation.

Cultural Differences in Attitudes about Animals

While it is important not to stereotype any one individual based on the culture or ethnic minority group with which they affiliate, it is important to be aware of potential cultural differences in how persons view animals. For instance, relatively few Koreans in their native country have dogs or cats as pets. In fact Koreans have long viewed dogs as a source of food; however, the government and other humane organizations are today actively trying to change these views (Shin, 2003). Also, many Koreans are afraid of large dogs because they so frequently are used as aggressive guard dogs in Korea.

Europeans and European-Americans have incorporated cats and dogs and other animals as pets into the family system for hundreds of years, and the concept of the household pet is very common. Europeans and European-Americans traditionally take individual or family ownership of a pet and assume private responsibility for the feeding, training, and care of a pet; neutering or spaying the pet; and typically confining the pet to the owner's home or property when the pet is not accompanying the owner on a leash or riding with the owner in a vehicle.

In contrast, Latino and Hispanic communities in North, Central, and South America have a very different attitude about pets than Europeans or European-Americans. Latino and Hispanic persons typically think of a dog or cat as a community pet, allowing the pet to wander freely and procreate at will, and people share in giving food to the dog or cat:

> The concept of the "community dog" is at the heart of Latino custom. Few people would have a personal pet but all would interact with the dogs and cats who lived within the village. Animals who were prized were the working animals who could help a family survive economically. In poor villages, stray dogs were often fed by many but belonged to none.
>
> (Richard, 2004, p. 2)

Native Americans also have a very different concept of pets from Europeans and European-Americans. Large numbers of dogs and cats are allowed to roam freely around Native American reservations. The tribe shares in the feeding and care of the reservation dogs and cats. Few of these animals, if any, are ever spayed or neutered. Native Americans have a special respect for an animal's spirit and purpose, and tradition and culture impose an informal noninterference policy of sorts for these animals:

> David Ortiz is a writer and anthropologist based in Flagstaff, Arizona. His work has taken him to the heart of the Navajo population — a patriarchal culture where elders still pass down traditions and customs, and shape the attitudes of younger generations. "Many older people on the reservation lands were brought up with the idea that animals are a resource," says Ortiz. "Dogs guard the hogan or house and herd sheep and goats. A cat's job is to kill mice and other smaller animals. When animal welfare people show up and start talking about altering the animals to control the population, they just can't relate to it. They feel in part that dogs and cats need to reproduce to provide food for coyotes and other predators. They're part of the cycle of life."
>
> (Munro, 2004, p. 1)

The cost of taking care of an animal also prohibits the idea of a family pet for many Native Americans:

> Many tribes are excessively poor, and some of the most basic human needs — food, medical care, and adequate housing — are not met. And that's often the biggest stumbling block when trying to change attitudes about animals. Add to that the belief that all of life will begin and end as it is intended, as part of the natural world, and the resistance to animal welfare is understandable.
>
> (Munro, 2004, p. 2)

AAT-C with Elderly Clients

Elderly clients may have special needs that must be considered when engaging in AAT-C. Many seniors may not see or hear as well as they used to, thus when counseling someone with sensory disability you must explain right away that a therapy animal is present and the role and purpose of the animal. Otherwise, if the animal is not expected by the client and cannot be seen or heard, contact or interaction with the animal may startle the client. A visually impaired client who wishes to touch or pet a therapy animal may need assistance. Always receive permission before touching a client, but having received such permission you might need to take the hand of a visually impaired client and guide it to the pet. An elderly client may not be agile and may even be in a wheelchair, so reaching down or over to pet a therapy animal may be physically difficult. A small pet may be placed in the lap of elderly clients with their permission. If you will be placing a therapy pet in a client's lap, you might first want to place on the lap a clean towel or cushion the pet is familiar with to minimize the amount of fur that gets onto the client's clothing. A thick foam cushion is usually best because it is light and also firm enough to provide a soft yet sturdy platform for the small pet to keep it from sliding between the client's legs or off the side of the client's lap. A medium-sized therapy animal like my Cocker Spaniels, Rusty and Dolly, is too big for a client's lap but too small to be reached from the floor. A medium-sized therapy animal can be placed on a couch with a client and sit or lie next to the client or may be placed in a steady chair next to the client so it is easier for the client to reach the pet. Make sure the chair that you place the therapy animal in does not have wheels, or if it does have wheels, hang on tightly to the chair and keep it steady for the animal's safety. Usually, large therapy animals, like large dogs, can still be easily reached even when they are sitting on the floor. I highly discourage placing a large dog on a couch or bed with any client since the weight of the dog may injure the client. Dementia is common in older seniors, thus extra supervision may be required to insure the safety of a therapy animal around a client with dementia. Dementia clients prone to aggression should probably not be considered for AAT. Memory impairment from dementia or aging memory processes is common in older seniors. Thus, the counselor may have to reintroduce himself or herself and the therapy animal many times when counseling this population.

The presence of a therapy pet in the therapy room may serve as a source of comfort for the elderly client who may wish to pet the therapy animal. The presence of a therapy animal in a room with an elderly client may be effective in enhancing the client's focus and attention during a counseling session and encourage the client to be more expressive. There are also some animal assisted structured interventions that may be helpful for an elderly client. Walking, petting, grooming, and interactive play with the therapy animal can be performed during a counseling session to help stimulate physical and neurological pathways of the client. The animal's presence may encourage the elderly client to recall personal life stories about previous pets. Life story telling has the therapeutic benefits of enhancing an elderly client's mood and reinforcing a sense of self-worth. Sharing photographs of the therapist's pets with an elderly client may also encourage the client to tell life stories. Many elderly no longer have opportunities to provide something meaningful to others, and this can be damaging to their self-worth. Thus, an elderly client may want to give something to the therapy animal to make the therapy animal feel good. Provide healthy treats for the client to share with your therapy pet. Also, offer a soft grooming brush that is easy for the client to grip and brush the animal. Describe for the client the animal's favorite spots to be petted or massaged. Clients get a real kick out of watching Dolly's head roll way over to one side and her eyes droop closed when they scratch under her collar. She is in "doggy heaven" when you do this for her. Likewise, Rusty considers anyone who rubs the tops of his ears a best friend for life.

He will lean his head heavily into your hand, close his eyes, and make repeated deep sighs of pleasure. Dolly's and Rusty's obvious reactions of appreciation inevitably elicit a smile or laugh in a client. The ability to do something meaningful for someone else reinforces in the client that they still have positive value.

AAT-C with Hospitalized and Hospice Clients

Clients with a serious illness that requires lengthy hospitalization are isolated from the rest of the world. A counseling session involving a therapy animal offers a warm and inviting interaction that is very different from the sterile hospital atmosphere. The therapy animal may brighten the client's mood, making them more receptive to counseling; the brightened mood may carry over long after the counseling session is over. Clients in a hospital for a long time may miss their pet at home, and time spent with a therapy animal may substitute somewhat for the time they miss with their own pet. It may even encourage the client to talk about their pet at home. The therapy animal may encourage the client to talk not only about their pet at home but also about how they miss home and how they are experiencing the difficulties of hospitalization or struggles with their illness. And, pleasure experienced from interacting with a therapy animal may actually help to counteract some of the physical pain or discomfort resulting from the client's illness. Playing with a therapy animal or walking a therapy animal may assist in getting or keeping a client mobile if that is deemed a healthy element for recovery. There are many hospital programs that incorporate AAA and AAT as part of the patient's recovery process. Three well-known hospital AAT programs are: The National Institutes of Health in Washington, D.C.; Warm Springs Rehabilitation Hospital in San Antonio, Texas; and Summa Health Systems in Akron, Ohio (Ptak & Howie, 2004).

Hospice clients are terminally ill and often are provided "end of life care" at home by qualified health professionals. Counseling clients in the final stages of their life is indeed a special type of counseling. A therapist must help the client maintain the highest possible quality of life during this final journey. Therapy animals bring an exuberant energy into what could be a gloomy environment for a client who is dying. Therapy animals are playful, funny, and entertaining. They offer unconditional, nonjudgmental, and endless affection and nurturance — all of which are much needed by a hospice client. A therapy animal can also offer relief for visitors and family members of the hospice client as well as other health professionals assisting a terminally ill client.

A therapist providing counseling services for a hospice client can assist by providing counseling sessions that include a therapy animal as well as by providing other types of animal-related counseling services for the client. For example, the therapist can guide the development of a bird feeding center out a window or in an accessible garden. A butterfly garden can be planted with nectar flowers to attract butterflies to feed on, and garden plants such as passion vine, dill, and fennel for the butterflies to lay eggs in. The therapist can help the client harvest the caterpillar chrysalises and create a butterfly hatchery in the home of the client and arrange a counseling session with the client centered on the actual release of the hatched butterfly. The butterfly and caterpillar transformation life cycle is a powerful metaphor for a client who is dying and may be wondering about a hereafter. The therapist working with a hospice client may also assist the client in making provisions for the transfer of care of the client's own pet once they are too ill to take care of it themselves and assist the client in setting up adoption procedures for the client's own pet once they have died.

A therapist who is providing AAT-C in a hospital or hospice environment must be especially careful to follow established policies and procedures for infection control to protect both the client and the therapy animal. In addition, the therapy animal must be healthy, without open wounds, and parasite free. The animal must be clean and bathed and groomed within 24 hours of the counseling session. Be sure the animal's claws are clipped and filed to a dull state. Be careful the animal does not come into contact with any body fluids of a client with a contagious illness. Make sure all items that may have contacted body fluid are not in reach of the animal: tissues, bed clothing, undergarments, eating utensils, leftover food, and so forth. And, have clients wash their hands with an antibacterial soap or gel before and after visiting with the therapy animal. Make sure any pet items the client may interact with are clean before you begin the therapy session (collar, leash, toys, pet cushion, etc.). When you get home, carefully clean all pet items to remove any potential germs they may have accumulated. Be sure and disinfect the pet items with substances nontoxic to your therapy pet and clients you may work with next.

AAT-C with Clients in Prisons or Detention Centers

Sometimes it is difficult to gain the trust of a client confined in a prison or detention center. Detainees are suspicious of all authority figures and are hesitant to express themselves honestly and sincerely for fear of repercussions. It may be easier for this type of client to trust a counselor working with a therapy animal because the client can judge the counselor based on observing the positive and trusting relationship between the therapy animal and the counselor. Detained clients typically do not get opportunities to interact with animals, so being able to spend time with a therapy animal can motivate the client to attend counseling sessions as well as maintain good behavior so as to be allowed to continue to interact with the therapy animal. Structuring time for the detainee to pet, interact with, and play with the therapy animal will be very welcome to the client. Also, the detainee has limited opportunity to be outdoors, so gaining permission to spend some counseling sessions with the client outside in a secure recreational area is usually appreciated by these clients. As with all clients one is working with, the therapist should never leave the therapist's animal alone with the detainee. Detainee clients who participate in AAT should be carefully screened for aggressive tendencies as some detainees may not be appropriate for this type of therapy because of their aggression. Also, the counselor working in a prison or detention facility must be very aware of and carefully follow security procedures as well as maintain a constant awareness of where security personnel are and how to contact them in case of an emergency.

There are several types of AAT programs in prisons and detention centers in the U.S. Many of these programs are not necessarily counseling programs, but the programs do have positive emotional and behavioral benefits for inmates. Inmates have assisted rescue organizations with domesticating and training wild horses for adoption. Detainees have assisted humane societies with training unruly dogs so the dogs could be more easily adopted by approved families. Detainees have raised and trained dogs for preparation as service animals to help the disabled. Detainees have worked with animals to learn vocational skills that may be helpful once the inmates are released, for instance veterinarian technician skills, grooming and bathing of dogs and horses, and exercising and training dogs and horses. In many of these instances, the dogs in these programs are housed in kennels on site at the facility or some even live with the detainees in their cells. When keeping therapy animals on site, extensive monitoring and supervision measures must be in place to insure the safety of the animals 24 hours a day. The goals of residential type AAT programs at prisons and detention centers are to provide mutual assistance for the therapy animal and the detainee. Residential AAT program goals to assist detainees include decrease behavior problems, decrease manipulative behaviors, decrease the frequency of conflicts between detainees, increase the frequency of prosocial behaviors like cooperation and sharing, increase positive interactions between detainees and facility staff, increase detainees' attention to task, increase life skill development, enhance mood, and increase positive attitudes.

Residential AAT Programs in Prisons

Pet therapy programs in prison have been shown to uplift the spirits of detainees and reduce violence in the facility (Haynes, 1991). Pet therapy programs in correctional facilities can be a mutually beneficial coalition between humans and animals who need the type of assistance that each can offer the other.

> Taffy is just days away from euthanasia. The young heeler/beagle mix needs obedience training and socialization, and his luck is running out. A few days later, Taffy is relaxing in the cell of Eric Roberson, an inmate at the Mansfield Correctional Institution, a maximum security prison in Ohio. Taffy and Roberson are one of 30 inmate/shelter dog pairs participating in the Tender Loving Dog Care program at Mansfield. The program provides the inmates with the opportunity to train and socialize otherwise doomed dogs, who are then adopted into good homes. Roberson, who is serving 24 years for a 1992 murder conviction, has given a new life to 22 dogs; an additional 200 have also been saved [since the program began in 1998].
>
> (Rhoades, 2001, p. 24)

The television station called *Animal Planet* broadcast in the year 2004 a program series called *Cell Dogs* that demonstrated the benefits of animals interacting positively with inmates in prisons. One particular episode was especially touching. A local humane society in Nevada brought several dogs to the prison for the inmates to assist. Some were adult dogs that had been neglected by their owners and were never properly socialized, trained, or housebroken. Some of the dogs had been badly abused by previous owners and were so afraid they would just cower in a corner and shake. Two litters of puppies too young to be kept at the humane society shelter were also included in this group. Inmates kept the dogs for 6 weeks and spent time providing affection and nurturance for all of the dogs and training the adult dogs. The dogs stayed in the inmates' cells with them so they were together for 24 hours a day. The outcome of the program was delightful. The little puppies whose lives had been on the edge of survival at the time they arrived became healthy and robust balls of bouncing fur. The adult dogs became happy, friendly, and obedient animals. Two of the dogs were socialized and trained around prison horses that had been rescued from the wild and were undergoing training and socialization by prisoners so the horses could go to a good home; both of the dogs were adopted by local ranchers. All of the puppies and dogs were adopted by the time the program ended after several weeks, and many of the dogs were actually adopted by facility staff. A father of one of the inmates visited with the inmate and with the puppies the inmate was caring for. When the father lost his own dog from age-related illness, he adopted one of the puppies the inmate cared for. It seemed to mean a great deal to the inmate and to the father because the inmate could provide something very meaningful to his father that he and his father could connect with for many years to come. At the conclusion of the program, the inmates described the experience as very positive, feeling as though they had done something very worthwhile.

There are several animal welfare and rehabilitation programs in correctional facilities in the U.S. The Ohio Reformatory for Women in Marysville and the Marion Correctional Institution for Men work in cooperation with the Ohio Wildlife Center (Rhoades, 2001). The wildlife center was finding it difficult to care for over 4,000 sick, injured, or orphaned wild animals per year. Then they set up branch programs within the two correctional facilities. The inmates are trained by wildlife rehabilitators to provide 24-hour nursing care for a variety of wildlife, including hand-feeding mealworms to birds and tube-feeding baby opossums. Once rehabilitated, the animals are returned to the wild. The effects of the program are reflected by one inmate, Sharon Young, who is serving time for aggravated murder, "Our goal is to get as many animals healthy and back into their natural habitats as we can....It's difficult to see them go, but it makes you feel proud to know that you've done something good and really miraculous" (p. 25).

Animal care programs in correctional facilities provide many useful services for both inmates and the animals they care for (Rhoades, 2001). Dog grooming is taught in a number of prison programs including the Women's Correctional Institute in Purdy, Washington. The Hutchison and El Dorado facilities in Kansas serve as foster facilities for greyhounds that were destined to be euthanized after being retired from racing. The Hutchison correctional facility also works with the National Wild Horse and Burro program by gentling and socializing wild horses to be adopted by the public. The Animal Cruelty unit of the Maricopa County Sheriff's Office in Phoenix, Arizona, works with inmates to rehabilitate animals rescued by the unit so the animals can be adopted out to the public; inmates learn basic animal first aid and veterinary skills, as well as animal socializing and obedience training, as a by-product of this program.

Juvenile Detention Programs with AAT

The juvenile detention center of Denton County, Texas, has thoroughly incorporated AAT into their Post Adjudication Program. All of these juveniles are repeat offenders with theft and drug possession as common offenses. I visit with my two dogs and cat for social visits with the juveniles almost every week. In addition, I volunteer or work with one of my therapy animals as a cotherapist in weekly individual counseling with some of the juveniles. Some of the juveniles volunteer to go on supervised trips to local horse ranches for horse-riding lessons in exchange for community service at the ranch. Most of the juveniles in the Post Adjudication Program have an opportunity to participate in an intensive equine assisted counseling program at the Rocky Top Therapy Center located approximately 25 miles away. And this Post Adjudication Program recently became involved with a foster care and rescue group that rescues and finds homes for parrots. The juvenile facility now provides a foster home for a giant multicolored parrot named Romeo and a cockatoo named Tut. The birds' cages are rotated between the juveniles' sections so all of the juveniles have an opportunity to spend time with the birds. The juveniles are in charge of caring for and socializing with the birds, under supervision. Caseworkers report that the AAT has benefited the juveniles greatly in progressing through their rehabilitation program. The daily life skills that are taught as a basic part of postadjudication rehabilitation are reinforced by the juveniles' participation in the various AAT programs. In addition to opportunities to build and reinforce self-confidence and self-esteem, the AAT lends opportunities to practice teamwork, leadership, communication, and appropriate socialization. The therapy animals are also highly valued as a source of affection and comfort for the juveniles.

There is a juvenile detention AAT program in Dallas County, Texas, sponsored by the Dallas SPCA that is most beneficial for the adolescents in the program as well as the dogs who participate. Some of the dogs at the SPCA shelter are unruly and thus difficult to get adopted by the public. Volunteers transport these selected dogs

Figure 8.1 Therapy dog Dolly is a comfort for juveniles in a detention facility: Her quiet and affectionate personality has a calming influence.

to the juvenile facility once a week for a 2-hour training session by the adolescents in residence there. The dogs had previously been evaluated as not being aggressive so they were safe to work with the juveniles. The adolescents at the detention facility taught the dogs basic obedience commands and introduced the dogs to agility training. The volunteers who trained and supervised the juveniles with the dogs were experienced dog trainers. At the completion of the several-week program, the juveniles presented their dog at a graduation ceremony in front of a large group of facility staff and other juveniles. The presentation included an introduction and description of the dog and a history of its breed and what the dog was like when it began the training program along with a demonstration of what the dog could do now. Then the juvenile handed the dog over to a new owner who was adopting the trained dog from the SPCA. This last process was especially moving to observe. The juvenile was given an opportunity to say goodbye to the dog they had worked with for several weeks and see it placed with a new owner. Most of the dogs find new owners to adopt them and take home with them after the dog graduates from the juvenile training program because the program is so successful in training the dogs to be good companions. In my observation of this program, I overhead juveniles talk about how they related to the dog and felt they were helping the dog have a better chance in life by training it. The dog was locked up like they were and needed help to be able to function better in society so they could be free again. Rehabilitating these unruly dogs so they could be adopted was a powerful metaphor for the juveniles to work hard in their own rehabilitation, and they seemed to truly understand this about their participation.

There are several successful equine therapy programs designed to assist troubled teens (Rhoades, 2001). The Charles H. Hickey School in Baltimore, Maryland, a residential institution for young men, pairs troubled students with thoroughbreds. The students are responsible for all aspects of care for the farm's many horses, including grooming, feeding, exercise, first aid, and studying about horse physiology and horsemanship. The effects of the program are reflected by the comments of two 16-year-old participants in the program. Samuel: "When I came here, I had an anger problem....Working with horses has really helped me out. It's given me a good perspective on animals, on how to treat them properly" (p. 25). And, Allen: "You really want to go out there and work. I'd never been around an adult horse before. I like working with them" (p. 25). Similar equine therapy programs are in place at the Blackburn Correctional Complex in Lexington, Kentucky, and at Marion County Correctional Institution in Ocala, Florida.

Chapter 9

Crisis Response Counseling with Therapy Animals

Therapy Dogs Make the Best Crisis Response Pet Practitioners   140
The Nature of Crisis   141
Crisis Response Safety   141
Become a Recognized Crisis Response Counselor with Your Pet   142
The Nature of Crisis Response Counseling   143
Form an Animal Assisted Crisis Response Counseling Team   147

"If there are no dogs in Heaven, then when I die I want to go where they went."

— Will Rogers

Search and rescue dog teams have been working for many years in crisis situations all over the world. They assist in the recovery of lost persons and even bodies. These brave and dedicated animals risk their own lives working long hours in all types of weather, terrain, and dangerous environments to provide a valuable service to the human community. The successes of search and rescue dogs have more than proven the ability of dogs to provide invaluable aid in the face of tragedy.

There are well-known instances of therapy dogs assisting with crisis response in the aftermath of great tragedy in the U.S. Cindy Ehlers and her dog Bear of Eugene, Oregon, worked with students traumatized by the 1998 shootings at Thurston High School in Springfield, Oregon; they also assisted with crisis response following the violence in 1999 at Columbine High School in Littleton, Colorado (Rea, 2000). Numerous therapy dog teams volunteered crisis response services through the American Red Cross in New York providing comfort and stress relief to victims and families following the World Trade Center terrorist attack of September 11, 2001 (Teal, 2002).

Therapy Dogs Make the Best Crisis Response Pet Practitioners

Therapy dogs can be especially helpful as part of a crisis response team. They offer a sense of normalcy to a very abnormal situation. Seeing and interacting with something familiar like a dog can provide some reassurance that, although the world has been turned upside down, somehow things are going to be okay. Thus, the therapy dog is a powerful grounding mechanism for a client in crisis. The therapy dog can provide safe, unconditional, nurturing touch and affection at a time when it is needed the most to comfort the victims and survivors of tragedy. Being social animals, dogs have a fairly constant natural smile and tail wag that are universally known by all as friendly canine gestures; these gestures can relieve tension in the observer. Several studies have shown that the presence of a dog or another type of companion animal can help reduce the physiological stress response and alleviate anxiety and distress, thus petting a therapy dog can soothe rattled nerves (Barker & Dawson, 1998; Friedmann et al., 1983; Friedmann, Locker, & Lockwood, 1993; Hansen, Messinger, Baun, & Megel, 1999; Katcher, 1985; Nagengast, Baun, Megel, & Leibowitz, 1997; Odendaal, 2000; Robin & ten Bensel, 1985).

I recommend the use of therapy dogs over other types of companion animals for work in a crisis response situation. Dogs have a calmer demeanor and have more predictable behavior than other animals. Canines are more easily trained to obey direction and commands, imperative when in the center of disorganization and chaos that may erupt after a tragedy has occurred. Dogs can be trained and socialized to accept hurried crowds, intense emotions, loud noises, large equipment, blaring sirens, fast moving emergency vehicles, and disrupted physical environments such as building ruins and rubble. And, many medium- to large-sized dogs are robust and can sustain long and stressful working hours if they are in good physical condition.

The Nature of Crisis

The National Organization for Victim Assistance (NOVA, 2004) describes in their *Community Crisis Response Team Training Manual* a number of characteristics of a crisis. Crises are typically caused by three categories of disaster: naturally occurring, human-made, or technologically based. Naturally occurring include tornadoes, floods, hurricanes, lightning-instigated fires, earthquakes, and so on. Human-made would involve terrorist attacks, suicide, or homicide. Technological disasters would be train wrecks, building collapses, chemical spills, and so forth. The reactions to a crisis are both physical and emotional. Physical reactions include immobilization (frozen by fear), mobilization (fight, flight, or adapt), and exhaustion. Emotional reactions include shock, disbelief, denial, and emotional numbness. A cataclysm of emotion may occur that involves anger, fear, confusion, frustration, shame, humiliation, and grief. It is important to note that persons in crisis are trying to reconstruct some sort of equilibrium after their world has been plummeted into turmoil.

NOVA describes three stages of crisis intervention. The first stage is safety and security. The crisis response team must help the client experience physical safety and emotional security. The second stage of crisis intervention is ventilation and validation. The crisis response personnel validate for the client the client's crisis reactions. It is important that the client feel normal in this abnormal situation. Crisis response personnel must encourage clients to tell their stories to help them process through the event. The third stage of crisis intervention is prediction and preparation. The crisis response team must help the client anticipate the future and prepare to cope with the impact of the tragedy on the client's life.

Crisis Response Safety

Special precautions must be undertaken to insure the health and safety of the therapy dog in a crisis situation. Given the intensity and duration of such a situation, the dog may need more short breaks during the working day such as brief walks away from the crisis scene if possible and brief naps. During a crisis event, the dog may tend to change its eating and sleeping habits or get an upset stomach as a response to stress. Thus pay special attention to the dog's nutrition and its digestive responses. Make sure the dog gets lots of water and positive praise and affection from its handler. Give the dog a daily massage to help the dog relax after a hard day's work involving crisis counseling. Be careful when working in the aftermath of an event that has destroyed buildings because dust particles released into the air when a structure was damaged can be toxic for the therapy dog; this includes fires, tornadoes, and explosions. And remember, after the crisis has passed, your dog and you will both still be significantly impacted by the stress from having worked in a crisis situation, so take good care of yourself and your dog, eat well, and take a long rest.

It is vitally important to carry a doggy care bag with you when you and your dog are working as a crisis response team. Include fresh, bottled water; clean containers for food and water; dog food or snacks; a blanket, bed, or crate the dog is familiar with for resting and naps; a dog first aid kit; supplies to clean up after the dog goes to the bathroom; a dog toy for play breaks; and a dog chew toy to use during breaks for the dog's stress relief. Include cloths or antibacterial wipes to wipe the dog's fur in between visits with clients to minimize the animal's exposure to infectious germs and to help keep the dog's fur clean if there is dust in the air. Include a spare leash and collar for your dog in case the original ones choose this time to wear out on you.

For animal assisted crisis response counseling, I also recommend carrying a crisis response bag for the therapist, meaning the dog's owner or handler. You will want snacks for yourself, bottled water, and antibacterial wipes to clean your hands and for clients to clean their hands before and after visits with the dog. Include a lint brush to keep fur off of your clothing and for clients to remove fur from their clothing after visiting with your dog. You may not mind fur on your clothing, but others might be put off by it. You may want to include a first aid kit for yourself for minor injuries that may occur to you. Do not offer medical treatment to your clients unless you are a trained medical professional and are acting in an officially recognized capacity to provide such aid. It is best that if your client needs medical attention you seek that for your client by finding the nearest medical care provider on the scene or by asking for assistance from a police officer or firefighter. Include in your crisis bag for yourself at least a one-day change of clothes, in case you get caught on the scene for a long time or your clothes get soiled, and any medication or hygiene toiletries you may need within a 24-hour period. Include in the bag a cell phone and battery charger, flashlight with extra batteries, and money or a telephone service card for a pay telephone (because cell phone service may get too busy to access during a crisis). You might also want to place a paperback book in your bag because there actually may be long waiting periods at a crisis scene before you are called in to perform your counseling services. You may want to include rain gear and a weatherproof jacket or maybe a blanket for yourself in case the weather turns cold or you have to sleep in your car or stay in a community shelter overnight. Be sure and include pencil and paper for taking notes that may be necessary for a report later on. Add to the bag any small counseling tools that you may need, such as dog puppets or dog toys for the children to use to interact with the therapy dog during counseling sessions. You may even want to give the children you counsel in a crisis response session a small, inexpensive, stuffed dog toy to keep and take away with them after the session as a continued source of comfort. All of this is a lot to pack, so the real trick will be configuring the dog's care bag and your care bag so that they can be toted around easily. And, a lightweight, collapsible dog crate is much easier to travel with. Technology has advanced such that some dog crates are made to fold up to be quite small and extremely light, weighing only a few pounds.

When working in a crisis response situation, wear comfortable clothing appropriate for the environment or scene where you will be providing the crisis counseling with your pet. Also, you and the therapy dog should both wear visible identification that clarifies your role as a crisis response counseling team. This will reduce the likelihood of being confused with curious bystanders that may be shooed away by security. Remember though, you are in fact no more than a bystander unless you have been officially invited to the scene to provide crisis response counseling with your pet. Thus, let us examine some ways to become officially involved in animal assisted crisis response counseling.

Become a Recognized Crisis Response Counselor with Your Pet

If you have not had formal training in crisis response counseling, then before becoming involved as a crisis response counselor you should pursue crisis response training at a local, state, or national conference or continuing education seminar. If you have not had crisis response training for many years, you might want to get some current training in this area. Crisis response training is provided by the American Red Cross (2004) and NOVA (2004). Informative publications in crisis response include *A Practical Guide for Crisis Response in Our Schools, 5th edition* (Lerner, Volpe, & Lindell, 2004a), *A Practical Guide for University Crisis Response* (Lerner, Volpe, & Lindell, 2004b), and *Acute Traumatic Stress Management* (Lerner & Shelton, 2001). Animal assisted crisis response training is offered by K-9 Disaster Relief, a nonprofit humanitarian foundation (Shane, 2004). A highly recognized national network of therapy team crisis responders is called HOPE: Animal Assisted Crisis Response (HOPE, 2004); this nonprofit organization also offers training and continuing education in animal assisted response to crisis and disaster.

In the case of a community tragedy, the American Red Cross organization is often a primary respondent. Thus, many community crisis response service providers coordinate their efforts through the Red Cross response structure. To become a crisis response service provider for the Red Cross, you must take their standardized training then register with your local Red Cross organization as a crisis response counselor with your therapy pet. In the instance of a local school tragedy, many schools have in place their own existing crisis response team. Contact your local school district office to find out how to become part of that school district's crisis response counseling team. Whether you are a crisis response counselor for the Red Cross or a local school district, you may need to check in with them from time to time to make sure you are still listed as an active service provider and keep your telephone numbers and other contact information current. In the time of a real tragedy, things will need to happen quickly, so advance preparedness is the best approach. Many well meaning people will want to help out in a crisis, but the fact is that you will most likely only get in the way unless you are part of an established response structure with a clearly identified chain of command. You must know whom to contact to obtain your crisis response counseling assignment, including names and contact information of back-up supervisors if you cannot reach your assigned supervisor.

The Nature of Crisis Response Counseling

Victims and survivors of tragedy experience and display an array of emotions. Each child and adult will deal with the crisis in a unique way, but there are some common experiences that help us to prepare as professionals to provide counseling services in response to a crisis. Victims and survivors of tragedy are likely experiencing some form of emotional shock. This may be exhibited as a sense of disorientation and confusion, difficulty with communication, finding it hard to focus attention or concentration, and trouble with making decisions. Some clients will be very quiet and some will be very emotional and talkative. Demonstrating empathy, immediacy, and sincerity while listening attentively or sitting quietly with clients can be comforting for them. Despair, sadness, and anger are common emotions expressed in a crisis situation. Sometimes client anger may be directed at service personnel, so it is important not to take things said to you personally. All clients in a crisis situation are likely experiencing some level of anxiety. Their psychophysiological stress level will be significantly aroused. Thus, strategies to help calm a client can be implemented.

Lerner & Shelton (2001) describe four categories of responses commonly experienced by persons who have been exposed to a traumatic event; these are emotional responses, cognitive responses, behavioral responses, and physiological responses. A number and variety of emotions are possible; some examples for each category of response are listed below:

Emotional Responses

- Shock and numbness
- Fear and terror
- Anxiety
- Anger
- Grief and guilt
- Uncertainty
- Irritability
- Sadness or depression

Cognitive Responses

- Difficulty concentrating
- Confusion and disorientation
- Difficulty with decision making
- Short attention span
- Suggestibility
- Vulnerability
- Blaming self or others
- Forgetfulness

Behavioral Responses

- Withdrawal and isolation
- Impulsivity
- Inability to stay still
- Exaggerated startle response

Physiological Responses

- Rapid heartbeat and elevated blood pressure
- Difficulty breathing
- Chest pains
- Muscle tension and pains
- Fatigue
- Hyperventilation
- Headaches
- Increased sweating, thirst, and dizziness

If a client is perceived as needing medical attention, such as having chest pains, difficulty breathing, injury, and so forth, assist them in obtaining medical assistance immediately by locating a nearby, onsite medical emergency provider.

A crisis response counselor must attend to the many needs of a client that are unique to a crisis response situation. It is important to help clients feel that they are currently safe by reassuring them that the immediate tragic event is over. To help clients process the intensity of the experience, the crisis counselor encourages clients to express emotions and talk about how they feel and how they have been impacted by the event. If someone has died, processing the shock and grief of the death is important for the client. Processing the loss of property and pets is also very meaningful for the client. Because a client may not be thinking clearly, a crisis counselor may assist the client through some imminent decision-making process appropriate to the situation, although significant life-changing decisions should be postponed if possible until the client is thinking more clearly. Guiding the client through some brief relaxation exercises can calm the client's nerves. These exercises take only a few seconds each but can have significant positive impact. They can be practiced several times a day every day to alleviate stress. Following are some brief relaxation responses that are helpful to teach a client:

- Deep breathing. Have clients place their hands just above their belly buttons and take slow deep breaths while focusing on how their hands gradually rise and fall as they breathe. Also, have clients imagine inflating an imaginary balloon inside their stomachs beginning with filling up the bottom near the belly button and finishing with the top near the chest. Then deflate the imaginary balloon by reversing the process. Coach the client to take smooth, easy breaths and to not hold their breath, especially in between inhales and exhales. Proper, diaphragmatic breathing is a key to good health. The entire body responds positively to it. The blood is oxygenated, feeding the vital organs, muscles, and brain that aid in clearer thinking and more energy and health. Dogs have a nice natural diaphragmatic breathing process. So, to facilitate the slow breathing exercise for a client, I have my dog Rusty lie down with his belly showing. I have taught Rusty to respond to the word "relax" during our daily massage time so he can relax upon command in most situations, having associated the word with relaxation. I tell Rusty to relax, and as he lies there calmly, breathing slowly and deeply, I ask clients to put their hands on Rusty's warm belly, breathe deeply, and count how many of Rusty's breaths they can fit into one inhale and one exhale of their own, because dogs have faster breathing patterns than humans. I instruct the client to sense the warmth of the skin and relaxation of the stomach muscles on Rusty's tummy while doing this exercise.
- Shoulder shrug. Have the clients reach for their ears with the tops of their shoulders while taking a long, deep breath and then drop the shoulders like a ton of bricks falling on the exhale. This will aid in releasing tension that inevitably builds up in the shoulder region at times of stress.
- Shoulder roll. Have the client slowly roll the shoulders backwards and forwards to release tension.
- Slow neck stretch. Have the client slowly let the head fall to one side down toward the top of the shoulder without raising the shoulder to meet it, gradually stretching the neck muscles while taking deep breaths. Then repeat on the other side.
- Relax the dog. After clients have practiced the above exercises, I ask them to continue their slow breathing and release as much of any remaining tension in

their bodies as they can while they slowly pet Rusty, thereby trying to get Rusty as still and relaxed as possible. I tell the client that the dog can pick up on their emotional and physical stress so they have to relax themselves to get the dog to relax.

- Humor the dog (or funny face). The point of this exercise is to have the client stretch their facial muscles to help tight muscles relax. I ask clients to stretch their facial muscles by making as funny a face as they can, without touching their faces, to see if they can get my dog Rusty to respond to their funny faces in a positive way, such as him giving a responsive tail wag or walking over to the client and sniffing or licking their faces, and so on.

Extreme or constant psychophysiological arousal is very detrimental to emotional and physical well-being. When a threat is perceived, a chain of events occurs that sends a variety of stress-related hormones cascading into the bloodstream. In response, the heart rate increases, blood pressure rises, muscles become tense, and digestive processes are interrupted. The stress hormones, such as cortisol, have toxic effects on the immune system, thereby making us more susceptible to illness. Even after the tragic event is over, the client's rumination on the event continues the re-experiencing of it and thus maintains psychophysiological arousal. The presence of a therapy dog has been found to counter the stress response by reducing the amount of stress hormones released and increasing the release of health-inducing hormones, such as endorphins and oxytocin (Odendaal, 2000). Helping a client manage and control the stress response as part of the crisis recovery process is vitally important. Simply petting or playing with the therapy dog can help a client in crisis relax and feel better. Holding or hugging a friendly therapy pet can make the client feel more secure and grounded because of the familiarity that a therapy pet presents to an otherwise strange and upsetting situation.

Frank Shane of K-9 Disaster Relief (Shane, 2004) has written heartrending stories that epitomize the value of making it possible for a client to pet or hug a therapy pet during a crisis response situation. A brief reiteration of two of these stories follows. A woman and her child were seeking financial assistance from the Red Cross disaster headquarters after the woman lost her husband in the World Trade Center attack on September 11, 2001. The woman was visibly emotional upon seeing a therapy dog, saying that she missed her dog very much that had died of cancer a few months before September 11. The woman requested to pet the therapy dog. The animal's handler, who was a mental health provider trained in animal assisted techniques, facilitated an interaction between the woman and the dog. The woman petted the therapy dog and talked about her own pet loss, the dog, which her husband had named Ginger. She went on to process her grief from losing her husband. Then the woman's child spent time with the therapy dog and handler while the mother went to complete the forms for gaining financial assistance. The therapy dog lay underneath the table near the child as the child drew pictures of the former family dog, Ginger, playing ball with the child's now deceased father.

In a second incident described by Shane (2004), a volunteer AAT team was working just outside of the World Trade Center disaster site, very near "ground zero." Several exhausted firefighters and other rescue personnel were resting in this area. At one point, a firefighter knelt down next to the therapy dog and started crying. The firefighter spent nearly half an hour with the therapy dog. He told the dog's handler that the dog's reddish hair was the same color as a young man he had just taken off of a building. The firefighter spent time processing with the animal's handler the many terrible days working in the aftermath of the September 11 terrorist attack. The firefighter then asked the handler to come back the next day so he could give the dog something special.

Form an Animal Assisted Crisis Response Counseling Team

If your local school or community does not have a crisis response counseling team, then you may want to form one that includes several therapists working with their therapy animals as part of the team. Form your crisis response counseling team in cooperation with local school districts and community emergency management officials such as police, fire, and medical personnel. Make sure all of your crisis response counseling team members receive or have had crisis response training, such as may be provided by the American Red Cross organization or NOVA. Also, only therapy animals, preferably therapy dogs, that have been evaluated as being appropriate for crisis response work should be allowed to be part of the crisis response team. A crisis response therapy animal needs to have a high tolerance for stress, have a very even temperament, be very well behaved, demonstrate very predictable behaviors, and have a quick and efficient response to commands.

The NOVA *Community Crisis Response Team Training Manual* suggests guidelines for establishing a crisis response team. Based on NOVA guidelines, following is a step-by-step procedure for establishing an animal assisted crisis response counseling team. Step one for developing an animal assisted crisis response counseling team is to develop (a) a contract of agreement; and (b) a policy and procedures manual for each team member outlining responsibilities, duties, and obligations. Include in the contract and the policies and procedures information that clarifies the increased potential risk of injury and stress involved with crisis response counseling for both the counselor and the therapy pet. State clearly in the policies and procedures the chain of command for community contact of the team, including back-up contacts, procedures for disseminating crisis response assignments, procedures for on-site supervision of crisis response counseling team members, procedures for recording and reporting activities performed during the crisis response counseling, and procedures for debriefing and processing after the crisis has passed.

Step two for developing an animal assisted crisis response team is to designate at least two coordinators who will serve as initial contact persons for your response team. Two coordinators are necessary so that one coordinator is always available locally to be contacted by school or community emergency response supervisors in the event of a tragedy. These coordinators will provide to school and community emergency response management supervisors and to other appropriate emergency response personnel a description of the service your team offers and contact information for the two designated coordinators of the response team. The response team coordinators will be the initial persons contacted when the school or community emergency management system supervisor calls upon the services of your crisis response counseling team. In fact, it might be a good idea to have a team coordinator on 24-hour call at all times as it is never known when tragedy may occur. Make sure school or community emergency management supervisors continue to be aware of your team, how to contact the team coordinators, and when to call upon the team's service. Periodic communication with school and community emergency managers will more likely assure that your crisis response team will be utilized even though a certain amount of disorganization and chaos rules the aftermath of a tragedy. Your crisis response team coordinators will contact team members to organize a response to the tragedy, oversee the response, and organize a process and debriefing session regarding the crisis response once the crisis is over. Also, response team coordinators will be the designated contact persons for crisis response team members to check in with after a tragedy has occurred to find out if their services will be called upon. The response team coordinators also serve as group communication personnel, directing communication among response team members during a crisis as well as coordinating communication with outside agencies, organizations, and facilities. The designated response team coordinator must not provide direct client services with or without their pets during a crisis because they will be busy coordinating and communicating the response effort. Response team coordinators can also organize crisis response training for potential new members and coordinate community outreach activities between team members and the community for education about the service the team provides.

Step three is to designate at least one team member as a team assessor who is an on-site supervisor of all the crisis response team members. This assessor will not provide direct services to clients and will not work with his or her pets but will supervise the services of the active team members with their pets. The team assessor oversees the services being provided at the crisis site and serves as a feedback resource to both the crisis response counseling team coordinator and the school or community emergency management supervisor. The team assessor is often the person who initially evaluates team members with their pets to approve them as crisis response team members. Thus, it is most helpful if the team assessor is a counselor and a trained animal evaluator. All response teams must, with their animals, check in with the team assessor once they reach the crisis response site. The team assessor screens team members at the crisis site in advance of the team reporting for duty and continuously monitors each team's capacity to cope with a specific population, trauma, or environment. If a team becomes overwhelmed or fatigued, the assessor makes recommendations to remove the team from the site. The team assessor can cooperate with the team coordinator to provide ongoing emotional support for crisis response team members who respond to disaster. The team assessor should definitely be an important participant at the debriefing and processing session or sessions that are organized by the team coordinator after the crisis has passed that all response team members must attend.

Step four in developing an animal assisted crisis response counseling team is to designate at least one team member whose role will be to locate and alert an on-call veterinarian in case his or her services will be needed by the responding therapy animals. Step five is to develop and maintain an up-to-date resource directory of approved team members and their approved therapy pets with names and contact information with multiple phone numbers for each team member. Designate in the directory at least two coordinators who will serve as the initial contact persons for community emergency managers who wish to call upon the response team for services. All key personnel for the response team should be designated in the directory. Step six is to come up with a recognizable team name that can easily become familiar to emergency management personnel. Step seven is to develop and distribute recognized identification badges and clothing for team members to wear at the crisis site.

The therapy pets should all wear visible identification, such as a neck scarf or vest of the same colored material and team markings, to clearly identify the animal as a crisis response team therapy animal. And human team members should also wear recognizable clothing, such as a team vest or jacket. All human team members should also wear a laminated team identification badge with the name of the crisis response team, the names of the therapist and the therapy pet, and a photograph of both the human and animal team member on it. In a crisis situation, it is the duty of on-site security to make sure you belong there. You must be cordial and cooperative with any and all requests to check your identification.

Keys to effective crisis response counseling include preparation and organization as well as ongoing coordination and supervision. No tragedy can be predicted, and sometimes the best laid plans can have hitches given the nature of a tragedy. Following the terrorist attack on the World Trade Center of New York on September 11, 2001, the American Red Cross was contacted by hundreds of personnel wanting to donate their services. One enthusiastic response team was a group of faculty and student play therapists from our graduate program in counseling at the University of North Texas. Upon their return the therapists described the designated site in New York for counseling services as a hastily created, large common area where families and individuals would come for free counseling services. The manner in which it was arranged was chaotic and intrusive with a significant lack of privacy for the client and multiple impositions upon the therapists. Professionals readily invaded the space of other professionals while volunteers stumbled into counseling sessions interrupting therapeutic process. As it was described to me, in one instance a play therapist was working with a child using a portable play therapy kit when over walked a volunteer with a therapy dog interrupting the counseling session and inviting the child to play with or pet the dog. This happened on multiple occasions. In another instance, a play therapist was working with a child using play therapy and a psychologist walked over, interrupted the counseling session, and started directing the child to respond to the psychologist's inquiries. It seems obvious that both the volunteer with the therapy dog and the psychologist neither recognized nor respected the work of the play therapist. It is easy to understand how a nonprofessional community volunteer might make such an error, but even professionals were stumbling all over one another. The well-meaning volunteers and professionals may have been more effective had there been better coordination of facilities and services in this crisis situation.

Chapter 10

Establishing a School-Based Program for Animal Assisted Therapy and Education

Guidelines for AAT Program Development   152
Types of AAT School-Based Programs   153
How to Solicit Funding for Your AAT Program   154
How to Report on the Progress of Your AAT Program   157

"To educate our people, and especially our children, to humane attitudes and actions toward living things is to preserve and strengthen our national heritage and the moral values we champion in the world."

— John F. Kennedy

There are many schoolteachers and school counselors across the U.S. who work successfully with their pets at their schools. The purpose of this chapter is to describe some recommended procedures for establishing such a program. The recommendations apply whether it is just one professional who wishes to work with a pet or an entire group of professionals or volunteers with their pets.

Guidelines for AAT Program Development

The first step is to develop a proposal that clearly outlines the program you wish to develop. The proposal should include:

- A program mission statement and educational or therapeutic objectives
- Expected benefits of the program
- Any potential risks of the program and how they will be prevented/managed
- Which adults and animals will participate in the AAT program
- Which students will participate in the AAT
- What types of activities are expected to take place in the AAT program
- The training, evaluation, and credentials of the persons and animals to provide the AAT
- Where the AAT will take place
- All relevant persons who will be consulted about the development of the AAT program (i.e., school nurse, custodial services, facilities management, grounds maintenance, other teachers, other counselors, other administrators, parents, and so forth)
- Intent to develop a set of policies and procedures for the AAT program with consultation with relevant school personnel

It is imperative that you consult with all relevant personnel that may be impacted by the program. The persons you leave out of the loop will inevitably be those who complain about the program or try to sabotage the program. This is usually because they do not understand the program's implications and fear it will interfere with their work or add to their workload. Also, consulting with them may make them feel more a part of the program, thereby adding to its chances for success.

Policies and procedures for the AAT program you develop should be as comprehensive as necessary. Some recommendations for items to include are:

- Procedures for obtaining informed consent to participate from parents and informed assent from students
- Procedures for keeping the environment clean — cleaning up and disposing of animal excrement; cleaning up animal fur from the floor, furniture, and participants; and making available safe, nontoxic cleaning materials in case of an accident (e.g., the animal poops or vomits indoors)
- Procedures for injury prevention for human and animal participants

- Procedures for handling and reporting injuries to humans and animals
- Procedures for infection prevention for humans and animals
- Dress code for human participants and grooming code for animal participants
- An appropriate behavior code for human and animal participants

Present the proposal at a meeting with the school principal. Briefly explain in person the basics of the program you wish to offer, answer any questions, and leave the written proposal for the administrator to read. You might also want to leave a public relations video that shows AAT in action so the administrator gets an image of what AAT looks like. A video like this, along with an introduction kit, can be obtained from Delta Society (2003). It is important that all therapy teams get proper training and certification prior to offering services.

Types of AAT School-Based Programs

A common simple application of AAT in the school is the school counselor who brings a pet to work. Children can appreciate the novelty of the pet's presence and use it as an excuse to drop by and visit with the counselor without feeling awkward. A child who needs some nurturing touch or affection can safely get that by hugging a therapy pet. A child who feels dejected can feel affirmed by the way the therapy pet responds positively to the child. A child who may have difficulty expressing his or her needs or hurts may find it easy to talk to the therapy pet or may find it therapeutic to just spend time quietly petting the therapy animal. There is an abundance of school counselors in the Dallas, Ft. Worth, Denton metro area who work with their pets. They have communicated to me that their therapy pets become popular, unofficial mascots for the school children, teachers, and staff. The presence of the therapy animals actually lifts the spirit of the school. Many teachers and administrators as well drop by for a moment's visit with the therapy pets to get their mood lifted.

Another popular school-based program is AAT for classroom and instructional enhancement. Math and reading teachers have shared with me that having a dog in the classroom seems to have a calming effect on the students. The students seem to have fewer behavior problems and pay greater attention to the lesson when the teacher's therapy dog is in attendance. In addition, students who are otherwise anxious to read out loud seem more motivated to participate and less anxious when they can pet the therapy dog while engaged in the exercise. Having animals in the classroom to facilitate the educational process for students is a growing interest across the country.

Therapy pets can aid in vocational training for students. Participants can learn skills in grooming, obedience training, agility training, tracking, and so forth. Community professionals can volunteer to teach these skills to the students with their pets. Getting students involved with existing dog training and performance groups in the community can provide a healthy outlet for recreation. In addition, students can become trained to provide community service with their pet by completing a certification program like Delta Society's Pet Partners Program. Then, under adult supervision, student Pet Partners Teams can visit nursing homes, hospitals, and younger students at the school. Providing community service can teach a student the benefits of community caring and involvement. It can enhance the student's relationship skills and contribute to teaching and reinforcing moral and humane values.

Volunteer work at the local animal shelter or animal rescue facility can contribute to the education and development of the student and could save the life of many animals. Some dogs are difficult to place because they lack obedience training or are hard to handle. As long as the dogs have been evaluated to be nonaggressive, student training groups can work with these unruly dogs and teach them in a matter of weeks to be obedient and socially responsive and, thus, more attractive for adoption.

A school can also partner with an existing AAT program. For instance, students can attend a nearby equine facility to learn horsemanship and enhance social skills. It is important that the school thoroughly investigate the credentials and reputation of the community program with which the school affiliates. The rapidly rising popularity of equine assisted therapy in Texas has led to such programs popping up all over the state. There are already a huge number of horse ranches in Texas, and turning a ranch or part of a ranch into a therapy program can offset the huge costs incurred in owning and running a horse ranch. Unfortunately, a few of these equine therapy programs do not follow standardized guidelines established for the protection of participants. A rule far too often broken by less reputable programs is all equine therapy clients should always be required to wear a helmet when mounted on the horse. Also, many of the so-called therapeutic staff are not qualified to provide equine assisted therapy. Recognized educational programs for training persons who wish to offer equine therapy exist, such as EAGALA (2003) and NARHA (2003), and it is essential that staff offering therapy services have adequate training. There is one equine therapy facility in the north Texas region that has a very poor reputation among other more reputable programs. The owner continuously "thumbs his nose" at safety procedures and claims he offers certain therapeutic services, yet the therapy service performed is below par of what the service should be and the so-called therapy staff do not have the proper training and credentials to offer the therapy service. The general public does not know that his practices are substandard and potentially dangerous because they are unaware of what a really good and reputable equine program should look like. There are several equine assisted programs in the same north Texas geographic region that are excellent and go above and beyond established standards of training and service provision. It is the substandard programs like the one described that may damage the public's opinion or slow the public's acceptance of AAT. NARHA and EAGALA are two organizations that can assist the public in their investigation of reputable equine therapy programs and in the examination of standards of practice that should be followed by these programs.

Another fun school program idea that involves animals is a nature or wilderness study program. Supervised field trips to bird sanctuaries, wild game preserves, and wild life and wilderness areas can help students get in touch with nature and learn science lessons. Students can participate in the annual Audubon Society bird count. This is a fun 1-day activity held once per year that contributes to an important database for tracking birds and determining whether they are endangered. Our environment is facing ever-increasing pollution and global warming, and sensitizing students at an early age about nature preservation is of vital importance for current and future generations.

How to Solicit Funding for Your AAT Program

An AAT program design can be simple and not incur much cost, especially if most of the work is done by volunteers with their pets. However, sometimes funds are required to achieve certain goals of some types of school-based programs for such things as supplies, transportation, and training of animal therapy teams or for contracting with established outside professional therapy or education programs. I would classify program funding resources into three basic categories: (a) local or regional private companies or foundations, (b) government-sponsored programs (city, state, or federal), or (c) large, national private companies or foundations. For small program cost requirements, the best approach would be to go to local businesspeople or community organizations for funding in exchange for public recognition of their contributions, such as a write-up in the local paper and a service award plaque they can hang on the wall of their business. This type of school–community relations is very traditional and a commonly accepted practice.

Applying for and receiving a government-sponsored grant is probably the most difficult route to take for getting funding. These types of grants usually have very specific application formats, strict application deadlines, and a large number of applicants making the process very competitive. This type of grant is highly labor intensive, with a small percentage of applicants often receiving awards. And, while a government grant process is supposed to be fair, many researchers who have gone this route, even the successful ones, will tell you that it is a highly political process. You are more likely to get a government-sponsored grant if, in addition to having an outstanding idea and proposal, you also have a great deal of experience in the area of the program you want to start and if you are well known, either by reputation or personal contact, by persons who are part of the decision-making process. The advantage to this type of grant is that some can provide a significant amount of money, in the thousands and sometimes millions of dollars. However, the more money you go for, the stricter the rules and the more closely the program is monitored. Precise documentation of how every single cent is spent is required as well as detailed, periodic progress reports. Sources on how to find out about government-sponsored research grants include a local library, a college or university library, or searching the internet on the computer.

My favorite route to take when I need a significant amount of money to initiate or maintain a program is to approach a large, national private corporation or foundation. These can be discovered through the same process as finding a government-sponsored grant — through a library resource person or a computerized internet search. Also, you can get creative and just think of some companies or organizations that might be interested in your project because of the product they sell, such as veterinary supply companies, dog food companies, and so forth. If these companies offer grants, then they might be interested in sponsoring your program. Some of these types of private granting resources have a formal proposal format and some do not. Some have strict application deadlines and some do not. Some advertise their grants nationally and some do not. Some have pre-established giving amounts and some are more flexible and will base the award on the judged merits of your program. It is important to remember that if you receive funds from a private company or foundation they will want some type of recognition, and how that is to be accomplished should be described in your proposal to them. A common way to recognize a funding agency is to print on program material a statement much like "This program is made available by a generous grant from (company/foundation name)," or a similar statement. Recognition formats can be negotiated with the company. I would not describe myself as having been greatly successful in getting funding for my programs over the years, but I have had a little success, and when you have to you can make a little success go a long way. For example, I put together a proposal for one company that resulted in getting a few thousand dollars used as seed money to start a Center for Animal Assisted Therapy at the University of North Texas where I work (see Sample Funding Proposal to Establish a Center for Animal Assisted Therapy in the appendix). The basic components that should be in a funding proposal typically include:

1. The name of your program and a brief introduction of the idea
2. Contact information for you and appropriate team members in leadership positions
3. A description of community support for the idea with accompanying letters of support (from schools, parents, administrators, students, teachers, counselors, collaborating organizations, etc.)
4. A description of the community to be served by the program, i.e., students or clients
5. Information about you and other team members in a position of leadership (also, attach copies of professional resumes or vitas)
6. An in-depth description of your proposed program including a mission statement and detailed procedures
7. A description of expected outcomes and outcome measures to be used for program evaluation
8. A detailed budget estimate over a designated time period

Some funding agencies may require more information than what I just described. Also, some funding organizations may require that you obtain from your organization or school board permission to use human subjects in research if you are planning on publishing your results at some point. Most application review processes to use human subjects in research require a copy of your complete funding proposal along with a description of:

1. How participants will be recruited to receive services
2. How informed consent to participate in the program will be obtained from participants and legal guardians
3. How the safety of participants will be appropriately maintained
4. How the identity of participants will be kept confidential (where appropriate)
5. What the potential risks and benefits of the program to participants will be
6. How and to whom program results will be disseminated

After reading this section on obtaining funding for your program idea, you may be a bit overwhelmed. But if you break the process into steps and complete it one step at a time, it becomes quite manageable. Once you have written a good proposal, you can submit it to a number of different funding agencies and resources. And when you do get some funding, you will see that your efforts were valuable. As one colleague said to me recently when reflecting upon the grant writing process, "This ain't easy, but it's worth it."

How to Report on the Progress of Your AAT Program

Once you have your program up and running, you will need to complete periodic progress reports. Hopefully, you will not need to do this but once per year. I have included a sample progress report I recently did for my program, the Center for Animal Assisted Therapy, that I hope you may find helpful (see Sample Progress Report for the Center for Animal Assisted Therapy in the appendix). Basic components typically included in a program progress report are:

1. Name and title of your program
2. Your contact information
3. An introduction and brief description of the program
4. Program goals that have been established
5. Goals that have been completed
6. Outcome measures and results and any adjustments to program services or goals based on these outcome measures
7. Goals in progress and their current status
8. Future goals

For reportable outcome measures, it is very useful to conduct statistical analysis on the collected data. If you are not interested in doing this yourself, you can probably hire someone to do it for you, such as a professor or a graduate student from a local college or university.

Once you have collected sufficient data and analyzed them, you might want to publish your results. There are many professional journals available for this. A visit with a college or university librarian can point you in the right direction. Guidelines for submission are usually printed in the back or front of the journal but not necessarily in each volume, so you may have to look through several copies before you find it. In most cases, you will receive no money for publishing your data in a professional journal. But it is nice to be a published author, and you perform a great service by sharing the success of your program with the rest of the world.

I highly encourage you to present your results at a regional, state, or national conference in your field. Your own professional organization probably has an annual meeting, and you can submit a presentation proposal for the meeting or conference program board to review. Most organizations that sponsor conferences these days have a website on the internet with downloadable conference program proposals, so you can do the whole submission online using your computer. Usually program presentation proposals must be received months in advance of the actual conference date. Typically, one does not receive any money for presenting at these conferences, but it is a great opportunity to network.

Chapter 11

Establishing and Maintaining a University-Based AAT Training Program

Seeking Approval and Establishing Policy for an AAT Program   160

Obtaining AAT Credentials   161

Being a Role Model: Practicing AAT-C   162

Developing a University Course   162

Involving the Community   163

Establishing a Center   164

Creating Student Internships in the Community   164

Serving as an Educational Resource   165

Gaining National and International Recognition   165

"For horses can educate through first hand, subjective personal experiences, unlike human tutors, teachers, and professors can ever do. Horses can build character, not merely urge one to improve on it. Horses forge the mind, the character, the emotions and inner lives of humans. People can talk to one another about all these things and remain distanced and lonesome. In partnership with a horse, one is seldom lacking for thought, emotion and inspiration. One is always attended by a great companion."

— Charles de Kunffy

There are certainly a number of ways to approach establishing a university-based AAT-C training program. I will describe what worked for me in establishing the AAT-C program in the College of Education at the University of North Texas. The tasks presented in this chapter required approximately 3½ years to accomplish.

Seeking Approval and Establishing Policy for an AAT Program

First, I presented a proposal to the department chair. The primary components of the proposal were:

1. I wanted to begin searching for a puppy to buy and to raise and train to be a therapy dog (the current family dog was old, arthritic, and grumpy and therefore not appropriate as a therapy dog). All expenses regarding the therapy dog would be my own because I wanted the dog to be my personal pet and family member.
2. I wanted to be able to bring the puppy to work for early socialization training. The dog would continue to accompany me to work during appropriate activities, such as all class lectures, office hours, and some meetings. I made reassurances that the dog would not be brought to work until the dog had learned the social graces of relieving itself outside on the ground and not inside on the floor.
3. I would train the dog in obedience, and the dog and I would achieve national registration as a therapy team by a recognized organization.
4. I would develop a course of instruction in AAT to train students in our program and other related programs. The course would also be open to professionals seeking training in AAT-C.
5. I would provide a few weekend workshops per year to train volunteers and professionals in the community in basic introductory animal assisted techniques.
6. I would seek external funds to establish a Center for Animal Assisted Therapy that would support the training and research of AAT-C.
7. I would seek approval for all of the above from the dean of the College of Education and other appropriate administrative offices.

The department chair gave me his endorsement for my proposal. I am very fortunate to work with a department chair who is a progressive thinker and trusts my judgment. I was further fortunate in that the dean and associate dean of the College of Education were also very supportive of my proposal. After consultation with me, the dean's office wrote an official letter to the university facilities and risk management office to inform them of the purpose and presence of therapy pets on campus as part of an academic training program. It clearly outlined that:

1. The pets were owned by their handlers and would not be housed on university property.
2. The pets would be on a leash or in a crate at all times and under supervision.
3. The pets would be in training or trained in basic obedience and professional AAT techniques.
4. The pets' handlers would clean up after the pets, and the pets would pose no additional work for ground or facility maintenance crews.
5. All pets were certified healthy and disease free.
6. The therapy pets should be allowed in classrooms and, where appropriate, meeting rooms.
7. The therapy pets would not be allowed in food services facilities on campus.

Facility and risk management recommended that the university legal office also be informed of the new animal therapy program. Communication and consultation with legal affairs led to the development of an official university policy recognizing the presence of certified therapy dogs on campus.

One big step was to take the proposal for developing an AAT-C training program to my fellow faculty members in the counseling program for their approval. This turned out to be the most difficult of all steps. We had over a dozen faculty members in our program at the time. I am lucky to have as colleagues a group of highly talented faculty members with national reputations in their field. The potential downside to this is sometimes it is difficult to get professionals with clearly established ideas about the value of their own area of specialty to be accepting of a new area of specialty. For instance, in discussion about the topic it was said, "Animal assisted therapy? I don't get it. What's the point?" and, "Pet assisted therapy has no proven record in the literature and therefore should not be allowed." After a brief debate, the proposal passed in the faculty meeting by a narrow margin. For the most part, I have received support and encouragement by my fellow faculty members with regard to the AAT program. The therapy dog is allowed to accompany me most everywhere in the faculty suite and on campus. And in fact, when the dog is not with me, faculty, staff, and students often act disappointed, ask all about the dog, and request I bring the dog by soon for a visit. I even have doctoral students whose advisory and dissertation committee I serve on request that Rusty be present at their dissertation proposal or defense to relieve the student's anxiety about his or her presentation. It may not always be easy to start a new specialty area in an academic program, but it can be done, and it is rewarding.

Obtaining AAT Credentials

I eventually found a red-on-white colored Cocker Spaniel puppy with the "right stuff" (see the section on selecting a puppy in an earlier chapter). I named him Rusty. The first year of Rusty's life was full of socialization, obedience, and special skills and trick training. When he was 1½ years old, he and I became a nationally registered Delta Society Pet Partners Team. I had spent the first year of Rusty's life investigating therapy registration/certification programs in the U.S. I settled on Delta Society because it had the most rigorous training and screening requirements and had published a number of educational and research resources that would be beneficial to a training curriculum. I continued my training with Delta Society and became a Delta Society Licensed Pet Partners Instructor and Licensed Animal Team Evaluator and AAT Instructor. With these credentials, I could train and evaluate my students and persons in the community to become registered Delta Society Pet Partners Teams and animal assisted therapists. Rusty served as my co-instructor and co-evaluator. Since that time, I have added two more therapy team members to my family, a cat named Snowflake and a Cocker Spaniel named Dolly.

Being a Role Model: Practicing AAT-C

Because I had given up my private practice a few years prior, I had no avenue to practice AAT-C. A good friend of mine was therapeutic programs coordinator at the Denton County, Texas, juvenile detention center. Soon after Rusty and I were credentialed, we accepted an invitation from her to volunteer our counseling services at her facility. We still volunteer for a few hours a week, providing individual AAT-C and group AAAs to the teens in the postadjudication program of juvenile detention. This relationship with the juvenile detention center later resulted in additional joint operations regarding research and intern training in AAT-C. Rusty can hardly wait to get out of the car to go see the teens when we pull up in the parking lot of the juvenile detention facility. It is one of his most favorite things to do. Snowflake, my therapy cat, and Dolly, my other therapy dog, work together with Rusty in the group activities at the juvenile center. Graduate students trained in AAT meet me at the facility to assist.

Developing a University Course

I designed a course called Animal Assisted Therapy and offer it through the counseling program where I am a faculty member. Students do not have to have a pet to take the course. The course is open to counseling students, related majors, and professionals in the community. The course description and objectives are as follows.

Course Description

AAT is the incorporation of qualified animals into a therapeutic environment. The course explores techniques to facilitate animal assisted therapeutic interventions in a variety of settings, including schools, counseling agencies, hospitals, nursing homes, hospices, prisons, detention centers, and facilities for the developmentally disabled. A variety of animals are suitable for therapy programs. You need not have an animal or pet to take the course.

Course Objectives

The course objectives are the acquisition of knowledge and skills necessary to facilitate AAT in a variety of professional settings in a fashion that is both safe and humane to the client and the animal.

Course Content and Resources

I incorporated a number of Delta Society materials as resources as well as a conglomeration of other books and articles on the subject. One of the reasons I am writing this book is so I will have an appropriate textbook to use for my course because none existed. I have covered in this text most of the content information that I covered in the course, but now it will be more accessible in one location. I will still require and cover the Delta Society texts *Pet Partners Team Training Course Manual* and *Animal Assisted Therapy Applications I: Student Guide* so that students taking the course can register for those two national certifications upon completion of my course. That is another really good reason for the instructor of the course to have the instructor and evaluator credentials from Delta Society, so that your students can receive those national certifications. The course includes field trips for the observation of AAT-C with dogs, cats, and horses. The course includes an end of the semester Delta Society Pet Partners Team Evaluation for students who are ready for that next step. Because I offer several dates for evaluations per year, there is always ample opportunity for students to be evaluated at a later date if they are not ready by the end of the class.

I first offered the course as a special topics course once a year over 2 years to test the interest level. After two successful offerings, I completed and submitted the paperwork to the curriculum committee to establish it as a permanent course with its own number and title. The course is now listed in the University of North Texas Graduate Catalog as COUN 5530 Animal Assisted Therapy. Undergraduates often have an interest in the course and take it as a Special Problems Course, COUN 4900. (A sample copy of the course syllabus for COUN 5530 is provided in the appendix.)

Involving the Community

The greatest visibility of a new program comes from integrating it into the community. For this reason, I offer two to three weekend workshops per year to the community for volunteers and professionals. The Saturday portion is 4 hours long and is basically the Delta Society Pet Partners Team Training. The following Sunday, I evaluate the handlers with their pets based on Delta Society evaluation standards. Over the first 3½-year period, I organized and presented at 13 Pet Partners workshops, training over 200 Pet Partners teams. Enrollment at the workshop was limited to 15 to 20 (and 15 therapy teams was the maximum number of dogs I felt I could evaluate the following day).

The majority of attendants at the workshop were elementary and junior high school teachers, school counselors, agency counselors, librarians, and community volunteers. Reading teachers and librarians were interested in starting a reading assistance dog program. Math teachers were interested in starting an animals in the classroom program. As a result of these workshops, we assisted in the initiation of AAT-C, reading assistance dogs, and canine classroom dog programs in several schools in several cities in the Dallas, Ft. Worth, Denton, Texas, area, and the number continues to grow. Those who experienced our training programs shared affirmative feedback with others, and we got many more requests for training. Largely due to the community workshops, our AAT program experienced broad recognition in a three county area. We also have frequent attendants from across the state of Texas and three bordering states.

One of the teams that completed our weekend workshop training was professional counselor Pam Flint and her blond Labrador Retriever, Roxy. After Roxy and Pam completed their Delta Society Pet Partners certification, Roxy began joining Pam at her place of employment, the University of North Texas Student Counseling and Testing Center. Roxy was welcomed with open arms by clients and staff. Staff often sought Roxy out for a hug or a pet to relieve job stress and requested her at staff meetings to relieve some of the tedium. After only 1 year of service together in the counseling center, Pam and Roxy received the annual University Staff Service Award. This was the first time an animal had ever won a University of North Texas award. Roxy is considered a regular part of the counseling staff and is included in the department staff photo. Roxy receives no stipend for her work and is not on the university payroll. I don't think she minds having no salary. Based on the expression on her face and the wag in her tail, she is just happy to be at work with her owner Pam.

Establishing a Center

Establishing a center at our university to serve as a central hub for our training and research activities was somewhat difficult to achieve, as it requires external funding. Government grants are difficult to come by, and many grant review boards are not familiar with the educational and therapeutic benefits of AAT. Thus, I felt the best avenue for funding would be with private foundations or corporations, even though most animal foundations respond to projects focused on animal health and protection or spay and neutering programs. Iams's Paws to Share Foundation gave us $33,000 in start-up money in 2001, and thus was established the Center for Animal Assisted Therapy at the University of North Texas (see Sample Funding Proposal to Establish a Center for Animal Assisted Therapy and Sample Progress Report for the Center for Animal Assisted Therapy in the appendix).

Creating Student Internships in the Community

A key to a thriving AAT program in a university is having established internships in the community. The easiest place to start an AAT internship program is with agencies or schools that you have a prior relationship with. I had been volunteering at our county juvenile detention center providing AAT for a couple of years, and they were very receptive to the idea of starting AAT-C internships. Interns who work with their dogs must have first completed my university course in AAT and be a certified Delta Society therapy team. In addition, interns and their dogs must interview with the therapeutic programs coordinator at the juvenile detention center and be willing to submit to a background check. Each intern must adhere to the policies and procedures of the juvenile detention center. Other juvenile detention centers in Texas and the neighboring states of Oklahoma and Louisiana have sought information from our AAT program on how to start such a program at their juvenile facilities.

I also occasionally volunteer at Rocky Top Therapy Center with their equine assisted counseling program. My positive history and relationship with them has led to the establishment of internships there as well. This is an ideal setting for interns who enjoy doing group therapy outdoors that involves the integration of a therapeutic challenge course with horsemanship activities. I serve as the faculty supervisor for most of our students who perform AAT at this internship site.

Serving as an Educational Resource

AAT-C has not been incorporated into very many university-based programs in the U.S. Thanks to our university website that describes our AAT program, a lot of people find out about us (http://www.coe.unt.edu/CDHE/AAT). For this reason, I spend a lot of time every week answering e-mails and phone calls about that subject area. I receive requests for information from all over the U.S. and from other countries as well. I get a lot of e-mails from high school and college students who ask how to make AAT their career. Of course, as part of my advising I always tell them about our counseling program at our university and have recruited some undergraduate, master's, and doctoral students to our program. I answer requests on how to establish an AAT program in an elementary or secondary school or at a university or college. I respond to inquiries on how to start reading assistance dog programs or other types of animals in the classroom programs. I receive a number of requests from high school and college students who are doing a paper on AAT and want my opinion on where to look for resources. I am always careful with this last request not to do their research work for them but try to at least get them pointed in the right direction by recommending a few well-known books and articles. Although it is fun to be a resource person because of the number of people I speak with, it is also very time-consuming. This type of community service is not rewarded or recognized very well by the department. Its own reward is getting to speak with people with a vast array of interests and from a variety of places.

Gaining National and International Recognition

To assist in the growth and development of AAT in counseling, I make it a point to present on the subject at as many national and state conferences as I can. I encourage the involvement of graduate students in my research and offer them copresentation opportunities as a way of increasing the number of recognized resource persons in the field. I actively engage in research projects on AAT and encourage graduate students to do likewise, especially doctoral students who focus their dissertation on the area.

The efforts put forth to establish an AAT training program at the University of North Texas were greatly rewarded when Samsung Corporation of South Korea sent one of their staff to study in our program for a summer session and then invited me to South Korea to speak on and consult about the development of AAT in Korea. I had the honor of speaking on the history of AAT in the U.S. at the First International Symposium on the Human Animal Bond held in Korea in November, 2003. While in Korea, I toured the country, consulted with Samsung Corporation Animal Assistance Services staff, and spoke with students and professors at the veterinary school at Cheju University. In addition, I had the privilege, through instruction and evaluation, of certifying the first two Delta Society Pet Partners teams in Korea, Dr. Angela Kim and Juyeon Lee, both with the same dog, a Cavalier Spaniel named Lulu.

Chapter 12

An Intercultural AAT Experience: Examining the Human–Animal Connection in South Korea

A History of the Human–Animal Connection in South Korea   169
The Human–Animal Connection in the 21st Century:
A New Era for South Korea   170
International Information Exchange and Relationship Building   172
Defining the Role and Scope of AAT in South Korea   173

"The greatness of a nation and its moral progress can be judged by the way its animals are treated."

— Mohandas Ghandi

The human–animal connection construct embraces the ideology of mutual companionship, assistance, and affection between humans and domesticated animals, and as the ruling species, humans have an obligation to demonstrate infinite compassion and appropriate protection for all animals. The human–animal connection is different from the construct of human dependence on animals. The latter encompasses utilization of animals for protection, labor, food, and shelter and exploitation for experimentation and entertainment.

The U.S. has a long history of human dependence on animals. For many centuries, the Native Americans shared their camps with dogs that provided early warning for danger in exchange for food scraps. Native Americans used for transportation horses brought over from other continents by European explorers. Native Americans relied on buffalo, antelope, and other animals of the wilderness as sources for food and clothing. The utilization of animals for food and shelter in pretechnological eras is viewed as justifiable; however, today with many more options available to people for meeting basic survival needs, the essentiality of human dependence on animals becomes more difficult to defend.

The evolved concept of the human–animal connection in the U.S. was inherited from the European immigrants of the 17th and 18th centuries. By the time that the U.S. declared its independence from England in 1776, the concept of the family household pet with access to home and hearth was firmly established. The cultural position on the human–animal connection in the U.S. is by no means a paragon. The majority of our society consumes animal meat products, incidents of animal cruelty or neglect are still too prevalent, far too many stray pets are euthanized in so-called animal shelters, and many animals are victims of the controversial practice of experimentation. The U.S. made significant progress in the 20th century in complying with an ethical duty as compassionate protector of animals. States enacted and enforced laws against animal cruelty, including the outlawing of dog fighting and rooster fighting. Laws were passed to protect the sanctity of the household pet, primarily the dog and the cat. Various regulations incorporated more humane ways of killing farm animals prior to meat processing. Today, there are numerous volunteer groups that rescue stray animals from animal shelters and find them loving homes. Although experimentation on animals for research purposes continues, there is an increase in consciousness-raising efforts about this concern.

The purpose of this chapter is not to examine the history or political correctness of the U.S. cultural position on the human–animal connection. The purpose of this chapter is to share a wondrous cultural movement regarding the human–animal connection in the country of South Korea. But, such is difficult to do without having first reflected on the state of the culture of the human–animal connection in the U.S. Although not completely satisfied with ourselves, most U.S. citizens are fairly comfortable with the state of the cultural position on the human–animal connection in the U.S., viewing existing laws and ethical standards as mostly sufficient for handling failures to meet humane obligations.

A History of the Human–Animal Connection in South Korea

Animals have a long history as beasts of burden and a food source in South Korea with little concern for animal cruelty, and the generally accepted idea of companion animal, or family pet, is yet to evolve in this country (Shin, 2003). Conversations with various South Korean officials revealed an abundance of concerns regarding the current cultural position on the human–animal connection for this country (Y. Kim, D. H. Lee, J. Lee, and S. Lee, personal communications, November 2–12, 2003). Only a small handful of pet dogs can be seen walking with their owners, and the uniqueness of this draws a good deal of attention from passersby. Pet dogs are typically purchased from privately owned pet stores that line up in groups of about four or five, side by side along a busy city street; it looks like puppy row. Small pet dogs are the most popular in South Korea, especially the American Cocker Spaniel, Cavalier Spaniel, Yorkshire Terrier, Boston Terrier, Pomeranian, and Miniature Poodle. South Korean pet owners have a high incidence of quickly turning pet dogs into shelters after discovering that dog ownership requires more than they expected. Due to an ever-increasing population and absence of space, most persons in major cities in South Korea live in a conglomeration of apartment skyscrapers (referred to by locals as "apartment forests"), and this makes exercising pets inconvenient. Animal shelters in South Korea are typically not very sanitary and are overcrowded, and many are privately owned. Most pet owners do not train or socialize their dogs very well, or at all, which further adds to the lack of attraction for them as pets. Most of those who do have trained dogs have sent the dog away to training school and thus have little understanding of continuing training or reinforcing what the pet has learned. Typical South Korean pet owners do not pick up after their dogs relieve themselves, and city officials are hesitant to pass laws compelling them to do so. As a result, city officials ban dogs from many parks where they could meet people and other dogs and exercise. Some large dogs have historically been used as guard dogs, and most South Koreans are afraid of large dogs as a result. Other types of large dogs are still raised as a food source, and the killing of such animals is done in cruel ways. Cats are not a popular choice as pets, and the very few cats visible in South Korea run wild in the streets. The most common horse in South Korea is the native, small JeJu pony, which was frequently observed to have good physical health but whose role was mostly relegated to giving pony rides around a very small arena or being mounted for brief photo opportunities for tourists.

The enactment of laws to protect animals from cruelty in South Korea is new to the current generation and met with reluctance from older generations. Common companion dog activities in the U.S., such as obedience training and trials, agility and fly ball trials, and work by service and therapy animals for the emotionally and physically challenged, are extremely new to South Korea and very rare. In fact, community acceptance and employment of disabled persons is a relatively new concept in South Korea. Public service announcements on television are frequent right now in South Korea that encourage the acceptance and employment of disabled persons, and there are numerous animal activity and animal education television programs that discuss proper care for pets. It is interesting how increased attention to and advocacy for these two diverse groups, disabled persons and animals, seem to parallel one another in this country right now.

The Human–Animal Connection in the 21st Century: A New Era for South Korea

Like unto the immortal words from *2010*, the movie sequel to *2001: A Space Odyssey*, "Something is about to happen … something wonderful." On November 2, 2003, the First International Symposium on the Human Animal Bond was held in South Korea. The symposium sponsor was the South Korean Veterinary Medical Association, and it was organized by Samsung Assistance Dog Services and held at Samsung Everland, a combination cultural center and theme park owned by Samsung and located on a vast expanse of beautiful land in heavily wooded mountains approximately 1 hour's drive from Seoul. The importance of this symposium to the people and animals of South Korea must not be underestimated, and the significance of this event as an official send-off for another major effort to shift the South Korean culture toward a more humane concept of the human–animal connection deserves sharing with the rest of the world. The stated purposes for the First International Symposium on the Human Animal Bond held in South Korea were to encourage veterinarians and other professionals to educate the people of South Korea about the negative connotations of eating dogs and animal cruelty, the benefits of pet ownership, and the responsibilities of pet ownership — and having accomplished such tasks the eventual intention being to change the views of other countries toward South Korea to that of a less barbaric and more humane country (Shin, 2003).

Opportunities to witness a cultural shift are rare and to participate in one even rarer. My small part was the honor of being invited to South Korea for several days by Mr. D. H. Lee, operations manager of Samsung Assistance Dog Services, to advise and consult with Samsung executives and staff on developing AAT programs in South Korea, and to be a speaker at the international symposium as a representative of the U.S. view on the human–animal connection and the history of AAT. Other speakers at the symposium were Dr. Nam-sik Shin, professor of veterinary science, Seoul National University, who spoke on the history of the human–animal bond in South Korea; Dr. Hiroko Shibanai, former president of the Japanese Animal Hospital Association, who spoke of the history of AAT in Japan; Mr. Yoon-ju (George) Choi, general manager of Samsung Assistance Dog Services, who spoke of the Samsung animal facilities and services in South Korea; Dr. Yang Soon (Angela) Kim, professor, Cheju National University in South Korea, who started the first animal assisted play therapy program at her university after studying play therapy and AAT for 1 year at the counseling program of the University of North Texas in the U.S. in 2001; and Ju-yeon (Queenie) Lee, coordinator of Samsung Assistance Dog Services of South Korea, who spoke of her visit to the U.S. in the summer of 2003 to train in AAT at the counseling program of the University of North Texas, to visit the Green Chimneys AAT farm in New York, and to attend the Conference on Humane Education in New York. At the conclusion of the speeches, symposium participants were treated to a tour of the newly constructed, highly technological Samsung veterinary clinic by clinic manager Dr. D. H. (David) Chung; a demonstration of the Samsung guide dogs by head trainer and operations manager for the guide dog school, S. J. Lee; a demonstration of the Samsung search and rescue dog training exercise by the award-winning rescue dog team and trainers; and a demonstration at the newly completed Samsung hearing dog training facility by D. H. Lee and his staff. Samsung provided me with a very talented and personable language translator for the symposium, Soojung (Julie) Lee, Samsung public relations manager of the Office of International Relations.

The First International Symposium on the Human Animal Bond held in South Korea was a grand experiment so was only designed to last half of a day. As it turns out, the meeting was very well attended, mostly by veterinarians of South Korea. The success of the symposium led officials to begin right away to plan another symposium for the following year that will last more than 1 day and invite a broader audience. Samsung and the South Korean Veterinary Medical Association are jointly cooperating to move South Korea into the modern age by providing citizens with a greater understanding for and acceptance of the companion animal, service animal, and therapy animal.

Samsung has been actively engaged in numerous activities in South Korea to promote the welfare of animals over recent years (Choi, 2003):

> Since the late 1980s Samsung has been working towards creating a society of harmony and love where all life forms are respected. Samsung continues to work domestically as well as internationally to promote positive awareness of human animal relationships and to change the negative perceptions of Korea. Because Samsung believes that a society which protects and cares for its animals in effect enhances the quality of life for its people.
>
> (Samsung, 2003)

What is significant about the Samsung animal programs is that there is virtually nothing else like them in the rest of the country of South Korea. Residents in this country are solely reliant on Samsung for many animal related services. Samsung's interest in animal activity and welfare began in 1988 when Samsung built a beautiful state-of-the-art equestrian facility in South Korea and imported top-of-the-line horses to participate in equine sports. Samsung equestrian teams have been winning numerous honors and are rapidly moving up on the world respect ladder. Samsung built a beautiful dog kennel, dog training and animal care facility, and animal hospital nestled among the heavily wooded slopes at Samsung Everland.

Samsung began a Responsible Pet Ownership Program in 1992. Dogs raised in the kennel or rescued from shelters are provided to Samsung employees, and the welfare of the pet is tracked so that if proper care is not provided, the animal is withdrawn from the owner for better placement. The Samsung Guide Dogs for the Blind Program began in 1993. These dogs, mostly Labrador Retrievers, are imported by Samsung from other countries, trained by Samsung professional staff, and donated to visually impaired persons of South Korea. The Samsung Search and Rescue Dogs Program began in 1995. German Shepherds are trained at spacious indoor and outdoor facilities to track and find lost persons and buried victims. These dog teams have received international honors for their response to tragedies, such as a devastating earthquake in Taiwan. The Samsung AAA/AAT programs utilizing a variety of dogs were begun in 1995. The Samsung Riding for the Disabled Program was begun at the Samsung equestrian facility in 2001. This hippotherapy program is currently small, with a handful of staff and two therapy horses. The Samsung Hearing Dogs for the Deaf Program began in 2002. Samsung hearing-assistance dogs are typically small breed dogs that will be easily integrated into the typical Korean small-sized residence of the recipient of the donated dog. Samsung recently completed in 2003 at Samsung Everland a state-of-the-art training facility for the hearing dog program that includes apartments for the recipients of the dogs to stay in during the last training and owner transition days of the hearing dog. From an outside observer's view, it seems as if Samsung, typically known for their electronic products and more recently car manufacturing, is attempting to almost single-handedly bring South Korea into the modern age regarding the culture of the human–animal connection. And each of these Samsung animal programs is nonprofit. Samsung spends millions a year to support these programs and receives nothing in return except the gratitude of its people and appreciation of other world observers. Other world business corporations could learn from the charitable example set by Samsung.

International Information Exchange and Relationship Building

The additional days I spent in South Korea after the human–animal bond symposium were very special for me. Not only did the gracious and warm reception lead me to feel that I had made a number of new friends, but the concentrated interest in numerous small meetings set up between me and a variety of Samsung executives and staff offered opportunity for sharing information and ideas that could aid Samsung in the development of their AAA/AAT programs in South Korea. Samsung is currently most interested in designing their AAA and AAT training programs on the Pet Partners Team Training model of Delta Society (2003).

Following the symposium, a whirlwind of activity proceeded over the next few days. I was given a personal tour of the beautiful and spacious Samsung Noble County Nursing Home by associate therapist Sang Hoon Lee and invited to a private meeting with Noble County director Ho Kap Lee. Noble County Nursing Home, another Samsung project, was occupied in 2001. It is a state-of-the-art retirement community that serves persons aged 60 years and older of varying abilities, including patients with Alzheimer's (Noble County, 2003). Samsung is leading the way in South Korea in providing care for their elderly. I observed AAA with Noble County residents provided by five human-therapy animal teams directed by Ju-yeon (Queenie) Lee, coordinator of the Samsung AAA and AAT programs. Back at Samsung Everland, lunch was hosted by John C. U. Kim, vice president of international relations of Samsung. I was given a personal in-depth tour of the Samsung animal care and training facilities by D. H. Lee, operations manager of Samsung Assistance Dog Services. I was also treated to a private demonstration of the Samsung Agility Dog Team, currently the only one of its kind in this country. That afternoon, I gave a demonstration of a standardized animal evaluation and met with the Samsung therapy staff to advise and consult on AAA and AAT.

The next day, I was given a personal tour of Samsung Everland Theme Park, which is very similar to Disneyland in the U.S., except I did not have to wait in any lines as a personal guest of Samsung. That afternoon, I toured the very beautiful Samsung equestrian facility and met with assistant director Young-Bum Woo and physical therapist of the hippotherapy program, Amy J. Lee.

The next 3 days, I toured South Korea under the guidance of Dr. Yang Soon (Angela) Kim of Cheju University. Our tour included museums of ancient relics, historical palaces, and shopping at the In Sa-Dong arts district in Seoul. Then we took a day-long train ride down the length of the country to the south through heavily wooded mountains shrouded in brilliant fall colors. We toured Buddhist temples and burial grounds in the ancient city of Gyeongju (also spelled Kyongju) and flew over to visit the beautiful island of JeJu (referred to as "Honeymoon Island" by locals). It was tangerine season on JeJu, and I don't think I have ever tasted them so rich and delicious. With a translator's assistance, I spoke to a class of about 100 veterinary medical students and a handful of professors at Cheju National University in JeJu on the history of the human–animal connection and AAT in the U.S. I also gave a demonstration of a typical Delta Society standardized animal evaluation in front of this very large crowd. Through this demonstration, the first ever Delta Society Pet Partners team was certified in South Korea. Afterward, a private lunch was hosted by the dean of the College of Natural Sciences of Cheju National University, Dr. Young-Oh Yang.

In the afternoon, I evaluated for certification a second therapy dog team who shared the same dog as the first team certified that morning. Thus was born the first two Delta Society Pet Partners teams in South Korea, first was Dr. Yang Soon (Angela) Kim with a Cavalier Spaniel named Lulu and then Ju-yeon (Queenie) Lee with the same dog. Ju-yeon (Queenie) Lee flew down to JeJu that day for the animal evaluation because, although Ms. Lee works at Samsung Everland near Seoul, she has the opportunity to work with Lulu on occasion. After the evaluations, I was invited to observe an animal assisted play therapy session by Dr. Kim with an autistic child.

Defining the Role and Scope of AAT in South Korea

I was very impressed with the work being done by all Samsung staff at the animal facilities near Seoul and with the animal assisted play therapy established at CheJu National University in JeJu by Dr. Yang Soon (Angela) Kim. I do see that South Korea has miles to go to bring the culture of the human–animal connection up to the level of countries such as the U.S. Included among the growing pains is that there are two different and competing approaches to the development of AAT programs in South Korea. One thrust is to develop AAT as an independent profession trained through the colleges of veterinary medicine. This is the path that Ju-yeon (Queenie) Lee was trained on as she has a degree in veterinary medicine and part of her professional title is a PAT (Pets as Therapy). Ms. Lee performs AAA at a juvenile detention center and an elderly care residential facility. The benefit of the professional animal therapist training model offered through veterinary medicine is that veterinarians have the most contact with, access to, and understanding of animals in South Korea. Remember that household pets are not a common occurrence in the country and relatively few professional mental health or physical therapists own a pet or know how to train a pet. The problem with the veterinarian-focused AAT model is that veterinarians do not have expertise in human health fields and thus are not qualified to perform therapy outside of their field, such as not being trained in physical therapy, recreational therapy, counseling or psychology, speech therapy, and so forth.

The second thrust for the practice of AAT in this country is for professional educators and health therapists in a variety of human health fields to receive training in AAT by organizations inside or outside of South Korea, such as the training at the University of North Texas or Delta Society programs in the U.S. This is the

approach chosen by Dr. Yang Soon (Angela) Kim, a practicing registered play therapist at Cheju University who incorporates AAT into her work. The benefit to this
approach is that the best person to provide human therapy services within that field
is a trained, credentialed therapist and it parallels a proven, successful model in the
U.S. The obvious problem is of course that few professional therapists in South
Korea have or have access to a qualified therapy animal. AAT training programs in
South Korea are very limited, and few human health services providers have the
resources to travel outside of the country to get the proper training in AAT.

I was frequently asked by various Korean officials and staff my opinion of how
to resolve the dilemma of two differing philosophies on the development of AAT in
South Korea. My position was to offer a compromise of mutual cooperation. It is
obvious that professional educators and human health therapists in this country
need the animal expertise and resources of the veterinarians, and it is further obvious that the veterinarians need professional educators and human health therapists
to perform AAT within human health and educational fields. It is my opinion that a
most beneficial working model for South Korea regarding the provision of AAT
could have two categories of professionals: (a) the animal assisted therapy specialist
technician (AAT-ST) and (b) the AAT health or education professional. The AAT-ST
would be trained by animal specialists, such as those found at schools of veterinary
medicine or the Samsung Animal Assistance Center. The AAT-ST would make their
services available to human health and education professionals who would establish
the goals and plans for students and patients and design animal assisted interventions with the advice of the AAT-ST. And then the AAT-ST would perform the animal
assisted educational and therapeutic interventions under the guidance and supervision of the professional human health therapist or educator. This model is ideal for
educators or human health therapists that choose not to have their own therapy pet
but still would like their students or patients to have access to AAT. This model also
legitimizes the establishment of an independent profession of AAT within the South
Korean veterinary schools, that of the AAT-ST.

The second category of professional would be the animal assisted therapy educator or health professional (AAT-EP or AAT-HP). This health or education professional would have received proper training and credentialing for their specific
education or human health field, such as teaching, physical therapy, speech therapy,
psychology, counseling, and so on. And then those educators and human health professionals interested in providing AAT with their own pet could receive training in
AAT from schools of veterinary medicine and organizations such as the Samsung
Animal Assistance Center. They could also adopt a pet through these organizations,
and be monitored and researched by these organizations. These two categories of
AAT professionals, AAT-ST and AAT-EP or AAT-HP, would seem to satisfy the needs
of two competing groups in South Korea who have an interest in providing AAT.
Clear guidelines and standards for training and credentialing for these two branches
of AAT practice would need to be established. But whatever decisions are made
regarding the development of AAT in South Korea, officials in that country are making great strides in promoting a progressive shift in the culture of the human–animal
connection.

I chose to include this chapter in the book because I feel that the efforts to
enhance the human–animal connection in South Korea by the members of the
Korean Veterinary Association as well as the staff of the privately owned company
Samsung are like pushing a very large rock up a very high hill. Changing cultural

values takes time, money, and the efforts of many dedicated people. I believe that these efforts deserve the recognition and support due them by the U.S. and other countries that believe in the preservation and enhancement of the positive relationship between humans and animals.

If you wish to contact some of the hardworking persons at Samsung mentioned in this article, you may do so through the Samsung Animal Assistance Center (website: http://mydog.samsung.com/eng/) or e-mail the coordinator of the AAA/ AAT program, Ju-yeon (Queenie) Lee at queenie.lee@samsung.com.

Appendix A

University Centers Promoting Animal Assisted Therapy and Related Topics

- Colorado State University, Human-Animal Bond in Colorado program (HABIC), School of Social Work. Founded in 1993 as a nonprofit service outreach program. It is comprised of volunteers from the community and university who volunteer with their pets at local schools, hospitals, long-term care centers, and hospice. Website: http://www.cahs.colostate.edu/sw/HABIC2003.htm. Telephone: (970) 491-2776. E-mail: habic @ cahs.colostate.edu.

- DePaul University, Animal Assisted Therapy and Education Certificate Program, School for New Learning. A collaborative program with People, Animals and Nature (PAN, Inc.) to train animal assisted therapy teams. Website: http://www.pan-inc.org. E-mail: coultis@umich.edu (current president of PAN, Inc.)

- Purdue University, Center for the Human-Animal Bond, School of Veterinary Medicine. Established in 1982 and renamed in 1997. Committed to expanding knowledge of the interrelationships between people, animals, and their environment including companion animals, farm animals, and wildlife. Website: http://www.vet.purdue.edu/depts/vad/cae/. Telephone: (765) 494-0854.

- Tuskegee University, Center for the Study of Human-Animal Interdependent Relationships, School of Veterinary Medicine. Tuskegee, Alabama, 36088. Established in 1993 to promote, through study and practice, health benefits that people and animals may derive from one another. Websites: http://www.tuskegee.edu/global/category.asp?c=51862 and http://www.tuskegeebond.com. Telephone: (334) 727-8122. E-mail: schaffer@tuskegee.edu.

- University of California – Davis, Center for Animal Alternatives, School of Veterinary Medicine. A resource center for the dissemination of information about animal welfare topics including human-animal interaction and animal assisted therapy. Website: http://www.vetmed.ucdavis.edu/Animal_Alternatives/main.htm. Telephone: (530) 757-8448.

- University of Minnesota, Center to Study Human-Animal Relationships and Environments (CENSHARE). Dedicated to improving human-animal relationships and environments through the mediums of education, research, and service including animal assisted therapy. Website: http://www.censhare.umn.cdu/. Telephone: (612) 626-1975.
- University of North Texas, Center for Animal Assisted Therapy (CAAT), College of Education, Counseling Program. Established in 2002 as a research and training center for the study and practice of animal assisted therapy in counseling, education, and related fields. Website: http://www.coe.unt.edu/CDHE/AAT. Telephone: (940) 565-2914 or (940) 565-2910. E-mail: chandler@coe.unt.edu.
- University of Pennsylvania, Center for the Interaction of Animals and Society (CIAS), School of Veterinary Medicine. Re-established in 1997 to promote understanding of human-animal interactions across a wide range of contexts including companion animals, farm animals, and wild animals. Website: http://www2.vet.upenn.edu/research/centers/cias/. E-mail: cias@lists.vet.upenn.edu.
- University of Tennessee, Human-Animal Bond in Tennessee (H.A.B.I.T.), School of Veterinary Medicine. A community group of volunteers working together to promote the human-animal bond and animal assisted therapy. Website: http://www.vet.utk.edu/habit/. Telephone (865) 974-5633.
- Virginia Commonwealth University, Center for Human-Animal Interaction, School of Medicine. Established in 2001 to promote education, research, and practice of activities related to the human-animal relationship. Website: http://www.chai.vcu.edu. Telephone: (804) 827-7297. E-mail: chai@vcu.edu.
- Washington State University, Center for the Study of Animal Well-Being, The People-Pet Partnership (PPP) Program, College of Veterinary Medicine. A public service program to research and educate the public about the human-animal bond and its applications. Website: http://www.vetmed.wsu/edu/depts-pppp/. Telephone: (509) 335-1303 or (509) 335-4569.

Appendix B

Client Screening Form for Animal Assisted Therapy

Name of potential client: _____ Date:_____

Age of client: _____ Gender of client: _____ Guardian's name: _____

Client's/guardian's address: _____

Client's/guardian's phone number(s): _____

Permission granted to contact via telephone: _____ yes _____no

Name of intake interviewer: _____

Does the client have any of the following?

_____ Animal allergies. Which animals?_____

_____ Animal fears or phobias. Which animals? _____

_____ History of aggression or abuse toward animals.

_____ History of aggression or abuse toward people.

_____ Hallucinations.

_____ Dementia.

_____ Emotional problems.

_____ Behavioral problems.

_____ Severe developmental disorder. Describe: _____

Animals the client has had as pets: _____

Any negative experiences with animals: _____

Would this person like to participate in animal assisted therapy? _____ yes _____ no

Additional information: _____

_____.

Based on the available information is this person appropriate for animal assisted therapy? _____ yes _____ no

Cynthia K. Chandler © 2005

Appendix C

Animal Assisted Therapy — Psychosocial Session Form

Client's Name: _____ Date of Session: _____ Session Number: ___

Location of Session: _____

Estimated Length of Session (hours and minutes): _____

AAT Type: Equine Assisted   Dog Assisted   Cat Assisted   Other (list)

Format: __ Individual Session __Group Session __ Family Session __ Other: _____

Therapist(s) Names: Human(s)- _____

Animal(s)- _____

Rating Comparison (check one): The client's behavior ratings are based on:

_____ (1) a comparison of the client with what is considered to be typical, normal, healthy functioning in society (this is the preferred format); or

_____ (2) a comparison of the client with self from the previous session (or if this is the first session this is a baseline rating based on ___(1) ___(3) or ___(4); or

_____ (3) a comparison of the client with other members of the group; or

_____ (4) other (describe) _____

For evaluation purposes the comparison category checked above should be consistent across all sessions for the client and for clients in the same group. This Psychosocial Session Form is designed to track client progress in a consistent and measurable format. If possible, the same therapist should complete the form for consistency in interpretation of client behaviors. If a treatment team is involved then as many team members as possible should give their input as to the client's scores on various behaviors below.

Circle the number that best describes the amount of client behavior that is listed below.

Positive Behaviors:	No Opportunity to Observe or Doesn't Apply	None	Very Low	Low	Medium	High	Very High
Participation	x	0	1	2	3	4	5
Positive Interactions	x	0	1	2	3	4	5
Cooperation	x	0	1	2	3	4	5
Appropriately Assertive	x	0	1	2	3	4	5
Attention to Task (Focus)	x	0	1	2	3	4	5
Follows Directions	x	0	1	2	3	4	5
Respectful	x	0	1	2	3	4	5
Integrity/Honesty	x	0	1	2	3	4	5
Leadership	x	0	1	2	3	4	5
Teamwork	x	0	1	2	3	4	5
Eye Contact	x	0	1	2	3	4	5
Active Listening	x	0	1	2	3	4	5
Open-minded	x	0	1	2	3	4	5
Accepts Feedback	x	0	1	2	3	4	5
Positive Feelings	x	0	1	2	3	4	5
Positive Vocalizations	x	0	1	2	3	4	5
Empathy	x	0	1	2	3	4	5
Sharing	x	0	1	2	3	4	5
Helpful	x	0	1	2	3	4	5
Problem Solving	x	0	1	2	3	4	5
Self-Confidence	x	0	1	2	3	4	5
Self-Esteem	x	0	1	2	3	4	5
Insight about Self	x	0	1	2	3	4	5
Insight about Others	x	0	1	2	3	4	5
Expression of Needs, Appropriately	x	0	1	2	3	4	5
Other Positive Behaviors (list):							
_____	x	0	1	2	3	4	5
_____	x	0	1	2	3	4	5

Negative Behaviors:

Belligerent	x	0	1	2	3	4	5
Resistant	x	0	1	2	3	4	5
Guarded	x	0	1	2	3	4	5
Manipulative	x	0	1	2	3	4	5
Deceptive	x	0	1	2	3	4	5
Negative Vocalizations	x	0	1	2	3	4	5
Argumentative	x	0	1	2	3	4	5
Angry or Agitated	x	0	1	2	3	4	5
Closed-minded	x	0	1	2	3	4	5
Overly Fearful	x	0	1	2	3	4	5
Fidgety/Hyperactive	x	0	1	2	3	4	5
Verbally Aggressive	x	0	1	2	3	4	5
Physically Aggressive	x	0	1	2	3	4	5
Overly Passive	x	0	1	2	3	4	5
Overly Submissive	x	0	1	2	3	4	5
Sad or Depressed	x	0	1	2	3	4	5
Withdrawn	x	0	1	2	3	4	5

Other Negative Behaviors (list):

_____	x	0	1	2	3	4	5
_____	x	0	1	2	3	4	5

Session Scores and Summary

Do not count the items marked "x" (no opportunity to observe) as scored items.

____ **Total Positive Behavior Score** (add scores and divide by number of items scored.)
An increasing total positive score across sessions indicates an increase in positive behaviors.

____ **Total Negative Behavior Score** (add scores and divide by number of items scored.)
An increasing total negative score across sessions indicates an increase in negative behaviors.

____ **Total Behavior Score** (subtract Total Negative Score from Total Positive Score).
An increasing total behavior score across sessions indicates overall improvement in positive behaviors relative to negative behaviors.

Other Notes

Any indication in the client of (check those that apply, if so explain):

_____ Suicidal Ideation _____ Crisis _____ Self-Harm _____ Harm to Others

Describe any progress by client toward existing goals:
_____

Describe any new issues presented or new goals established:
_____

Describe any changes or adjustments in conceptualization of client or diagnosis:
_____

Describe primary presenting problem(s) discussed or exhibited by client in this session:
_____

Therapeutic Intervention(s) Applied: _____
_____
_____
_____

Other Comments (continue on back if necessary): _____
_____
_____

Cynthia K. Chandler © 2005

Appendix D

Sample Funding Proposal to Establish a Center for Animal Assisted Therapy

Dr. Cynthia Chandler
Counseling Program
College of Education, University of North Texas, Denton, Texas
February 27, 2001

For more information please contact:

Dr. Cynthia K. Chandler	*Address: Counseling Program*
Professor	*P.O. Box 310829*
E-mail chandler@coe.unt.edu	*University of North Texas*
Phone: (940) 565-2910	*Denton, TX 76203-0829*
FAX: (940) 565-2905	

Introduction

Animal Assisted Therapy (AAT) is about pets helping people through the human-animal connection. AAT is practiced in hospitals, schools, prisons, nursing homes, counseling settings, rehabilitation clinics, and other environments. The presence of the trained therapy animal calms and motivates the person in need while planned, structured interaction with the animal facilitates learning and recovery.

We would like your support to establish a Center for Animal Assisted Therapy (CAAT) at the University of North Texas (UNT). The center would serve to support the study and training in AAT with two primary service programs:

- The UNT Reading Assistance Dogs (RAD) program to promote reading literacy in school-aged children; and

- The UNT Therapy Animal Team (TAT) program to train university students and persons in the community with their pets to be volunteer and professional teams providing animal assisted therapy in health-related and educational settings.

These two service programs would be highly interactive and mutually supportive. Additional information about each of the above listed programs is provided in the following pages. Total requested funding is $35,000 for both programs combined to cover a two-year period.

Community Support

This proposal is supported by the Denton County School District as well as the Juvenile Detention program. Letters of support are included in the appendix of the proposal. Many children, adolescents, and adults can be assisted through services offered by the Center for Animal Assisted Therapy at UNT.

About the Community

The University of North Texas is in the City of Denton and lies just 35 miles north of Dallas and Ft. Worth. There is a UNT campus in Dallas where counseling and education courses are also taught. The University of North Texas has outstanding programs in counselor preparation and reading education. The Counselor Education Program is among the highest ranked programs in the United States. It has won the Outstanding Counselor Preparation Program Award in the nation twice, the most recent time was the year 2000. You can learn more about our counseling program via your computer at the website: http://www.coe.unt.edu/CDHE.

About the Solicitor

Dr. Cynthia Chandler will serve as the director of CAAT. She is a professor of counseling at UNT. She holds a doctoral degree in educational psychology from Texas Tech University. She has earned awards for her work in counseling, biofeedback, and supervision. She is licensed and certified in the following areas: mental health counseling, marriage and family therapy, biofeedback therapy, and animal assisted therapy. She is also a certified supervisor and trainer in each of these fields. Dr. Chandler is a certified Pet Partner with her dog Rusty and cat Snowflake through the national therapy animal organization Delta Society. She developed and teaches the only animal assisted therapy course ever taught at UNT. The course is open to students from all academic programs at both the graduate and undergraduate levels. The course also attracts students from the other Denton University, Texas Woman's University, who are approved by their advisor to take this UNT AAT course. For more information see Dr. Chandler's professional vitae in the appendix.

Reading Assistance Dogs Program (RAD)

The proposed Reading Assistance Dogs (RAD) program will be an incorporation of certified therapy dogs into a new reading literacy program for children and adolescents in the following Texas counties: Denton, Dallas, and Tarrant (Ft. Worth). Children find it easier to read to a dog that is accompanied by its handler than to read to a person alone. The calm presence and nonjudgmental attitude of the animal help the child to feel more relaxed and reassured in his or her reading efforts.

Elementary and secondary school children of Denton County, Texas with reading difficulties will be invited to participate in reading sessions with a professionally trained therapy dog and handler at a school or library. Each time a child moves up a reading level the child will receive a gift of a book autographed with a paw print by their reading companion dog. Certified therapy dogs and their handlers will be recruited from local therapy animal organizations to volunteer for the RAD program. In addition, a significant number of new volunteers will be trained from the university and surrounding community to participate as volunteer therapy teams in the RAD program. Schoolteachers and school counselors will be especially encouraged to receive training in and participate in RAD, thereby establishing a sense of permanency to the RAD program within the schools. There is already a great interest by the schools of Denton County to participate in such a program as RAD should it be developed (see attached letters of support).

Mission of the RAD Program

The mission of the RAD program is to improve the literacy abilities of reading challenged students. In order to improve literacy skills, students need multiple opportunities to practice. Individuals who are below the literacy level of their peers often lack the opportunities to read, as well as lack the self-confidence to read in front of others. These factors lead to low self-esteem. Creating a risk-free environment that promotes literacy skills is at the forefront of the educational process for these individuals. According to research with therapy animals, children with low self-esteem are more willing to interact with an animal than with another person. This interaction allows children to learn in an environment that is relaxed and positive.

Procedures for the RAD Program

Children who need reading assistance will be identified by their classroom teacher. Pre and post assessment of a student's reading skills and reading level will be obtained. The RAD volunteers will not be teaching the students how to read, however, they will need to be knowledgeable of literacy strategies in order to assist the student when the student is having difficulty in reading practice and to ensure understanding of the material that has been read. Volunteers will be trained to provide several aspects of literacy, including identification of unknown words, comprehension, and response to the literature. Instruction will be delivered to RAD volunteers (animal handlers) in a 2-hour session prior to beginning with the students.

Each RAD volunteer will also be trained in basic therapy animal team (TAT) techniques. The TAT training program is outlined in greater detail in the TAT section of the proposal. The instruction for the TAT training will be based on the Delta Society Pet Partner Team Training Course. For more information on this program visit the website www.deltasociety.org. The combined RAD and TAT training for RAD volunteers will be accomplished in a 1-day (8 hour) workshop.

The RAD volunteers will have a copy of the book that the student is reading so they can listen and note the types of problems that the student is having. Demonstrations will be provided so that the RAD volunteers will learn how to give meaningful assistance that will not be invasive to the student. After the reading, the RAD volunteer and the student will discuss the reading and any of the difficulties that were noted.

Expected Outcomes of the RAD Program

The program will serve elementary and secondary school children in the public schools and also include children living in juvenile probation in-house facilities. Denton County is a highly populated area 35 miles north of Dallas and Ft. Worth. The county has several medium sized cities (50,000 or more population) within its boundaries. Thus, there will be a significant number of children with reading difficulties who can benefit from this program. The efficacy of the RAD program will be evaluated annually in the following ways:

- A pre and post "reading level" assessment for each child participant;
- A pre and post "attitude toward reading" assessment for each child participant;
- A pre and post "attitude toward animals" assessment for each child participant;
- The number of books within each reading level completed by the child;
- The number of reading levels achieved by each child;
- The number of children participating in the program;
- The number of RAD volunteers (reading assistance dogs and handler participants) in the program.

Expected outcomes include:

- Enhanced interest in reading by students with reading difficulties;
- Increased reading skills by student participants;
- Increased participation in the learning environment by community volunteers and their trained therapy dogs; and
- Enhancement of the learning environment by the presence of trained dogs.

The Therapy Animal Team Program (TAT)

This proposal also addresses the desire to establish a program to train person-pet therapy teams who will provide volunteer and professional services to those in health-related and educational environments.

Mission of the TAT Program

The Therapy Animal Team (TAT) program will provide university coursework and community workshops for training in Animal Assisted Therapy (AAT). Those who are trained will work with their certified therapy animal within the newly developed RAD program and/or in other settings that may include: hospitals, rehabilitation centers, nursing homes, and juvenile detention centers. The TAT program will also provide a speaker's bureau to enhance public awareness about the benefits of AAT through professional presentations.

Procedures for the TAT Program

The Counselor Education Program currently has in place a course in Animal Assisted Therapy. University students take this class if they plan to work as health professionals with their pets in educational or therapeutic environments. Scholarships could be offered through the TAT program to support the training of those interested in learning AAT and who need financial assistance for educational costs. In addition, the TAT program would offer weekend training workshops at no cost for persons in the community who desire to volunteer with their pets to visit various settings. In addition, persons who take the course or the workshop will be recruited to participate with their pets in the Reading Assistance Dogs (RAD) program to improve reading literacy in school-aged children.

Training material for the semester-long course and the 1-day workshop is material published by the Delta Society, a well-respected national therapy animal organization. The 1-day workshop format will be the basis for the training of volunteers and teachers for the RAD program.

The Delta Society Pet Partners Team Training Program will be the material used for the 1-day TAT instruction and will be provided by a certified Delta Society instructor. The Delta Society Pet Partners training will cover the following areas: assessing when AAT is appropriate, evaluating a facility, establishing a positive relationship with facility staff, animal skill and aptitude requirements, acting as the animal's advocate, preparing the animal for a visit, techniques for reducing risks for injury to animals and humans, and interaction and intervention techniques with a variety of populations.

The training for the person-pet animal teams requires that both the animal and the animal handler pass a formal evaluation before they can participate in the TAT program.

For more information on the Delta Society Pet Partner Team Training Program visit the following website: www.deltasociety.org.

The semester-long course in AAT will incorporate all of the 1-day TAT workshop material plus material more specific to professional health providers who want to work with their pets in health-related environments. This course includes training in: assessment guidelines, treatment planning and establishing treatment goals, treatment interventions specific to a variety of health fields, and evaluation procedures. Persons who take the semester-long course in AAT are studying to be professionals in fields such as counseling, psychology, therapeutic recreation, and physical or emotional rehabilitation. The semester-long course is already in place at UNT, having been taught for the first time in the year 2000. It was received with enthusiasm by faculty and students at UNT and Texas Woman's University.

Expected Outcomes of the TAT Program

The efficacy of the TAT program will be evaluated annually in the following ways:

- The number of newly trained professionals in AAT through the course;
- The number of newly trained volunteers in AAT through the workshops;
- The number of therapy teams in the RAD program trained by the TAT program;
- The number of newly created clinical practice internships in AAT in a variety of clinical practice settings, such as counseling clinics, school counseling offices, school classrooms, hospitals, prisons, juvenile detention halls, hospices, rehabilitations centers, and so forth;
- Post treatment assessment of "client evaluation of clinical service" by recipients of animal assisted therapy services;
- Post treatment assessment of "attitudes toward animal therapy" by recipients of the animal assisted therapy services.
- The expected outcomes of the TAT program include:
  - Increased quality of services provided in health-related and educational settings with the inclusion of therapy animals;
  - Enhanced relationship between professionals and their pets; and
  - Enhanced relationship between the public and animals.

Estimated Costs for the RAD and TAT Programs Combined

Requested total funding for two years is $35,000. See the following estimated budget and justification.

Estimated Budget Totals Over a Two-Year Period

Animal subject library books, grade specific $15,000
(To establish a library section for the reading practice by children)

Gift books for children and volunteers $ 5,000
(The children will get to keep the books they read)

Graduate student research fellowship $ 5,000
(To research the efficacy of the RAD program)

Assessments $ 2,500

Training materials for therapy animal teams $ 5,000

Supplies, travel, telephone, miscellaneous $ 2,500

Appendix of the Funding Proposal

Contents:

- Outside Letters of Support:
  1. Billy Ryan High School, Denton, TX
  2. The Colony High School, The Colony, Denton County, TX
  3. Woodrow Wilson Elementary School, Denton, TX
  4. Juvenile Probation, Post Adjudication Program, Denton County, TX
  5. D.I.S.D. Special Education Supervisor, Juvenile Coordinator, Denton, TX
- Professional Vitae of Dr. Cynthia Chandler
- Professional Vitae of Rusty, The Therapy Dog

Appendix E

Sample Progress Report for the Center for Animal Assisted Therapy

Cynthia K. Chandler, Ed.D.
Professor of Counseling and
Director of the CAAT

University of North Texas, College of Education
P.O. Box 310829, Denton, Texas 76203-0829

Unit: Center for Animal Assisted Therapy (CAAT)   *Date: February 19, 2004*
Person Completing the Information: Cynthia Chandler   *Email: chandler@coe.unt.edu*
Head of the Unit: Cynthia Chandler   *Phone: (940) 565 2910*

Introduction

The CAAT was established with a $33,000 grant from Iams, Paws to Share Foundation. Activities to develop and operate the CAAT began in the year 2002. In gratitude, the CAAT has given credit to this donor, Iams Paws to Share Foundation, at all presentations and on the internet website for the CAAT. The website address for the CAAT is http://www.coe.unt.edu/CDHE/AAT. Photos of just a few of the CAAT activities are on the website under the icon "AAT in Action."

The Center for Animal Assisted Therapy (CAAT) and the supporting animal assisted therapy programs are new and expanding rapidly. AAT is a field with accelerating interest nationwide and internationally as well. Creative efforts in marketing our program and making it more accessible to others will insure its success. The CAAT at UNT is the only one of its kind in a counseling program in the State of Texas or in the nation. It is one of only nine like centers in the U.S., the others being in the fields of education, social work, and veterinary medicine.

I. Mission

The mission of the Center for Animal Assisted Therapy (CAAT) at the University of North Texas is to train professionals and volunteers to work with their pets to: 1) facilitate the development of students in kindergarten through 12th grade with pet-assisted educational programs; and 2) enhance the emotional well-being of persons of all ages through positive human-animal interactions. To fulfill its objectives, the CAAT has the following areas of focus:

Goal 1: Provide training in the field of animal assisted therapy to graduate students and professionals seeking national certification in animal assisted therapy.

Goal 2: Conduct animal assisted therapy research, establish funding for animal assisted therapy, and provide laboratory facilities for conducting research in animal assisted therapy.

Goal 3: Network with agencies and schools to promote and provide high quality animal assisted therapy services in the North Texas region and throughout the state.

Goal 4: Assist graduate students in obtaining graduate training and national certification in animal assisted therapy and promote diversity among students seeking training through the provision of scholarships.

The Center for Animal Assisted Therapy achieves the above-stated goals through the provision of two primary programs: the RAD program and the TAT program.

RAD Program

This stands for Reading Assistance Dogs program. This program provides adult supervised reading practice for children who are reading challenged. Volunteers and professionals spend a few hours or more a month with their pets at various public libraries and schools to assist children with reading skills or other pet-assisted educational activities. The therapy dog serves to motivate the child to attend and participate in reading practice and other educational programs.

TAT Program

This stands for Therapy Animal Teams program. The CAAT is in partnership with the national certification organization Delta Society, headquartered in Renton, Washington, to provide volunteer and professional certification training for Pet Partner teams and Animal Assisted Therapy. Volunteers and professionals can complete a weekend workshop to become volunteer Pet Partner teams who visit with their pets at schools, nursing homes, agencies, hospitals, and so forth. Graduate students and professionals can take a graduate training course in Animal Assisted Therapy to learn how to integrate their pets into the professional setting, such as counseling or rehabilitation. The therapy pet is a co-therapist, or pet-practitioner, that assists in the provision of professional services. The pet's presence also is a considerable motivating force for the client in their recovery process.

II. Completed Goals of the Center for Animal Assisted Therapy 2002–2003

Goals completed:

Professional, Volunteer, and Graduate Student Training

- We offered the course as COUN 5800, Special Topics in Summer 2001 and again in Summer 2002, and as an approved course COUN 5530, Animal Assisted Therapy in Summer 2003.
- Over twelve Pet Partner Team Training workshops have been offered across 2 years; trained over 175 participants. The first 11 workshops were free to participants, now an individual participant fee of $45.00 is assessed to cover the cost of the workshop and provide support for the operation of the CAAT. Also, persons must maintain their national certification and be re-certified every 2 years and we charge $25.00 to provide that recertification process.
- The UNT CAAT program is 1 of only 2 national certification programs for community volunteers in the entire North Texas Region and the only national certification program for counseling professionals in the state of Texas. Thus, the CAAT fulfills a great need for this type of training.

Research and Funding

- Received $33,000 gift from Iams, Paws to Share as start up money two years ago.
- Established funding for the endowment of a student scholarship using own personal money, salary contributions by Dr. Cynthia Chandler, toward a $10,000 endowment to be completed by the year 2006. Name of endowment in progress is Dr. Cynthia Chandler, Professor, and Rusty Chandler, Therapy Dog Scholarship.
- Hired a graduate student to gather research data at approved sites participating in CAAT activities. This consists of five schools and two agencies.
- Currently gathering data for 3 separate research projects: 2 at Rocky Top Therapy Center and 1 at Juvenile Detention Center.
- Professional presentations on Animal Assisted Therapy were given at the Hawaiian International Conference on Education in 2003; Texas Counseling Association 2003; and the American Counseling Association in Anaheim, California in 2003; and at the 1st International Meeting on the Human Animal Bond in South Korea in 2003.

Network with Agencies and Schools to Provide Services

- Established RAD (Reading Assistance Dogs) programs in local schools and libraries. (RAD programs established at the following sites: Razyor Elementary, Denton; Hedrick Elementary, Lewisville; Flower Mound Library, Flower

- Mound; and Montclair Elementary, Garland). Many who live outside of our service area have come to our trainings and have started their own RAD programs in their region, such as Austin, Abilene, Bridgeport, Houston, etc.
- Many teachers from this North Texas region and all from all over the State of Texas who completed our Pet Partner training integrated their dogs into their classroom for motivational purposes. These include teachers in a variety of subjects such as math, science, and English. These teachers report the dog is a calming and motivating presence in the classroom.
- Many school counselors from the North Texas region and from all over the State of Texas who attended our Pet Partner training incorporated their dogs into their school counseling service. The counselors report much popularity of the dogs and report the dogs' presence as co-therapist has increased the participation and motivation of students to seek out and benefit from counseling.
- Networked with local agencies to set up internship sites for graduate students providing AAT. (Current sites: Denton County Juvenile Detention – Post Adjudication Program, contact person Laura Prillwitz; Rocky Top Therapy Center, Right Trail Program, contact person, Deborah Bond.)
- Provided a link from CDHE department to a new website page describing the AAT program. (Completed: Spring 2003, see www.coe.unt.edu/CDHE/AAT. This website provides much international publicity. I answer 30 to 40 inquiries per week regarding our AAT program from website contacts, including from other countries, i.e., South Korea, Wales, India, and Argentina.) Many interested parties are requesting information on enrolling in our graduate program in counseling just to study Animal Assisted Therapy.
- Developed regional, state, and national/international reputations in AAT. Completed and ongoing: 1) We are listed on the national website for Delta Society as an AAT provider at www.deltasociety.org; 2) TCA newsletter (2003) referenced our program as the only university training program in Texas for AAT; 3) Presented at both state and national counseling/education conferences on AAT; 4) Samsung corporation sent their director for their new AAT program in South Korea over here to the U.S. to study at our AAT program for 7 weeks (summer 2003); 5) The director of the CAAT accepted invitation to South Korea to speak at an AAT symposium in November 2003 and consult for 2 weeks with Samsung Assistance Dog Services in Seoul and the College of Veterinary Medicine at Cheju University in JeJu, Korea. While there I evaluated and certified the first 2 therapy dog teams in Korea. I submitted an article to a national magazine about the Korean trip and it is under review; 6) AAT workshop participants have traveled from as far away as Oklahoma, Louisiana, Austin, Houston, Abilene, and Lubbock.

Assisting Students and Promoting Diversity

- Dr. Cynthia Chandler will continue to provide her personal monthly donation for the purpose of the eventual endowment of a $10,000 student scholarship for the study of animal assisted therapy at UNT, The Dr. Cynthia K. Chandler, Professor, and Rusty Chandler, Therapy Dog Scholarship. Endowment should be completed by the target date end of December, 2006.

- Provided animal assisted therapy services to a diverse population. Many of the persons who benefited from animal assisted therapy research and services of the CAAT are disabled persons, elderly persons, at risk children, or ethnic minority children. Animal assisted therapy workshops and courses provided by the CAAT at UNT train persons to work with their dogs in schools, libraries, nursing homes, hospitals, juvenile detention centers, rehabilitation centers and therapy centers.
- The director of the CAAT works closely with the directors of the internship sites and school programs to gain feedback on how well these programs are functioning.

III. Statement of Expected Outcomes for 2003–2004

Future Professional, Volunteer, and Graduate Student Training

- Continue to offer a graduate course in AAT once a year that provides national certification in AAT for graduate students and professionals.
- Continue offering community weekend training workshops at least twice per year that provide national certification as a Pet Partner team for community volunteers and professionals. Will charge a small fee of $45.00 for workshop participants that includes the initial animal team evaluation for national certification. Those just requesting re-certification evaluations will be charged the small fee of $25.00.
- The UNT CAAT program is one of only two national certification programs for community volunteers in the entire North Texas Region and the only national certification program for counseling professionals in the state of Texas. Thus the CAAT fulfills a great need for this type of training.

Future Research and Funding

- Continue to solicit additional funds to support the operation of the CAAT. Workshop fees will continue to be used to support the operations of the CAAT. In addition, grants will be sought from Iams, Paws to Share Foundation (and other resources if necessary) to support the operations of the CAAT.
- Continue to hire graduate students to gather research data at approved sites participating in CAAT activities.
- Continue to perform research to study the clinical efficacy of AAT.
- Continue to present research results at professional meetings and prepare manuscripts for publication in nationally refereed journals.

Future Networking with Agencies and Schools to Provide Services

- Continue to network with local school programs to establish RAD (Reading Assistance Dogs) in local schools and libraries.

- Continue to network with local agencies to set up internship sites for graduate students providing AAT.
- Continue to provide a link from CDHE department to a new website page describing the AAT program. Completed: Spring 2003, see www.coe.unt.edu/CDHE/AAT. This website provides much international publicity. I answer 30 to 40 inquiries per week regarding out AAT program from website contacts, including from other countries. Many interested parties are requesting information on enrolling in our graduate program in counseling just to study Animal Assisted Therapy.
- Continue to develop regional, state, and national/international reputations in AAT.

Future Assistance to Students and Promotion of Diversity

- Dr. Cynthia Chandler has provided and will continue to provide a personal monthly donation from her UNT salary for the purpose of the eventual endowment of a $10,000 student scholarship for the study of animal assisted therapy at UNT, **The Dr. Cynthia K. Chandler, Professor, and Rusty Chandler, Therapy Dog Scholarship.** Endowment should be completed by the target date December, 2006.
- Continue to solicit funding from additional resources for the establishment of additional scholarships and endowments for students to study animal assisted therapy at UNT.
- Continue to provide animal assisted therapy services to a diverse population. Many of the persons who benefit from animal assisted therapy research and services of the CAAT are disabled persons, elderly persons, at risk children, or ethnic minority children. Animal assisted therapy workshops and courses provided by the CAAT at UNT train persons to work with their dogs in schools, libraries, nursing homes, hospitals, juvenile detention centers, rehabilitation centers, and therapy centers.
- The director of the CAAT will continue to work closely with the directors of the internship sites and school programs to gain feedback on how well these programs are functioning.

IV. Measuring Expected Outcomes

- At the completion of each training workshop participants complete a standardized evaluation form designed by Delta Society, the national certification organization for animal assisted therapy. These evaluations are sent to Delta Society, which oversees the quality control of the UNT CAAT program.
- At the completion of each graduate course offering, students complete a standardized evaluation form designed by the University of North Texas, College of Education.
- Research involving the RAD program and the TAT program involves a number of assessment measures to measure the educational and clinical efficacy of these programs.

V. Use of Assessment Results

- The workshop and course evaluations are used to evaluate the effectiveness of the presenter and program information. The evaluations are tabulated and feedback is taken into consideration in organizing and presenting the topics. The Center for Animal Assisted Therapy strives to provide the most professional and educational training in animal assisted therapy in this area. This unique training opportunity provides students, professionals, and community volunteers with accessibility to leading information in the field of animal assisted therapy.
- Feedback that is gathered from supervisors at animal assisted therapy internship sites is used to adapt or modify animal assisted therapy services as deemed necessary.
- Outcome measures used to determine efficacy of AAT related programs (RAD and TAT) have been and will be presented and published at professional meetings for evaluation and critical evaluation by professionals in the field. All research conducted by the CAAT follows federal, state, and local regulations to protect the identity of research participants. All research participants are fully informed of their rights when agreeing to participate in research.

VI. Changes Made Based on Assessment Results

Decisions about the organization, structure, and content of each workshop and graduate course are adapted or modified based on the suggestions of the participants' evaluations.

Animal assisted therapy at internship sites is adapted or modified based on the feedback of field supervisors and is carefully tuned to the needs of the diverse populations being served.

Signature of Person Completing the Form:

_____ Date: _____

Dr. Cynthia K. Chandler, Professor of Counseling & Director, Center for Animal Assisted Therapy

Appendix F

Animal Assisted Therapy

Course Syllabus - COUN 5530
Counseling Program, University of North Texas, Denton, TX

Course Description

Animal assisted therapy is the incorporation of qualified animals into a therapeutic environment. The course will explore techniques to facilitate animal assisted therapeutic interventions in a variety of settings, including schools, counseling agencies, hospitals, nursing homes, hospices, prisons, and facilities for the developmentally disabled. A variety of animals can be suitable for therapy programs. You need not have an animal or pet to take the course.

Course Objectives

The course objectives are the acquisition of knowledge and skills necessary to facilitate animal assisted therapy in a variety of professional settings in a fashion that is both safe and humane to the animal.

Course Content Outline

I. An introduction to animal assisted therapy

Description of animal assisted therapy
The human-animal connection
Benefits of animal assisted therapy

Risks involved with animal assisted therapy
History of animal assisted therapy
Animal assisted therapy in counseling: A new frontier therapy

II. Research in animal assisted counseling

Psychophysiological health
Anxiety and distress
Dementia
Depression
Motivation
Self-esteem enhancement
Children in pediatric hospitals
Children with developmental disorders
Children with emotional and behavioral problems
The elderly and nursing home residents
Physically disabled persons
Psychiatric patients
Conclusions

III. Selecting an animal for therapy work

Therapy dogs
Therapy cats
Therapy horses
Small therapy animals
Therapy farm animals

IV. Preparing a pet for therapy work

Socialization
Touch desensitization
Obedience training
Teaching special skills and trick training

V. Evaluation of a pet for therapy work

American Kennel Club Canine Good Citizen Test
Therapy Dogs International testing requirements
Delta Society Pet Partners evaluation
    Pet Partners Aptitude Test
    Pet Partners Skills Test
Tuskegee Behavior Test

VI. Risk Management

Professional disclosure and informed consent to participate
Client screening for animal assisted therapy
Recognizing stress in therapy animals

Understanding your pet's communication
Preventing injury and infection
Preparing the pet for a therapy visit
Ethical considerations
 Dangers for animals in elderly residential care facilities
 Dangers for animals in institutionally based residential programs
 Concerns for animals in visitation programs
 Concerns for wild (nondomesticated) animal programs

VII. Animal assisted counseling techniques

Animal assisted rapport building
Animal facilitated life stage development
Animal assisted psychosocial goals and techniques
Introducing the pet practitioner
Basic relational techniques
Accessing feelings
Family history gathering
Animal assisted therapy and diagnoses
Animal assisted metaphor
Animal assisted play therapy
Equine assisted counseling
The therapeutic zoo
Termination of therapy
Documentation of counseling sessions
Program evaluation

VIII. Animal assisted counseling for populations with special needs and cultural
   concerns

Cultural sensitivity
Counseling elderly clients
Counseling clients in hospitals and hospice settings
Counseling clients in prisons and detention centers

IX. Animal assisted crisis response counseling

The nature of crisis
Crisis response safety
Getting started as a crisis response counselor
Crisis response counseling interventions

X. Establishing a school-based program for animal assisted therapy
  and education

Guidelines for program development
Types of programs
How to solicit funding for your AAT program
How to report on the progress of your AAT program

XI. Establishing and maintaining a university-based training program for animal assisted therapy in counseling

Seeking approval and establishing policy
Obtaining credentials
Being a role model: Practicing animal assisted counseling
Developing a university course
Involving the community
Establishing a center
Creating student internships in the community
Serving as an educational resource
Gaining national and international recognition

Course Activities

- Lectures
- Demonstrations and practice
- Audio-visual presentations (videos, PowerPoint presentations, transparencies)
- Field trips to observe animal assisted therapy
  Equine therapy ranch
  Juvenile detention
  Other field trips as they become available
- Guest speakers who practice animal assisted therapy

Course Evaluation Criteria

Class attendance	10%
Class participation in discussions and activities	15%
Completion of a final take-home examination	75%

Instructor Information

Cynthia K. Chandler, Ed.D., LPC, LMFT, BCIA-C & EEG
Professor, Counseling Program
Office: Stovall Hall, Room 155, phone (940) 565-2914, fax (940) 565-2905
E-mail: chandler@coe.unt.edu
Snail mail: P.O. Box 310829, University of North Texas, Denton, TX 76203-0829
Instructor's Summer I office hours: Mon & Tues. 2:30-5:30 p.m.

Dr. Chandler is a tenured graduate faculty member. She has been on the faculty of UNT since August of 1989. She is a licensed professional counselor, a licensed marriage and family therapist, and a nationally certified biofeedback and neurofeedback therapist. She is an approved supervisor and trainer in all four license and certification areas. She is registered through Delta Society as Pet Partners with her dogs Rusty and Dolly and her cat Snowflake. She is a Delta Society Pet Partners and AAT course instructor and licensed animal team evaluator.

Course Bibliography

Required

Chandler, C. K. (2005). *Animal assisted therapy in counseling.* New York: Routledge.
Delta Society (2003). *AAT applications I student guide.* Renton WA: Author.
Delta Society (2004). *Pet partners team training course manual.* Renton, WA: Author.

Recommended

Benjamin, C. L. (1985). *Mother knows best: The natural way to train your dog.* New York: Howell.
Delta Society (1999). Animals and Children. Renton, WA: Author.
Delta Society (1998). Animals in institutions. Renton, WA: Author.
Delta Society (1999). Animals in the Classroom. Renton, WA: Author.
Delta Society (1999). Health Benefits of Animals. Renton, WA: Author.
Fine, A. (ed.) (1999). *Handbook on animal-assisted therapy: Theoretical foundations and guidelines for practice.* San Diego: Academic.
Gammonley, J., Howie, A., Kirwin, S., Zapf, S., Frye, J., Freeman, G., & Stuart-Russell, R. (1997). *Animal-assisted therapy: Therapeutic interventions.* Renton, WA: Delta Society.

Appendix G

Animal Assisted Therapy
Animal Illustrations:
Instructions and Activities

Part I

These therapists' instructions are to be used with the illustrations of a dog, cat, horse, rabbit, and parrot. (Appendix G animal illustrations were drawn by Susan Decker.)

1. Have the client choose which animal illustration of the ones available that he or she wishes to color and provide the client with that animal illustration and a copy of the client's instructions page, "Animal Colors Activity."
2. Provide the client with nontoxic and preferably water-soluble color pencils or markers.
3. On the client's instruction page, "Animal Colors Activity," have the client label what colors will represent which feelings the client is experiencing right now. They can use the suggested colors as a guide or choose different emotions or different colors for each emotion.

Suggested Guide

Colors can represent the following feelings: sad = blue, afraid = yellow, happy = orange, relaxed = green, angry = red, frustrated = black, curious = gray, confused = brown, love = pink, like = purple, and hurt = white or no color.

Feelings	Colors
Sad:	
Afraid:	
Happy:	

Relaxed:
Angry:
Frustrated:
Curious:
Confused:
Love:
Like:
Hurt:
Other feelings:

4.   On the client's instruction page, "Animal Colors Activity," have the client label the body parts of the animal with certain important persons or situations in the client's life, such as family, friends, school/work, self, hopes/dreams, etc. The client can use the suggested body part labeling or choose different life areas or different body parts for life areas.

Animal Body Parts   Life Persons or Situations

Eyes:
Ears:
Head:
Neck:
Body torso:
Tail:
Legs:
Feet:

Suggested Guide

Body parts can represent the following topics: eyes = spirit, ears = school or work, head = family, neck = (left blank to be filled in by client), body = love, tail = friend(s), legs = fun or hobbies, and feet = myself.

5.   Now, have the client color in the animal's body parts that represent different persons or situations in the client's life with colors representing the different feelings the client currently has about those persons or situations.

6.   Have the client share the results of their artwork and discuss it in length.

Part II

The following instructions are to be used with the dog and cat expressions illustrations in the back of the book. This activity can follow the activity presented in Part I, or can be performed as a separate activity at a different time.

1.   Have the client look at the dog expressions or cat expressions illustrations and label each animal with an emotion the client thinks the animal is expressing. Five basic emotions are presented in the illustrations: sad, angry, happy, afraid, and content/calm/relaxed. The client is allowed to label the animals with other emotions than the suggested five presented. The client can then color each animal expression based on the color the client wants to represent

that emotion. Have the client discuss which dog or cat it most closely identi-
fies with as a primary or dominant emotion in the client's life.

2. Now have the client discuss at what times in the client's life he or she experiences each emotion in each life area based on the instructions provided to the
client in the "Animal Feelings Activity."

Animal Colors Activity

This exercise is designed to help you get better in touch with your feelings about different areas of your life. Look at the drawing of the animal that has been given to
you. You will be coloring this animal's body parts to represent different areas of your
life. You will have an opportunity to discuss your animal drawing when you are done.

Step 1

Based on the colors available to you, decide what color you want to represent each
emotion and write it down below. You can use the suggested guide if you prefer.

Feelings   **Colors**

Sad:
Afraid:
Happy:
Relaxed:
Angry:
Frustrated:
Curious:
Confused:
Love:
Like:
Hurt:
Other feelings:
a)
b)
c)

Suggested Guide

Colors can represent the following feelings: sad = blue, afraid = yellow, happy
= orange, relaxed = green, angry = red, frustrated = black, curious = gray, confused =
brown, love = pink, like = purple, and hurt = white or no color.

Step 2

Based on the body parts presented in the animal drawing, decide what body parts
you want to represent each area of your life and write them down below. You can use
the suggested guide if you prefer.

Animal Body Parts	Life Persons or Situations
Eyes:	
Ears:	
Head:	
Neck:	
Body torso:	
Tail:	
Legs:	
Feet:	

Suggested Guide

Body parts can represent the following topics: eyes = spirit, ears = school or work, head = family, neck = (left blank to be filled in by client), body = love, tail = friend(s), legs = fun or hobbies, and feet = myself.

Animal Feelings Activity

Step 1

Look at the expressions of the animals in the drawing that has been given to you. How would you label each emotion that each animal seems to be expressing? (Suggested guide: the animals could be expressing the five basic emotions of sad, angry, happy, afraid, or content/calm/relaxed, but you may see something different in the animals' expressions so describe the animals' emotions the way that you see them.) Write the emotion next to that animal. Color each animal based on what color you want to represent that emotion for the animal.

Step 2

What emotion do you feel more than any other emotion right now in your life?

Step 3

List below at what times in your life and under what circumstances you experience certain emotions in each of your major life areas.

A.   When do you feel each of the emotions when you are with your significant other (girlfriend/boyfriend, husband/wife, or life partner)?

Girlfriend/Boyfriend, Husband/Wife, or Life Partner
Sad:
Angry:
Happy:
Afraid:

Content/calm/relaxed:
Other emotion(s):

B.   When do you feel each of the emotions when you are with members of your family?

Family

Sad:
Angry:
Happy:
Afraid:
Content/calm/relaxed:
Other emotion(s):

C.   When do you feel each of the emotions when you are with friends?

Friends

Sad:
Angry:
Happy:
Afraid:
Content/calm/relaxed:
Other emotion(s):

D.   When do you feel each of the emotions when you are at work or school?

Work or School

Sad:
Angry:
Happy:
Afraid:
Content/calm/relaxed:
Other emotion(s):

E.   When do you feel each of the emotions in relation to yourself?

Self

Sad:
Angry:
Happy:
Afraid:
Content/calm/relaxed:
Other emotion(s):

F.   When do you feel each of the emotions in relation to your spirituality?

Spirituality

Sad:
Angry:
Happy:
Afraid:
Content/calm/relaxed:
Other emotion(s):

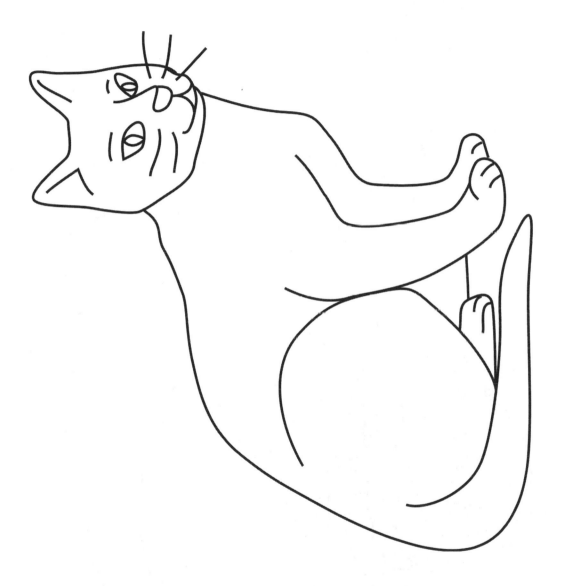

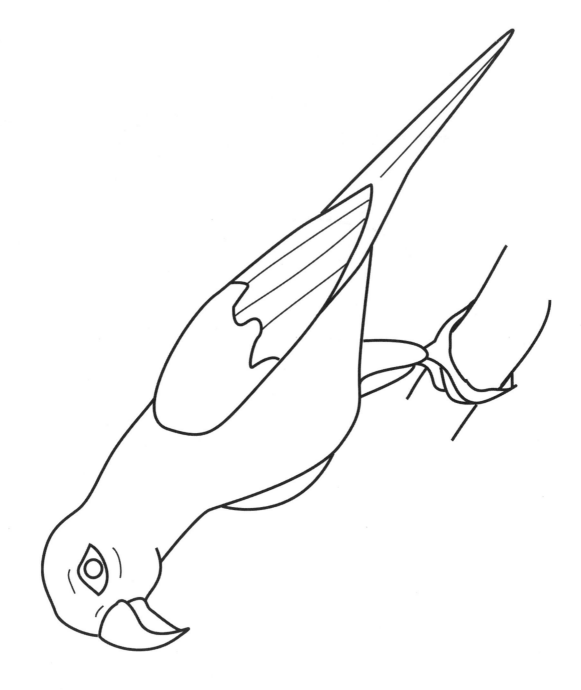

References

Achenbach, T. M. (1991). *The child behavior checklist.* Retrieved September 15, 2004, from Department of Psychiatry, University of Vermont Web site: http://www.uvm.edu.

Agnes, M. (Ed.). (2002). *Webster's new world dictionary* (4th ed.). Cleveland, OH: Wiley.

Alderton, D. (2000a). *Dogs.* London: Dorling Kindersley.

Alderton, D. (2000b). *Cats.* London: Dorling Kindersley.

American Kennel Club. (2003). *Canine good citizen test procedures.* Retrieved May 15, 2004, from http://www.akc.org.

American Red Cross. (2004). Retrieved June 23, 2004, from http://www.red-cross.org.

Ascione, F. R. (1989). *The intermediate attitudes scale.* Retrieved May 15, 2002, from Department of Psychology, Utah State University. Web site: http://www.usu.edu.

Bandler, R., & Grinder, J. (1975). *Patterns of the hypnotic techniques of Milton H. Erickson, M.D.* (Vol. 1). Cupertino, CA: Meta Publications.

Banks, M. R., & Banks, W. A. (2002). The effects of animal-assisted therapy on loneliness in an elderly population in long-term care facilities. *Journal of Gerontology, 57A*(7), M428–M432.

Barak, Y., Savorai, O., Mavashev, S., Beni, A. (2001). Animal-assisted therapy for elderly schizophrenic patients: A one-year controlled trial. *The American Journal of Geriatric Psychiatry, 9*(4), 439–442.

Barker, S., & Dawson, K. (1998). The effects of animal-assisted therapy on anxiety ratings of hospitalized psychiatric patients. *Psychiatric Services, 49*(6), 797–801.

Barol, B. (2002, May 13). Listen, Spot. *Time,* F14.

Batson, K., McCabe, B., Baun, M., Wilson, C. (1998). The effect of a therapy dog on socialization and physiological indicators of stress in persons diagnosed with Alzheimer's disease. In C. Wilson & D. Turner (Eds.), *Companion animals in human health* (pp. 203–215). Thousand Oaks, CA: Sage.

Benjamin, C. L. (1985). *Mother knows best: The natural way to train your dog.* New York: Howell.

Bernstein, B. E., & Hartsell, T. L. (1998). *The portable lawyer for mental health professionals: An A-Z guide to protecting your clients, your practice, and yourself.* New York: John Wiley & Sons.

Bernstein, P. L., Friedman, E., & Malaspina, A. (2000). Animal-assisted therapy enhances resident social interaction and initiation in long-term care facilities. *Anthrozoos, 13*(4), 213–224.

Burch, M. R. (1996). *Volunteering with your pet: How to get involved in animal-assisted therapy.* New York: Macmillan.

Burch, M. R. (2003). *Wanted! Animal volunteers.* New York: Howell.

Cameron, S. & turtle-song, i. (2002). Learning to write case notes using the SOAP format. *Journal of Counseling and Development, 80,* 286–292.

Choi, Y. (2003, November). History of the human–animal bond in Korea. Paper presented at the First International Symposium on the Human–Animal Bond, Samsung Everland, South Korea.

Christie, S. (2002). Standards of strength: Proportionate, powerful and agile, bully breeds share common physical traits and ancestry. *Popular Dogs Series: Bully Breeds, 21,* 19–33.

Clothier, S. (1996). *Understanding puppy testing.* Retrieved June 23, 2004, from http://www.flyingdogpress.com.

Coile, D. C. (1998). *Encyclopedia of dog breeds.* Hauppauge, NY: Barron's.

Cormier, S., & Nurius, P. (2003). *Interviewing and change strategies for helpers: Fundamental skills and cognitive behavioral interventions.* Pacific Grove, CA: Brooks/Cole.

Delta Society. (1997). *Animals in institutions.* Renton, WA: Author.

Delta Society. (1999). *Animals in the classroom.* Renton, WA: Author.

Delta Society. (2000). *Pet Partners team training course manual* (5th ed.). Renton, WA: Author.

Delta Society. (2003). Pet Partners Program. Retrieved June 22, 2004, from http://www.deltasociety.org.

Delta Society. (2004). *Pet Partners team training course manual* (6th ed.). Renton, WA: Author.

Deneen, S. (2002). Extraordinary bullys: Meet seven talented and athletic emissaries for their breeds. *Popular Dogs Series: Bully Breeds, 21,* 52–59.

DePrekel, M., & Welsch, T. (2000a). Animal-assisted therapeutic interventions. Unpublished manuscript.

DePrekel, M., & Welsch, T. (2000b). Hands-on animal-assisted therapy and education activities. Unpublished manuscript.

Therapy dogs have time for pupils. (1999, October 31). *Denton Record Chronicle,* p. A26.

Equine Assisted Growth and Learning Association. (2003). Retrieved June 21, 2004, from http://www.eagala.org.

Fawcett, N., & Gullone, E. (2001). Cute and cuddly and a whole lot more? A call for empirical investigation into the therapeutic benefits of human–animal interaction for children. *Behaviour Change, 18*(2), 124–133.

Fick, K. (1993). The influence of an animal on social interactions of nursing home residents in a group setting. *The American Journal of Occupational Therapy, 47*(6), 529–534.

Fine, A. H. (Ed.). (2000a). *Animal-assisted therapy: Theoretical foundations and guidelines for practice.* San Diego, CA: Academic Press.

Fine, A. H. (2000b). Animals and therapists: Incorporating animals in outpatient psychotherapy. In A. H. Fine (Ed.), *Animal-assisted therapy: Theoretical foundations and guidelines for practice* (pp. 179–211). San Diego, CA: Academic Press.

Fogle, B. (2000). *Cats: Portraits of over 70 pedigrees*. New York: Dorling Kindersley.

Folse, E. B., Minder, C. C., Aycock, M. J., & Santana, R. T. (1994). Animal-assisted therapy and depression in adult college students. *Anthrozoos, 7*(3), 188–194.

Friedmann, E., Katcher, A., Lynch, J., & Thomas, S. (1980). Animal companions and one-year survival of patients after discharge from a coronary unit. *Public Health Reports, 95*, 307–312.

Friedmann, E., Katcher, A., Thomas, S., Lynch, J., & Messent, P. (1983). Social interaction and blood pressure: Influence of companion animals. *Journal of Nervous and Mental Disease, 171*, 543–551.

Friedmann, E., Locker, B., & Lockwood, R. (1993). Perception of animals and cardiovascular responses during verbalization with an animal present. *Anthrozoos, 62*, 115–133.

Friedmann, E., & Thomas, S. (1995). Pet ownership, social support, and one-year survival after acute myocardial infarction in the Cardiac Arrhythmia Suppression Trial (CAST). *American Journal of Cardiology, 76*, 1213–1217.

Gammonley, J., Howie, A. R., Jackson, B., Kaufman, M., Kirwin, S., Morgan, L., et al. (2000). *AAT applications. I: Student guide*. Renton, WA: Delta Society.

Gammonley, J., Howie, A. R., Jackson, B., Kaufman, M., Kirwin, S., Morgan, L., et al. (2003). *AAT applications. I: Student guide*. Renton, WA: Delta Society.

Gammonley, J., Howie, A. R., Kirwin, S., Zapf, S. A., Frye, J., Freeman, G., et al. (1997). *Animal-assisted therapy: Therapeutic interventions*. Renton, WA: Delta Society.

Gosling, S., Kwan, V., & John, O. (2003). A dog's got personality: A cross-species comparative approach to personality judgments in dogs and humans. *Journal of Personality and Social Psychology, 85*(6), 1161–1169.

Guralnik, D. (Ed.). (1980). *Webster's new world dictionary, 2nd college edition*. New York: Simon & Schuster.

Hansen, K., Messinger, C., Baun, M., & Megel, M. (1999). Companion animals alleviating distress in children. *Anthrozoos, 12*(3), 142–148.

Hart, E. H. (1968). *The Cocker Spaniel handbook*. Neptune City, NJ: T.F.H. Publications.

Haynes, M. (1991, August). Pet therapy: Program lifts spirits, reduces violence in institution's mental health unit. *Corrections Today*, pp. 120–122.

Heindl, B. A. (1996). The effectiveness of pet therapy as an intervention in a community-based children's day treatment program. *Dissertation Abstracts International, 57*(4-A), 1501.

Heppner, P. P., Kivlighan, D. M., & Wampold, B. E. (1999). *Research design in counseling* (2nd ed.). Belmont, CA: Wadsworth.

Hoffman, M. (1999). *Dogspeak: How to understand your dog and help him understand you*. Emmaus, PA: Rodale Press.

Holcomb, R., Jendro, C., Weber, B., & Nahan, U. (1997). Use of an aviary to relieve depression in elderly males. *Anthrozoos, 10*(1), 32–36.

Holcomb, R., & Meacham, M. (1989). Effectiveness of an animal-assisted therapy program in an inpatient psychiatric unit. *Anthrozoos, 2*(4), 259–264.

Hooker, S., Freeman, L., & Stewart, P. (2002). Pet therapy research: A historical review. *Holistic Nursing Practice, 17*(1), 17–23.

HOPE. (2004). Animal assisted crisis response. Retrieved November 4, 2004, from http://www.hopeaacr.org.

Houghton Mifflin. (2001). *The American heritage dictionary* (4th ed.). Boston: Author.

Hoyle, R. H. (1999). *Statistical strategies for small sample research.* Thousand Oaks, CA: Sage.

Iannuzzi, D., & Rowan, A. N. (1991). Ethical issues in animal-assisted therapy programs. *Anthrozoos, 4*(3), 154–163.

Jewell, E., & Abate, F. (Eds.). (2001). *The new Oxford American dictionary.* New York: Oxford University Press.

John, O., & Srivastava, S. (1999). The big five trait taxonomy: History, measurement, and theoretical perspectives. In L. A. Pervin & O. P. John (Eds.), *Handbook of personality: Theory and research* (2nd ed., pp. 102–138). New York: Guilford Press.

Kaminski, M., Pellino, T., & Wish, J. (2002). Play and pets: The physical and emotional impact of child-life and pet therapy on hospitalized children. *Children's Health Care, 31*(4), 321–335.

Katcher, A. H. (1985). Physiologic and behavioral responses to companion animals. In J. Quackenbush & V. Voith (Eds.), *The human-companion-animal bond. The veterinary clinics of North America: Small animal practice, 15*(2), 403–410.

Katcher, A. H. (2000a). The Centaur's lessons: Therapeutic education through care of animals and nature study. In A. Fine, Ed., *Handbook on animal-assisted therapy: Theoretical foundations and guidelines for practice* (pp. 153–177). San Diego, CA: Academic Press.

Katcher, A. H. (2000b). The future of education and research on the animal–human bond and animal-assisted therapy, Part B: Animal-assisted therapy and the study of human–animal relationships: Discipline or bondage? Context or transitional object? In A. Fine, Ed., *Handbook on animal-assisted therapy: Theoretical foundations and guidelines for practice* (pp. 461–473). San Diego, CA: Academic Press.

Katcher, A. H., & Wilkins, G. G. (2002). *The Centaur's lessons: The companionable zoo method of therapeutic education based upon contact with animals and nature study.* Retrieved June 23, 2004, from http://www.PAN-inc.org.

Kogan, L. R., Granger, B. P., Fitchett, J. A., Helmer, K. A., & Young, K. J. (1999). The human–animal team approach for children with emotional disorders: Two case studies. *Child and Youth Care Forum, 28*(2), 105–121.

Kolander, C., Ballard, D., & Chandler, C. (2005). *Contemporary women's health: Issues for today and the future, 2nd ed.* St. Louis: McGraw-Hill.

Kottman, T. (2003). *Partners in play: An Adlerian approach to play therapy* (2nd ed.). Alexandria, VA: American Counseling Association.

Kraemer, H. C., & Thiemann, S. (1989). A strategy to use soft data effectively in randomized controlled clinical trials. *Journal of Consulting and Clinical Psychology, 57*(1), 148–154.

Kramer, S. H., & Rosenthal, R. (1999). Effect sizes and significance levels in small-sample research. In R. H. Hoyle, Ed., *Statistical strategies for small sample research* (pp. 59–79). Thousand Oaks, CA: Sage.

Landreth, G. (2002). *Play therapy: The art of the relationship* (2nd ed.). New York: Brunner-Routledge.

Lerner, M., & Shelton, R. (2001). *Acute traumatic stress management*. Retrieved July 1, 2004, from http://www.crisisinfo.org.

Lerner, M., Volpe, J., & Lindell, B. (2004a). *A practical guide for crisis response in our schools*. Retrieved July 1, 2004, from http://www.crisisinfo.org.

Lerner, M., Volpe, J., & Lindell, B. (2004b). *A practical guide for university crisis response*. Retrieved July 1, 2004, from http://www.crisisinfo.org.

Levinson, B. M. (1962). The dog as co-therapist. *Mental Hygiene, 46*, 59–65.

Levinson, B. M. (1969). *Pet-oriented child psychotherapy*. Springfield, IL: Charles C. Thomas.

Levinson, B. M. (1997). *Pet-oriented child psychotherapy* (2nd ed.). Springfield, IL: Charles C. Thomas.

Limond, J., Bradshaw, J., & Cormack, K. (1997). Behavior of children with learning disabilities interacting with a therapy dog. *Anthrozoos, 10*(2–3), 84–89.

Mallon, G. P. (1994a). Cow as co-therapist: Utilization of farm animals as therapeutic aides with children in residential treatment. *Child and Adolescent Social Work Journal, 11*(6), 455–474.

Mallon, G. P. (1994b). Some of our best therapists are dogs. *Child and Youth Care Forum, 23*(2), 89–101.

Marr, C., French, L., Thompson, D., Drum, L., Greening, G., Mormon, J., et al. (2000). Animal-assisted therapy in psychiatric rehabilitation. *Anthrozoos, 13*(1), 43–47.

Marshall, C., & Rossman, G. B. (1999). *Designing qualitative research* (3rd ed.). Thousand Oaks, CA: Sage.

Martin, F., & Farnum, J. (2002). Animal assisted therapy for children with pervasive developmental disorders. *Western Journal of Nursing Research, 24*(6), 657–671.

Maxwell, S. E. (1998). Longitudinal designs in randomized group comparisons: When will intermediate observations increase statistical power? *Psychological Methods, 3*(3), 275–290.

McKenzie, A. (2003, May 17). Sit, stay, HEAL: Therapist uses pets to lead patients down the road to recovery. *Dallas Morning News*, pp. 3E, 7E.

Mcvarish, C. A. (1995). The effects of pet facilitated therapy on depressed institutionalized inpatients. *Dissertation Abstracts International, 55*(7-B), 3019.

Munro, E. (2004, May 15). Minority report III: Reservation rescues. Retrieved June 21, 2004, from http://www.bestfriends.org/features/minority/minority-report-res1.htm.

Nagengast, S. L., Baun, M., Megel, M., & Leibowitz, M. (1997). The effects of the presence of a companion animal on physiological and behavioral distress in children during a physical examination. *Journal of Pediatric Nursing, 12*, 323–330.

National American Pit Bull Terrier Association. (2000, Spring/Summer). Delta Society award winner. *NAPBTA Bulletin*, 2.

North American Riding for the Handicapped Association. (2003). Retrieved June 21, 2004, from http://www.narha.org.

National Organization for Victim Assistance. (2004). Retrieved June 23, 2004, from http://www.try-nova.org.

Noble County. (2003). Noble County Nursing Home. Seoul, Korea. Retrieved May 15, 2004, from http://www.samsungnc.com/html/07_english_01.html.

Odendaal, J. S. J. (2000). Animal-assisted therapy — magic or medicine? *Journal of Psychosomatic Research, 49*(4), 275–280.

Orey, C. (2002). An American symbol: From a WWI poster dog to a movie star, bully breeds embody the American spirit. *Popular Dogs Series: Bully Breeds, 21*, 34–39.

Perelle, I., & Granville, D. (1993). Assessment of the effectiveness of a pet facilitated therapy program in a nursing home setting. *Society and Animals, 1*(1), 91–100.

Ptak, A. L. & Howie, A. R. (2004). Healing paws and tails: The case for animal-assisted therapy in hospitals. *Interactions, 22(2)*, 5–9.

Rea, J. L. (2000, July 31). Special therapy dogs learn how to heal. *The Register-Guard*, p. 1D.

Redefer, L. A., & Goodman, J. G. (1989). Brief report: Pet-facilitated therapy with autistic children. *Journal of Autism and Developmental Disorders, 19*(3), 461–467.

Reichert, E. (1994). Play and animal-assisted therapy: A group-treatment model for sexually abused girls ages 9–13. *Family Therapy, 21*(1), 55–62.

Reynolds, C. R., & Kamphaus, R. W. (1992). *Behavior assessment system for children.* Circle Pines, MN: American Guidance Service.

Rhoades, R. (2001, Summer). Sentence for salvation: Behind the walls of correctional institutions, inmates find a renewed sense of purpose through working with injured and rescued animals. *ASPCA Animal Watch*, pp. 24–27.

Richard, J. (2004, January 3). Minority report II: The humane movement in the Latino community. Retrieved June 21, 2004, from http://www.bestfriends.org/features/minority/minority-report-hisp1.htm.

Right TRAIL. (2001, September 13). *Right* TRAIL program. (Unpublished meeting handout). Retrieved June 21, 2004, from http://www.rockytoptherapy.org.

Right TRAIL. (2002, January 21). *Right* TRAIL lesson plan. (Unpublished meeting handout). Retrieved June 21, 2004, from http://www.rockytoptherapy.org.

Robin, M., & ten Bensel, R. (1985). Pets and the socialization of children. *Marriage and Family Therapy, 8*(3–4), 63–78.

Samsung. (2003). Creating a better future for all [Unpublished videotape]. Office of International Relations, Samsung Everland, Kyounggio-do, South Korea.

Schaffer, C. B. (1993). The Tuskegee behavior test for selecting therapy dogs. Tuskegee, AL: Center for the Study of Human–Animal Interdependent Relationships, School of Veterinary Medicine, Tuskegee University.

Schultz, S. (2000, October 30). Pets and their humans. *U.S. News & World Report*, pp. 53–55.

Shane, F. T. (2004). Canines in crisis: Mitigating traumatic stress through canine crisis intervention. (ATSS Workshop, April 14). Retrieved June 22, 2004, from http://www.K-9DisasterRelief.org.

Shin, N. (2003, November). Introduction of human–animal bond. Paper presented at the First International Symposium on the Human–Animal Bond, Samsung Everland, South Korea.

Steed, H. N., & Smith, B. S. (2002). Animal assisted activities for geriatric patients. *Activities, Adaptation and Aging, 27*(1),49–61.

Tangley, L. (2000, October 30). Animal emotions. *U.S. News & World Report*, pp. 48–52.

Tarrant, D. (2000, January 21). Teacher's pets: Lucy and Dottie are top dogs in the classroom. *Dallas Morning News*, p. 1C.

Taunton, S. & Smith, C. (1998). *The trick is in the training: 25 fun tricks to teach your dog.* Hauppauge, NY: Barron's.

Teal, L. (2002). Pet Partners help with the healing process. *Interactions, 19*(4), 3–5.

Tellington-Jones, L., & Taylor, S. (1995). The Tellington Touch: A revolutionary natural method to train and care for your favorite animal. New York: Penguin.

Therapy Dogs International. (2003). Retrieved June 23, 2004, from http://www.tdi-dog.org.

Thompson, B. (2002). "Statistical," "practical," and "clinical": How many kinds of significance do counselors need to consider? *Journal of Counseling and Development, 80*, 64–71.

Thornton, K. C. (2002). Famous bully breeds. *Popular Dogs Series: Bully Breeds, 21*, 10.

Tomaszewski, F., Jenkins, S., Rae, S., & Keller, J. (2001). An evaluation of therapeutic horseback riding programs for adults with physical impairments. *Therapeutic Recreation Journal, 35*(3), 250–257.

Volhard, J., & Volhard, W. (1997). *The canine good citizen: Every dog can be one*. New York: Howell.

Walsh, P., Mertin, P., Verlander, D., & Pollard, C. (1995). The effects of a 'pets as therapy' dog on persons with dementia in a psychiatric ward. *Australian Occupational Therapy Journal, 42*, 161–166.

Walsh, P. G., & Mertin, P. G. (1994). The training of pets as therapy dogs in a women's prison: A pilot study. *Anthrozoos, 7*(2), 124–128.

Wilkes, C. N., Shalko, T. K., & Trahan, M. (1989). Pet therapy: Implications for good health. *Health Education, 20*, 6–9.

Willett, J. B. (1989). Questions and answers in the measurement of change. In E. Z. Rothkopf (Ed.), *Review of research in education* (pp. 345–422). Washington, DC: AREA.

Willett, J. B. (1994). Measurement of change. In T. Husen & T. N. Postlethwaite (Eds.), *The international encyclopedia of education* (2nd ed., pp. 671–678). Oxford, UK: Pergamon.

Young, M. (2005). *Learning the art of helping: Building blocks and techniques* (3rd ed.). Upper Saddle River, NJ: Pearson.

Zeig, J. K., & Munion, W. M. (1999). *Milton H. Erickson*. Thousand Oaks, CA: Sage.

Zeigenfuse, M. & Walker, J. (1997). *Dog tricks: Step by step*. New York: Howell.

Index

A

AAT, *see* Animal assisted therapy

AAT-C, *see* Animal assisted therapy, in counseling

Abuse, of therapy animals, 70–71

Acute Traumatic Stress Management (Lerner and Sheldon), 143

Adjunctive therapy, 5

Administrative acceptance, of program establishment, 160–161

Adolescents, animal assisted counseling with, 110–120

Affect, recognition and expression of, 96–99

Affection and nurture, receiving, 87

Aggression, signs of
    in cats, 64–65
    in dogs, 63

Alzheimer's patients, studies of pet therapy with, 17–18

American Bulldog, 82–84

American Cocker Spaniel, 27, *see also* Dolly; Rusty
    breed description of, 98
    breed history of, 100–101

American Counseling Association, liability insurance, 58

American Guidance Service, contact information, 126

American Kennel Club, Canine Good Citizen Test, 50–51

American Red Cross, crisis response training by, 143, 147

American Staffordshire Terrier, 82–84
    breed description of, 98

Analysis of covariance (ANCOVA), 125

Analysis of variance (ANOVA), 125

Animal assisted counseling, 2–3, 12–14, 73–74, *see also* Animal assisted therapy
    clients of
        children, 106–110
        detention center residents, 133–134, 135–137
        elderly, 130–132
        hospice residents, 132–133
        hospitalized patients, 132–133
        juveniles, 110–120, 135–137
        prison residents, 133–136
    in crisis response, 139–149
    cultural considerations in, 129–130
    diagnoses treatable with, 101–102
    documentation of, 124–125
    evaluation of, 125–126
    family history gathering in, 99–101
    feelings assessment in, 93–99
    goals and techniques in, 79–85
    horses in, 110–120
    interventional activities in, 101–102
        group play therapy, 109–110
        metaphor, 102–106
        play therapy, 106–109
    in life stage development, 85–89
    listening responses in, 91–93
    rapport building in, 75–79
    research and studies in, 15–24
    risk management in, 57–71
    in special needs populations, 127–137

termination of, 123–124
therapeutic touch in, 74–75
therapy pet introduction in, 90–91
typical session of, 89–90
university training programs in, 159–165
zoo animals in, 120–123
Animal assisted therapy, 5
    as adjunctive therapy, 5
    and animal assisted activity, difference
        between, 5
    animal selection for, 25–33 (see also
        Therapy pet)
    benefits of, and studies, 4–5, 8, 11–12
    client screening for, 59
    client screening form for, 179–180
    construct of, 3
    in counseling, 2–3, 12–14 (see also Animal
        assisted counseling)
    course syllabus for, 201–205
    in crisis response counseling, 139–149
    description of, 5
    dynamics of process in, 3–4
    example of, 2
    health care settings incorporating, 4–5
    history of, 10–12
    human-animal interaction in, 5–7, 16
    illustration activity and therapy
        instructions in, 207–220
    and motivation to participate, 19
    psychophysiological benefits of, 4–5
    popularity of, 12
    promotion of, in university settings, 12,
        177–178
    psychosocial benefits of, 4–5
    psychosocial session form for, 181–184
    references for, 221–227
    risk management in, 57–71
    risks involved in, 8–10
    in schools, 151–157
    in South Korea, 167–175
    studies of, 4–5, 8, 11–12, 15–24
        in anxiety and stress, 17
        in child anxiety and stress, 17, 19
        in child emotional and behavioral
            problems, 20–21
        in dementia, 17–18
        in depression, 18–19
        in developmental disorders, 19–20
        in elderly people, 21–22
        in motivation to participate, 19
        in nursing home setting, 21–22
        in physically disabled people, 22–23
        in psychiatric patients, 23–24
        in self esteem enhancement, 19
    university centers promoting, 177–178
Animal care, vocational education in, 153–154

Animal Colors Activity, 207–220
Animal illustrations, 96–97
    and therapist instructions, 207–220
Animal rehabilitation, at correctional facilities,
    134–135, 136–137
Animal team evaluator, Delta Society, 162
Antisocial behavior, client, changing, 81–82
Anxiety, and stress, animal assisted therapy in,
    17, 19
ASEBA, contact information, 126
Assessment instruments, psychological, 126

B

Bates, Linda, 82
Bear (therapy dog), 12, 140
Beck Anxiety Inventory, 126
Beck Depression Inventory II, 126
Behavioral Assessment System for Children,
    126
Benjamin, Carol, 43
Beyond Limits service award, 82
Big Five Inventory, 66
Biofeedback therapy, 96
Birds
    in reducing depression, 18
    stress signs in, 61
    therapy, 136
Blackburn Correctional Complex (Lexington,
    KY), 137
Bloodhound, breed description, 98
Bond, Deb, 95, 110
Border Collie, breed description, 98
Boston Terrier, as therapy dogs, 76
Breed history, 100–101
Brie (therapy dog), 95–96
Bull Dog, breed description, 98
Bull Terriers, 82–84
Bully dog breeds, 82–84
Buros Mental Measurements Yearbook, 126
Burrill, Ken, 110
Buster (therapy dog), 109–110

C

Calming signals, 59–60
Canine Good Citizen Test, AKC, 50–51
Care kit
    human therapist, 142
    therapy animal, 69–70
    therapy dog, 141–142
Carselowey, Dena, 12
Cat(s)

behavior of, understanding, 64–65
species history of, 101
therapy, 18, 22, 30–31
   massaging, 39–40
   in play therapy, 107
   special skills for, 45–47
   stress signs in, 60
Tonkinese, 96
Cat Fancy, 85
Cats (Alderton), 85
Cats (Fogle), 100
Cell Dogs, 134
Center for Animal Assisted Therapy,
   University of North Texas, *see* University of
   North Texas
Charles H. Hickey School (Baltimore, MD),
   137
Cheju National University (South Korea), 173,
   174
Chihuahua, breed description of, 98
Child anxiety, and stress, 17, 19
Child Behavior Checklist, 126
Child developmental disorders, 19–20
Children, animal assisted therapy for, 106–110
Choi, Yoon-ju, 170
Chung, D. H., 170
Clarification, in counseling, 91–93
Client injury, preventing, 67–68
Client injury policy, of Delta Society, 67–68
Client-pet relationships, 84–85
Client screening, 9, 59
Client screening form, 179–180
Client-therapy pet relationship, 6–7
Cocker Spaniel, American, 27
Communication, animal assisted, 75–79, 80–81
Communication behavior, animal, 61–66
Community training, in animal assisted
   therapy, 163–164
Companionable Zoo program, 120–123
Competency and confidence, building, 87
Consulting Psychologists Press, contact
   information, 126
Correctional facilities, *see also* Detention center
   clients; Prison clients
      animal rehabilitation programs in,
      133–137
Corson, Sam and Elizabeth, 10
Course development, university, 162–163
Course syllabus, for animal assisted therapy,
   201–205
Crate containment, of therapy pet, 66–67
Credentials, program, 161–162
Crisis
   client needs in, 145–147
   emotions expressed in, 143–144
   nature of, 141

Crisis response counseling, 139–140, 143–147
   dogs as therapists in, 140
   kits for human and dog care in, 141–142
   safety of therapy dogs in, 141–142
   team formation for, 147–149
   training in, 142–143
Cultures, and attitudes regarding animals,
   129–130, 167–175

D

Dachshund
   breed description of, 98
   as therapy dog, 109–110
Dallas (TX) SPCA, juvenile animal assisted
   therapy program, 136–137
Decker, Susan, 207
Defense, signs of, in cats, 64
Delta Society, 11, 52
   AAT applications course offered by,
      79–81
   animal team evaluator status in, 162
   client injury policy of, 67–68
   licensed instructor status in, 162
   Pet Partners Evaluation of, 51–54
   Pet Partners program of, 11, 153–154,
      161–162, 163–164, 173
   public relations video of, 153
   registering with, 54
Dementia, clients with, 17–18
Denton County (TX) juvenile detention center,
   135–137, 162
   Rocky Top Therapy Ranch sessions for,
      110–120
Detention center clients, 133–134
Developmental disorders, 19–20
Diagnoses, treatment of, 101–102
*Diagnostic and Statistical Manual for Mental
   Disorders,* 4th edition, 101
Disabled people, physically, 22–23
Disabled therapy animals, handling, 61
Documentation, of animal assisted counseling,
   124–125
Dog(s)
   behavior of, understanding, 62–64
   breed comparisons of, 97–98
   fear of, 128–129
   sources of stories about, 85
   species history of, 101
   stories about, sharing, 81–85
   therapy
      advantages and disadvantages of, 28
      with anxious/distressed children, 17
      breed choices for, 27–28

in child developmental disorders,
   19–20
in child emotional and behavioral
   problems, 20–21
in counseling, 74–137 (*see also* Animal
   assisted counseling)
in crisis response, 140–149
with elderly people, 21–22
evaluating, 49–55
obedience training of, 40–43
with people with dementia, 17–18
personality traits of, 26–27, 28, 66
in play therapy, 106–109
with psychiatric patients, 23–24
puppy selection for, 29–30
in reducing depression, 18
rescued dogs as, 27
selecting, 26–30
in self esteem enhancement, 19
socialization of, 36–39
special skill training of, 43–46
stress signs in, 60
tests for potential, 49–55
touch desensitization of, 39–40
trick training of, 43–46
Dog Fancy, 85
Dog leash, double safety, 106–107
Dog Tricks: Step by Step (Zeigenfuse and
   Walker), 44
Dogs (Alderton), 85
Dogspeak (Hoffman), 63
Dolly (therapy dog), xv
   client interaction with, 111, 136, 162
   Delta Society evaluation of, 54
   overcoming car sickness, 37
   relational techniques with, 92
   socializing with horses, 38, 39
   touch desensitization with, 40
Dolphin swim programs, 71
Drawings, animal, and therapist instructions,
   207–220
Dude (therapy horse), 114, 115–116

E

EAGALA, *see* Equine Assisted Growth and
   Learning Association
Eden Alternative, 11
Ehlers, Cindy, 12, 140
El Dorado Correctional Facility (Kansas), 135
Elderly clients, 21–22, 88–89, 130–132
Elliot (therapy cat), 96
Emotional and behavioral problems, child,
   20–21

Emotions, in animals, 65
Encyclopedia of Dog Breeds (Coile), 85, 100
Equine assisted counseling, 95, 110–120, 137,
   see also Horses
Equine Assisted Growth and Learning
   Association, 11, 154
Equine assisted physical therapy, 10, *see also*
   Horses
Equine assisted therapy programs, school
   based, 154
Equine Facilitated Mental Health Association,
   10
Erickson, Milton, 102–103
Erikson, Erik, 86
   and stages of psychosocial development,
      86–89
Ethical considerations, 70
Evaluation, of animal assisted counseling,
   125–126

F

Faculty acceptance, of program establishment,
   161
Family tree exercise, 99–101
Farm animals, therapy, 10, 33
   and children with emotional and
      behavioral problems, 21
Fear
   of animals, 128–129
   in cats, signs of, 64
   in dogs, signs of, 63–64
Feelings assessment, animal assisted, 93–99
Ferrets, in animal assisted therapy, 23, 31–33
Fish, as therapy pets, 31–32
Flint, Pam, 164
Flower (therapy cat), 76
Frustration tolerance, learning, 115
Funding
   government sponsored, 155
   private corporation, 155–156
   proposal for, 156
   for school based programs, 154–156
   for university based programs, 164
Funding proposal, sample, 185–191
Fuzzy (therapy rabbit), 76

G

Gazette (American Kennel Club), 85
Genogram, 100
Gerbils/hamsters, as therapy pets, 31–33
German Shepherd, breed description of, 99

Goal directed activities, 5
Golden Retriever, 27
    breed description of, 99
Grant money, finding and applying for,
    154–156
Great Dane, breed description of, 99
Green Chimneys Children's Services
    (New York), 10, 21
Group play therapy, 109–110
Guinea pigs, in animal assisted therapy, 23,
    31–33

H

Harcourt Assessment, contact information, 126
Harper, Sara, 95–96
Hoffman, Matthew, 63
HOPE: Animal Assisted Crisis Response, crisis
    training by, 143
Horse grooming, 112
Horse riding, benefits of learning, 115–117, 122
Horsemanship, responsible, 119, 121
Horses
    in animal assisted counseling, 110–120,
      137
    feelings assessment using, 95
    obedience training, 40–43
    in physical therapy, 10, 22–23, 31
Hospice clients, 132–133
Hospitalized clients, 132–133
Human animal bond, 6
Human Animal Bond, First International
    Symposium on, 170–172
Human-animal interaction, 5–7
    physiologic changes in, 4–5, 16
Human-animal relationship, 167–175
Hutchison Correctional Facility (Kansas),
    135

I

Iam's Paws to Share Foundation, 164, 193
Identity development, 88
Illustrations, animal, and therapist instructions,
    207–220
Imagery, animal assisted, 102–106
Informed consent, 59
Injury, preventing, 66–69
Innis, Nancy, 76
Instructional enhancement, 153
Instructor, Delta Society Licensed, 162
Interactions (Delta Society), 85
Intermediate Attitudes Scale, 126

Internship establishment, student, 164–165
Interventions, animal assisted, 101–102
    group play therapy, 109–110
    metaphor, 102–106
    play therapy, 106–109
Intimacy, developing, 88

J

Juvenile clients, detention center, 135–137
    Denton County (TX), 110–120

K

K-9 Disaster Relief, 146–147
    crisis response training by, 143
Katherine (therapy cat), 96
Kim, John C. U., 172
Kim, Yang Soon, 170, 172–173, 174
Kit, care
    human therapist, 142
    therapy animal, 69–70
    therapy dog, 141–142

L

Labrador Retriever, 27
    as therapy dog, 95–96
Lane, Franklin K., 10
Learning disabilities, children with, 19–20
Lee, Amy J., 172
Lee, D. H., 170, 172
Lee, Ho Kap, 172
Lee, Ju-yeon, 170, 172, 173
Lee, Soojung, 171
Levinson, Boris, 10, 12–13
Licensed instructor, Delta Society, 162
Life review, 88–89
Life stage development, animal facilitated,
    85–89
Limit setting technique, play therapy, 107
Line drawings, animal, 96–97
Lulu (therapy dog), 173

M

Mable (therapy mule), 119–120
Mann, Denette, 77
Marion Correctional Institution for Men
    (Ohio), 135

Marion County Correctional Institution
(Ocala, FL), 137
Massage, animal, 39–40, 61
Measurement instruments, 126
Mental Hygiene (Levinson), 10
Metaphor, animal assisted, 102–106
*Mother Knows Best: The Natural Way to Train
Your Dog* (Benjamin), 43
Motivation, animal assisted, 19, 80, 81–82
Multivariate analysis of variance (MANOVA),
125

N

National Institute of Health (Washington, DC),
132
National Organization for Victim Assistance
(NOVA)
in crisis intervention, 141
crisis response training by, 143
crisis team recommendations by, 147–149
Nature program, school based, 154
North American Riding for the Handicapped
Association (NARHA), 10, 154
Nursing, animal assisted therapy in, 11
Nursing home residents, 21–22, *see also* Elderly
clients

O

Obedience training, of therapy dogs, 40–43
classes for, 40–41
length of practice sessions in, 42
practicing commands in, 41–42
reward and repetition in, 42–43
selective reading in, 43
tips in, 43
Ohio Reformatory for Women (Marysville), 135
Ohio State University Psychiatric Hospital, 10
Ohio Wildlife Center, 135
Oscar (therapy horse), 114, 115

P

Paraphrasing, in counseling, 91–93
Pawling Army Air Force Convalescent Hospital
(New York), 10
Paws to Share Foundation, Iam's, 164, 193
Pearson Assessments, contact information, 126
Perseverance, encouraging, 118
Personal fulfillment, 88

Personalities, of animals, 66
Pet-client relationships, 84–85
Pet Partners Evaluation, Delta Society's,
51–54
Pet Partners Team, Delta Society, 11, 153–154,
161–162, 163–164
in South Korea, 173
Pet practitioners, *see* Therapy pet(s)
Petting animals, 74–75
Physically disabled clients, 22–23
Pit Bull dogs, background of, 82–84
Play therapy, 106–109
group, 109–110
yard for, 109
Playfulness, signs of
in cats, 65
in dogs, 64
Poodle
miniature, breed description of, 99
as therapy dog, 77
Post Adjudication Program, Denton County
(TX), 110–120, 135–136
Postures
canine, 63–64
feline, 64–65
Practical Guide for Crisis Response in Schools
(Lerner, Volpe, Lindell), 143
Practical Guide for University Crisis Response
(Lerner, Volpe, Lindell), 143
Prison clients, 133–136
Professional disclosure, 59
Professional fulfillment, 88
Progress report, program, 157
sample, 193–199
Proposal, funding
funding, 156
sample, 185–191
Psychiatric patients, 23–24
Psychological assessment instruments, and
contact information, 126
Psychophysiological health, 4–5, 16
Psychosocial development, Erikson's stages of,
86–89
Psychosocial goals, and techniques, 79–81
Psychosocial Session Form, 125, 181–184
Puppet Theater, 110
Puppy selection, for therapy work, 29–30
PUPS program, 54–55

R

Rabbits, therapy, 22, 23, 31–33, 76
stress signs in, 60
RAD, *see* Reading assistance dogs program

Ramsey, Anetta, 76
Rapport building, animals in, 75–79, *see also* Communication
Reading assistance, animals in, 12, 163
Reading assistance dogs program, 187–188, 194
Reflection, in counseling, 91–93
Rehabilitation, animal assisted, 81–82
Reinforcement, of client behavior, 81–82
Relational techniques, basic, 91–93
Relaxation, signs of
    in cats, 65
    in dogs, 64
Reports, program progress, 157
Research, *see* Studies
Rewarding behavior, reinforcing, 87–88
Right TRAIL, 110
Risk management, 8–10, 57–58
    client screening in, 59
    communication behavior of animals in, 61–66
    ethical animal treatment in, 70–71
    informed consent in, 59
    injury/infection prevention in, 66–69
    preparation for visit in, 69–70
    professional disclosure statement in, 59
    stressed animals and, 59–61
Roberson, Eric, 134
Roberts, Tracy, 12
Rocky Top Therapy Center (Keller, TX), 110–120, 164–165
Ropes course, 111
Rosie (therapy dog), 77
Rowdy (therapy dog), 82
Roxy (therapy dog), 164
Rusty (therapy dog), xv
    allergic reactions to environment, 68–69
    client interaction with, 2, 9, 77–79, 162
    Delta Society evaluation of, 53–54
    Delta Society registration of, 161
    in feelings assessment in therapy, 93–95
    in play therapy, 109
    relational techniques with, 92
    socialization of, 37
    special training, 44–45, 46

S

Samsung
    animal welfare promotion by, 171
    charitable enterprises of, 171–172
    equestrian programs of, 171
    Responsible Pet Ownership Program of, 171–172
Samsung Animal Assistance Center, 174, 175
Samsung Assistance Dog Services, 170, 172
Samsung Veterinary Clinic, 170
School programs, with animal assisted therapy, 151–157, 163–164
    applications of, 153–154
    funding for, 154–156
    guidelines for, 152–153
    progress reporting in, 157
Self esteem enhancement, 19, 22–23, 81, 88
Shibanai, Hiroko, 170
Shin, Nam-sik, 170
Skill training, therapy dog, 43–46
Small animal therapy pets, 31–33
Smith, Cheryl, 44
Smith, Elaine, 11
Snowflake (therapy cat), xv
    allergic reaction to environment, 69
    client interaction with, 162
    empathy enhancement with, 32
SOAP plan, 124
Social interaction, providing, 88
Social skills, improving client, 80
Socialization, of therapy dogs, 36–39
South Korea, 167–175
    animal assisted therapy in, 172–174
    human-animal relationship in, 170–175
South Korea Veterinary Medical Association, 171, 174
Special needs clients, 127–137
St. Elizabeth's Hospital (Washington, DC), 10
Statistical analysis, 125–126
Steinmetz, Jennifer, 110
Stick (therapy horse), 114, 115–116
Stress
    hormonal release in, 146
    in therapy animals
        preventing, 107, 109
        recognizing, 59–61, 71, 96
Stress relief, in school based programs, 153
Student internship establishment, 164–165
Studies, of animal assisted therapy, 4–5, 8, 11–12, 15–24
    in anxiety and stress, 17
    in child anxiety and stress, 17, 19
    in child emotional and behavioral problems, 20–21
    in dementia, 17–18
    in depression, 18–19
    in developmental disorders, 19–20
    in elderly people, 21–22
    in motivation to participate, 19
    in nursing home setting, 21–22
    in physically disabled people, 22–23
    in psychiatric patients, 23–24
    in self esteem enhancement, 19

Submission, signs of
    in cats, 65
    in dogs, 64
Summa Health Systems (Akron, OH), 132
Summarization, in counseling, 91–93
Symptom Checklist 90-Revised, 126

T

Taffy (shelter dog), 134
TAT, *see* Therapy animal team program
Taunton, Stephanie, 44
TDI, *see* Therapy Dogs International
Tellington Touch, 61
Termination, of counseling, 123–124
Tests, for potential therapy dogs, 49–50
    AKC Good Citizen Test, 50–51
    Delta Society Pet Partners, 51–54
    Therapy Dogs International, 51
    Tuskegee Behavior Test, 54–55
The Canine Good Citizen: Every Dog Can Be One (Volhard), 43
The Trick Is in the Training (Taunton and Smith), 44
Therapeutic touch, animal surrogates for, 74–75
Therapeutic zoo, 120–123
Therapy animal team program, 188–190, 194
Therapy dogs, *see under* Dogs
Therapy Dogs International, 11
    evaluation tests of, 51
Therapy pet(s)
    assorted, 120–123
    cats as, 30–31 (*see also* Cats)
    client trust and affiliation with, 5–6
    communication behavior in, 61–66
    in counseling sessions, 73–126 (*see also* Animal assisted counseling)
    Delta Society testing of, 51–52
    disabled, handling, 61
    dogs as, 26–30 (*see also* Animal assisted counseling; Dogs)
    ethical treatment of, 70
    evaluating, 49–55
    farm animals as, 33 (*see also* Farm animals)
    horses as, 31 (*see also* Horses)
    identification and acceptance of, 5
    injury/infection prevention with, 66–69
    preparation of, for work, 69–70
    relationship with, nature of, 5–7
    safety and welfare of, 9–10
    selecting, 25–33
    small animal, 31–33, 51–54 (*see also* Birds; Rabbits)

stress in, recognizing, 59–61
    training, 36–47
Thomas, William, 11
Tom (therapy horse), 95
Tonkinese cats, 96
Touch desensitization, of therapy pet, 39–40
Toxic substances, reaction to, 68–69
Training, therapy pet, 36–47
    obedience training in, 40–43
    skill and trick teaching in, 43–47
    socialization in, 36–39
    touch desensitization in, 39–40
Transitional beings, 6
Trick training
    communication building in, 80–81
    therapy dog, 43–46
Trust, building, with horses, 112, 113–115
Tuskegee Behavior Test, 54–55

U

University centers, promoting animal assisted therapy, 177–178
University of North Texas, AAT-C program at, 159–165
    approval of, establishing, 160–161
    community involvement in, 163–164
    course development for, 162–163
    educational resources of, 165
    funding, 154
    instructor credentialing for, 161–162
    proposal for, 160–161
    recognition of, 165
    sample progress report for, 193–199
    student internship establishment in, 164–165

V

Vocational development, 88
Volhard, Jack and Wendy, 43

W

Walker, Jan, 44
Warm Springs Rehabilitation Hospital (San Antonio, TX), 132
Wilderness program, school based, 154
Women's Correctional Institute (Purdy, WA), 135
Woo, Young-Bum, 172

Y

Yang, Young-Oh, 173
Yorkshire Terrier, breed description of, 99
Young, Sharon, 135

Z

Zeigenfuse, Mary Ann Rombold, 44
Zoo, therapeutic, 120–123
Zoonoses, 69